The Atonement Creating Unions

The Atonement Creating Unions

An Exploration in Inter-Religious Theology

Godfrey Kesari

FOREWORD BY
Marius C. Felderhof

☙PICKWICK *Publications* • Eugene, Oregon

THE ATONEMENT CREATING UNIONS
An Exploration in Inter-Religious Theology

Copyright © 2019 Godfrey Kesari. All rights reserved. Except for brief quotations in critical publications or reviews, no part of this book may be reproduced in any manner without prior written permission from the publisher. Write: Permissions, Wipf and Stock Publishers, 199 W. 8th Ave., Suite 3, Eugene, OR 97401.

Pickwick Publications
An Imprint of Wipf and Stock Publishers
199 W. 8th Ave., Suite 3
Eugene, OR 97401

www.wipfandstock.com

PAPERBACK ISBN: 978-1-5326-5262-2
HARDCOVER ISBN: 978-1-5326-5263-9
EBOOK ISBN: 978-1-5326-5264-6

Cataloguing-in-Publication data:

Names: Kesari, Godfrey, author. | Felderhof, Marius C., foreword writer.

Title: The atonement creating unions : an exploration in inter-religious theology / Godfrey Kesari, with a foreword by Marius C. Felderhof.

Description: Eugene, OR: Pickwick Publications, 2019 | Includes bibliographical references.

Identifiers: ISBN 978-1-5326-5262-2 (paperback) | ISBN 978-1-5326-5263-9 (hardcover) | ISBN 978-1-5326-5264-6 (ebook)

Subjects: LCSH: Comparative theology | Christianity and other religions—Hinduism | Hinduism—Relations—Christianity | Religion—Theology—Hinduism | Religion—Theology—Christianity | Atonement

Classification: BT750 K271 2019 (print) | BT750 (ebook)

Scripture quotations are from The Catholic Edition of the Revised Standard Version of the Bible, copyright © 1965, 1966 National Council of the Churches of Christ in the United States of America. Used by permission. All rights reserved worldwide.

New Revised Standard Version Bible, copyright 1989, Division of Christian Education of the National Council of the Churches of Christ in the United Stated of America. Used by permission. All rights reserved.

Manufactured in the U.S.A.   01/29/19

Contents

Foreword by Marius C. Felderhof | vii
Preface | xi
Acknowledgements | xiii

Chapter 1: Introduction | 1

Chapter 2: Visistadvaitic Hindu Conception of the Means to Liberation (Salvation): With Special Reference to Ramanuja | 28

Chapter 3: An Analysis of Existing Theories of the Atonement in a Hindu-Christian Indian Context | 66

Chapter 4: Constructing an Atonement Model in a Hindu-Christian Indian Context: The Atonement Creating Unions | 118

Chapter 5: The Atonement Creating Unions: Potentialities and Problems | 164

Chapter 6: Conclusion. The Atonement Creating Unions: Its Nature and Use | 200

Abbreviations for Reference Works | 211
Bibliography | 213

Foreword

MOST HISTORIES OF PHILOSOPHY in the Western world begin with the works of Plato who lived some two and a half millennia ago (427–347 BC). What is most striking about Plato's philosophical contribution is his use of dialogues as the medium of thought. In effect, for him that sphere of human interest defined by a cluster of terms, such as, wisdom, knowledge and understanding, is grounded in human conversation. And ever since Plato's time, many of the most outstanding philosophical and theological thinkers have used the medium of a dialogue to explore ideas to deepen our understanding.

The reference to ideas makes it all sound rather abstract. Perhaps it is not only thought, but life itself that is deepened and enriched through conversation. Some of the conversations may be casual, others more formal and structured; some may be light-hearted, others deeply serious, but all contributing to a substantive depth in human life. The lack of conversation is a sign of shallowness, of anger, of indifference or of a passion for a single-minded commitment that blocks a genuine dialogue. It seems that the very character of life itself turns on the nature and quality of the conversations that are generated. So it is that conversation and dialogue, even by their absence, define the nature of human life and thought[1].

Where thought and life are intimately entwined, some of the great thinkers have wondered how understanding "the other" is possible at all, if one does not already share a form of life, culture or thought world. Thus the Christian theologian, F. D. E. Schleiermacher (1768–1834), sometimes known as the father of modern theology and hermeneutics[2], developed a whole theory of how one might go about understanding a deep and alien

---

1. It is an open question whether modern life with its access to the Internet, social media, and Twitter, have stimulated conversation or impoverished it, e.g., it is not unusual to observe couples in which each member of the pair is engrossed in his or her mobile phone rather than communicating with each other.
2. i.e. theory of interpretation.

text, whether written or spoken by another. Whilst the Danish thinker, Søren Kierkegaard (1813–1855), the father of existentialism, wondered[3] how from one position in life, e.g., of being a non-Christian, one could join another, e.g., of being a Christian, when the life one lives determines what one could potentially understand. The transition from one world to another is not easy when one grasps that life and thought go hand in hand. His solution was simply to present these wholes side by side. His whole corpus of work is a grand polyphony, that is, a presentation of many different voices occupying different positions in life to show the character of the particular understanding of each.

The difficulty of gaining a deep understanding of "the other" in matters that touch the very character of our existence is addressed with three different strategies. The first is to avoid any deep conversations with "the other." This was relatively easy in times past by virtue of the fact that the people who lived a significantly different life also lived in a different part of the world. Real engagement was avoided. This is no longer a realistic possibility when we live in a "global village." However, such an easy method is still actively pursued today simply by providing descriptions of "the other" without letting it have any bearing on the life of the person doing the studying or the describing. Or for that matter, letting it have any bearing on the life of the reader. Voyeuristic descriptions are essentially monologues rather than dialogues.

A second strategy is to focus only on those elements in human life that are shared. It is this commonality which provides a basis for mutual understanding and a common life. Those elements that are singular and unique are then sometimes simply jettisoned to avoid incomprehension, misunderstanding or the potential offence that comes from claiming a truth that is apparently not accessible to the other. In the field of inter-religious studies, those committed to the position of pluralism, that values all people and forms of life equally, have not infrequently sacrificed precisely those elements which seem to mark off one faith from the other. For example, some of the contributors to the debate about "the myth of God incarnate" appeared to be embarrassed by the unique role that Jesus Christ was assigned in Christian Life and thought. They set this key church teaching aside, or dismissed it as best left in the past, an embarrassing legacy. Others felt that by setting aside the traditional teaching relating to Jesus, the heart was taken out of the Christian faith and life.

---

3. See Søren Kierkegaard, *Philosophical Fragments*. Princeton: Princeton University Press, 1967.

A third strategy is that adopted by Dr. Kesari, which is to take precisely that core controversial church teaching about Jesus Christ that causes offence and makes that the focus of discussion with "the other," who is here identified as the *Visistadvaitic* Hindu. A first step is to recognize the complex intra-Christian discussions and then gauge exactly where the offence might be and what possibilities might be pursued to enable the Hindu to grasp what is at stake. But it is a two way process in which the Christian tradition may be encouraged to benefit from, and be illuminated by, the thoughts, doubts and experience of the Hindu traditions, without the integrity of either party to the conversation being compromised. The exchange of ideas and the interaction brought about by the conversation deepens our common human life. Fresh ideas and related fresh ways of living that come from "the other" provides the means for moving forward in history.

Rather than seeing the other as the stranger, the unknowable, or as a threat to one's intellectual life and practical ways of living, the other is truly a gift, an opportunity to see one's own life and its intellectual constructions anew. The other offers a new pair of eyes! It is always to one's advantage to seek out 'the other" and to start a conversation about what matters most to one in life. Of course, "the other" may present in various guises. "The other" may most obviously be a neighbor, a stranger in one's midst, but "the other" might equally well be the inner self that speaks to you, or as in the case of St. Augustine's *Confessions*, "the other" is the God who challenges, and who leads to truth and the good. What matters is to engage in a genuine conversation rather than a sham conversation in which neither party really listens to the other to the point where they might admit the possibility of living differently.

What Dr. Kesari has shown in what follows is how a truly serious conversation might go and the insights to be gained from one very specific encounter—with the atonement at its core.

Dr. Marius C. Felderhof
Hon. Sr. Research Fellow
Department of Theology and Religion
The University of Birmingham, UK

Preface

THIS BOOK PRESUMES THAT the theology of the atonement needs to be made lucid in every context and in this work I attempt to make it intelligible to those who belong to the *Visistadvaitic* Hindu tradition, in effect taking an interreligious perspective. This is in conformity with a traditional Christian way of thinking because the New Testament writings use many insights from the Graeco-Roman and Jewish religious traditions to express its own meaning and to serve its own purpose. Hence, in a way, our work is going back to the New Testament in attempting to formulate a doctrinal theology of the atonement with a cross-cultural bearing. Thus, methodologically this book is in the nature of finding a direction towards formulating Christian theology in the *Visistadvaitic* Hindu context.

I have always been fond of atonement theology. Christians generally insist that we see the love of God in Christ in its fullness on the cross. Without denying that understanding, in this book, I am devising a theology in an interreligious perspective using the theology of the atonement as an exemplar. To put it succinctly, this work will make explicit the connections between Christian and *Visistadvaitic* Hindu thinking with the theology of the atonement at its heart. It will become clear to readers that this is a creative way forward for pursuing the doctrine of the atonement in a new direction. This line of thought of course will retain the historicity and uniqueness of the love of God in Christ revealed on the cross whilst linking clearly to the distinctive thoughtfulness that is encountered within *Visistadvaitic* Hinduism.

Further this work will carefully elucidate the potentialities and problems in constructing a theology of the atonement in this direction. It will be obvious that this work ultimately is an attempt to find a way of treating and shielding the centrality and significance of the cross of Christ, in a fresh way, with contextual relevance and it is presented as filling a gap in the literature of interreligious theology relating to Christianity and *Visistadvaitic* Hinduism with the concept of means to salvation at its core.

In recent years, there has been much interest in the theology of the atonement. This book, I anticipate, will add to that interest not only amongst scholars and students of theology but also amongst people interested in the theology of the atonement in general as well as interreligious theology in particular. My prayer is that this book will promote better understanding, reconciliation, unity and peace within and between religious cultures in a world of alienation. I hope that you will enjoy reading this book. May God bless you as you turn the pages.

Holy Week 2018
Southwater, West Sussex

Acknowledgements

THIS BOOK HAS BEEN blessed by the grace of God, who had given me the time and all resources I needed from the beginning until the conclusion of this work. Many people along my life journey have helped me to think clearly and encouraged me by sharing lessons they learned from their own life.

My sincere thanks goes to Dr. Marius C. Felderhof of the University of Birmingham, UK, the author of *Revisiting Christianity: Theological Reflections*. He is an inspiring teacher and supportive tutor and I thank him for his invaluable comments and suggestions. I have enormously learned to think clearly, critically and constructively from his sharp insights and thorough scholarship. He was my PhD supervisor and this book is a revised version of my work under his guidance. I am also grateful to my examiners Professor Alan Torrance and Dr. David Cheetham for their encouraging comments.

My gratitude also extends to my teachers at the Princeton Theological Seminary, particularly to Professor J. Wentzel van Huyssteen who was my admired guide in philosophical theology and science and to Professor Bruce Lindley McCormack, who taught me the history of the theology of the atonement.

I am also grateful to Rev. Dr. O. V. Jathanna, former Principal of the United Theological College, Bangalore, India, who first introduced me to the theology of the atonement and its beauty. My heart-felt thanks also goes to my other teachers and mentors at UTC Bangalore where I pioneered the joy of learning and living theology.

Further, I am indebted to many people in the UK, the USA and India for the information and experiences that are offered in this book. Many authors and friends have helped me with the materials, bibliography, and methodology. Particularly, I would like to thank the staff at OLRC and the Main Library of the University of Birmingham and the staff at the

Princeton Theological Seminary, and more recently the staff at the Chichester University library.

My grateful thanks also goes to my editors Hannah Harris and Dr. Robin Parry and all the staff at Wipf and Stock for their wonderful support and help in publishing this book.

Finally, I am deeply indebted to my parents for their prayers, support and encouragement. I also thank my wife, Pradhma and our children, Emy and Evans who generously and lovingly shared the burden, pressure and the blessings involved with publishing this book.

Being a deep committed Anglican Christian, if this work could enhance friendship and peace between religions, such as Christianity and *Visistadvaitic* Hinduism, and promote progressive theological communication on the theology of the atonement between the West and India, I would be more than happy.

1

Introduction

A Setback of the Theology of the Atonement Clarified

The theology of the atonement has been regarded by many as central to the Christian scheme of doctrines throughout the Christian tradition. It is in important respects the very nexus of Christian theology because it brings meaning to all aspects of our "lives" under the divine. But, it is also a fact that this theology of the atonement is one amongst all the different theologies that are most consistently disputed and rejected in many other religious traditions, including the Indian Visistadvaitic Hindu tradition. The words of Israel Selvanayagam, an Indian Christian theologian, powerfully portray the nature of the problem of atonement theology in India. In his words,

> Western missionaries working in the non-Western world, who were insistent on the atonement theories had to face the challenge of those who either could not understand their argument or were unwilling to subscribe to their view. Some thinking persons were questioning the logic of a wrathful God demanding the blood of an innocent person like Jesus in order to maintain justice. Some western missionaries changed their view and started to present the cross as revealing the eternal suffering of a loving God . . .[1]

Precisely, the theology of the atonement remains a singular problem in Hindu-Christian contexts right up to the present time. This is because the whole concept of a God dying as a divine human being is not only alien but difficult to integrate into the Visistadvaitic Hindu Philosophy.

Of course, the atonement is an alien concept to other religious traditions such as Islam or Buddhism, too. However, since our endeavor is to understand the atonement using one another tradition we will limit ourselves

1. Selvanayagam, *Relating to People of Other Faiths*, 51.

to the Visistadvaitic Hindu tradition here. A similar study might be possible using other religious traditions.

The fact is many theologians within Hinduism, in general, accept the teachings of Jesus, but no Hindu has ever accepted the theology of the atonement as explained by the traditional theories. Mahatma Gandhi, Swami Vivekananda, and Raja Ram Mohan Roy are amongst the many of those who could be mentioned in this regard. We will very briefly highlight the problems posed by Gandhi, Vivekananda, and Ram Mohan Roy in their opposition to the atonement concept. It may also be pointed out here that Hindus form the vast majority in India. There are about 80 percent Hindus, whilst Christians form only about 2.3 percent of the population. Now, we will very briefly look at the difficulties that Mahatma Gandhi raised in understanding the atonement concept as accepted within traditional Christianity.

Mahatma Gandhi

Although Gandhi admired the Sermon on the Mount by Jesus, he had rejected the concept of the atonement in its traditional forms. On the Sermon on the Mount, Gandhi writes, "When I read in the Sermon on the Mount such passages as 'Resist not him that is evil: he who smiteth thee on thy right cheek turn to him the other also, and love your enemies, pray for them that persecute you that ye may be the sons of your Father which is in heaven,' I was overjoyed."[2] But, on the atonement, he says,

> I could accept Jesus as a martyr, an embodiment of sacrifice and a Divine teacher and not as the most perfect man ever born. His death on the cross . . . that there was anything mysterious or miraculous virtue in it my heart could not accept. The pious lives of Christians did not give me anything that the lives of other faiths had failed to give me. I had seen in other lives just the same reformation that I had heard among Christians. Philosophically, there was nothing extraordinary in Christian principles. . . . It was impossible for me to regard Christianity as a perfect religion or the greatest of all religions.[3]

Gandhi held the view that we need to seek redemption not from the consequences of sin but from the idea of sin itself. He writes, "I seek to be redeemed from sin itself, or from the very thought of sin. Until I have attained

2. Gandhi, *Autobiography*, 92.
3. Gandhi, *Autobiography*, 136.

that end, I shall be content to be restless."⁴ A good Christian, from Manchester, remarked that man must sin, that it was impossible in the world to live sinlessly, and it was for this that Jesus suffered and made atonement. Gandhi replied, "The brother proved as good as his word. He voluntarily committed transgressions and showed me that he was undisturbed by thought of them."⁵ As we noted, Gandhi's idea of redemption was different. In this regard he shared the view of most Vaishnava⁶ Hindus for he was not the only one amongst that group of Hindus with such views. We now turn to Swami Vivekananda's thought on the atonement.

Swami Vivekananda.

Swami Vivekananda also attacked the doctrine that Christ died to save people. For him, experience, not doctrine, was the fountainhead of Christianity, as with other religions (i.e. the experience of Christ and his disciples in meeting God).⁷ However, on the atonement, Vivekananda writes,

> The Christians believe that Jesus Christ died to save Man. With you it is belief in a doctrine, and this belief constitutes your salvation. With us doctrine has nothing whatever to do with salvation. What difference does it make to you whether Jesus lived at a certain time or not? What has it to do with you that Moses saw in the burning bush? . . . Records of great spiritual men of the past do us no good whatever except that they urge us onward to do the same, to experience religion ourselves. Whatever Christ or Moses or anybody else did does not help us in the least, except to urge us on.⁸

In fact, for Vivekananda, the teachings of Christ are part of Indian thought as well. More precisely, he finds many similarities between the

---

4. Gandhi, *Autobiography*, 124–25.
5. Gandhi, *Autobiography*, 125.
6. In this book, I will not use diacritical marks for the transliteration of Sanskrit or Tamil words because our study is focused on theological issues and not on exegetical issues.
7. Vivekananda, *Collected Works*, 126.
8. Vivekananda, *Collected Works*, vol. 6, 98–99. According to Vivekananda, one atonement cannot bring salvation to all. In his words, "The fault with all religions like Christianity is that they have one set of rules for all. But Hindu religion is suited to all grades of religious aspiration and progress." It may be noted that the aspirant in Hinduism, with his guru's assistance, can choose the path which is best suited to his nature or even combine two or more.

thoughts of Buddha and Christ.⁹ However, according to him, the concept of the atonement is alien to Indian thought. Like many Hindus, Vivekananda too is reluctant to accept the atonement as understood in its traditional forms. In short, the problem, which atonement theology faces in India, with regard to its acceptance, is clearly evident in Vivekananda's writings.

Raja Ram Mohan Roy

Another thinker who has rejected the atonement concept, as understood in traditional ways, is Raja Ram Mohan Roy. For him, Jesus' mission on earth was not to die a substitutionary death but "to preach and impart divine instructions."[10] Probably, it is difficult and enigmatic to account for Christ's suffering. Ram Mohan Roy interprets the parable of the wicked Husbandmen (Mark 12:1–9) as follows:

> This parable and these passages give countenance to the idea, that God suffered his Prophets, and Jesus, his beloved Son, to be cruelly treated and slain by the Jews for the purpose of taking away every excuse that they might offer for their guilt.[11]

The anti-Semitic bias in this explanation is unfortunate. It may in fact reflect Ram Mohan's uncritical deference to those Christian interpreters, who are inclined to cast the Jews in the role of "Jesus' crucifiers."

Nevertheless, Ram Mohan raises the traditional question of whether Jesus suffered death and pain in his divine nature or human nature? For him, on the one hand, the divine cannot suffer. On the other hand, if Jesus suffered in his human nature it has grave moral problems. Whereas on the notion of an atonement for the offenses of others, Ram Mohan says,

> ... it seems totally inconsistent with the justice ascribed to God, and even at variance with those principles of equity required of men; for it would be a piece of gross inequity to afflict one innocent being, who had all the human feelings, and who had never transgressed the will of God, with the death of the cross, for the crimes committed by others, especially when he declares such great aversion to it.[12]

---

9. Vivekananda, *Collected Works*, vol. 6, 98–99.
10. Nag and Burman, *The English Works*, 31.
11. Nag and Burman, *The English Works*, 33.
12. Nag and Burman, *The English Works*, 33.

We could possibly offer some traditional solutions to the problems which Ram Mohan raises. Nevertheless, our intention in this chapter is only to point out that atonement theology still remains problematic for Visistadvaitic Hindus amongst others.

Other notable Hindus who have rejected the atonement concept, the details of which we will not note here, are Sri Ramakrishna, Sri Aurobindo and Sri Radhakrishnan. We will examine some of the criticisms focused on atonement theology later in this book. Here, it is worth noting that even Indian Christian theologians find it difficult to accept the traditional understandings of the theology of the atonement. Indian Christian theologians criticize the view of the work of Christ as propitiation to satisfy an angry God and refuse to accept the work of Christ as reconciliation between God and human beings achieved through sacrifice.[13] The common questions, amongst many others, raised by the theologians in India are: *Why does God need an innocent's blood for forgiveness?* and *Is God not more powerful than evil?*

Generally, the problem which atonement theology faces in many other cultures is not merely one of communication but also of its inherent inadequacy to explain it logically.

As mentioned in the preface, I had the privilege of attending a fully-fledged course on the theology of the atonement at Princeton Theological Seminary, and I acknowledge that the course has influenced my thoughts on atonement theology. I was taught that the three basic motifs in New Testament teaching on the atonement are reconciliation, redemption, and propitiation/expiation. The course included the doctrine of the atonement as espoused in the early church and in the Middle Ages analyzing pre-Irenaean positions, Irenaeus' recapitulation theory, Athanasius and divinization, Gregory of Nyssa's dramatic view, Anselm's satisfaction theory, Peter Abelard's Moral Influence theory, Thomas Aquinas' Modified Anselmianism, and the Penal Substitution theory. Furthermore, the atonement in the reformation period and in modern theology were discussed in detail. Martin Luther's theology of the cross, John Calvin's threefold office of Christ, Hegel's reconciliation of the finite and the infinite, Schleiermacher's "Person-Forming" theory of redemption, Gustav Aulen's reaction to nineteenth century historiography, Dorothee Solle's Principle of Representation, D. M. Baillie's Evangelical liberalism, and the insights of yet other theologians (like Karl Barth, Dillistone, Pannenberg and Moltmann) on the atonement were all discussed. Having been given a thorough exposure to the theology of the atonement, we were asked to critically evaluate the various works on it.

---

13. For example, see Devasahayam and Sundarisunam, *Rethinking Christianity*, 57.

This is when I found that there had been no in-depth attempt to construct a theology of the atonement using other religious traditions. The sophisticated and well-designed course on the atonement, which was taught, supposed that the existing theologies of the atonement addressed the people of other religious traditions equally well. However, finding the truth to be just the opposite was stimulating and challenging. This book is an attempt to bridge that gap in theology.

Finally, why does atonement theology remain problematical in an Indian Christian-Hindu context? The simple answer is, as we will see in the next chapter, the Visistadvaitic Hindu notions of "sin" and "salvation" imply a different logic. Hence, the atonement theology fails to address significant concerns in that context. In this book, we will attempt to construct a fresh model of atonement that would be more readily understandable and applicable to the Vivistadvaitic Hindu context. Interestingly, this attempt will also help Christians in the West and worldwide to perceive the atonement in a different way and draw out fresh dimensions. We will call the fresh model of the atonement, which we will outline in chapter 4, as the *atonement creating unions*.

The Problem of Alienation Which the Theology of the Atonement Can Address

Indubitably, alienation in its manifold dimensions is one of the crucial problems, if not the central problem of our world. The word, alienation, is often used to describe social estrangement. Vince says that the vast disorientation caused by World War II and the writings of Weber, Kierkegaard, Tillich and Marx have a bearing on the extensive use of the word, alienation in contemporary society.[14] In general terms, alienation is treated as undesirable because it is the experience of being away from home and living as a stranger in the society.

Alienation is the immense quandary that has affected humanity throughout history. Hegel, in particular, dealt with the concept of alienation at length. He, in fact, sees a positive dimension to our minds being in a state of alienation with itself. For him, alienation stimulates the creative ardour of the mind; it is alienation that makes civilization.[15] However, it was Marx and Engels who were amongst the first to provide a comprehensive approach to alienation as a problem. Though they regarded the dynamics of self-alienation as inevitable and necessary in terms of growth from childhood

---

14. Vince, "Alienation," 15.
15. Hegel, *The Phenomenology of Mind*, 509–10.

to adulthood, they thought that the negative side of alienation during adulthood should not be overlooked. They held that alienation is self-denying and self-contradictory.[16] In Marx's early writings, alienation (*entfremdung* or *entäusserung* in German) refers to the separation of things that naturally belong together, or to antagonism between things that are properly in harmony. In fact, Marx bases his theory of alienation on economic disparity. For him, the evidence of alienation is the misery and poverty that abounds in this world of potential abundance. It is likely that this sense of alienation became a dominant theme after Marx.

However, although alienation can help in understanding the dynamics of the development of an individual against others, the work of Christ does not deal with the growth of the individual at a cost that is detrimental to others, but overcoming it has to do with collective growth. In this context, alienation, no doubt, needs to be viewed as a hurdle on the path of harmonious growth, mutuality, and development. We need to assert that alienation is a crucial problem because 1) it is against our nature, 2) it is against peace and harmony, 3) it denies growing together, 4) it is a product of a fall from unity, 5) it is morally evil, 6) it is against union, and 7) it denies the self.

In fact, alienation is a problem with a four-fold dimension. There is the divine-human alienation, the human-human alienation, the human-nature alienation, and the one-oneself alienation. This problem, as we shall see in the next chapter, is already well explored by Ramanuja, a noted Vaishnava Hindu theologian.

The Bible affirms that in the beginning God and human beings were in union with one another. Thus in Genesis 2, it is recorded that God walked with Adam and Eve in the Garden of Eden. Conversely, our alienation from the divine is understood as a fallen state which we need to overcome. How does the atonement help in overcoming this alienation? This book will seek to answer this question.

Secondly, there is the human-human alienation. We live in a world of competition and hatred. The alienation, which Marx points out, is human-human alienation and for him, it is largely based on the disparity in economic distribution. However, both Christianity and Visistadvaitic Hinduism desire a human-human union. The question of how the atonement would help in this regard will be explored in this book.

Thirdly, human-nature alienation is evident in our world of growing ecological crisis. Global warming, deforestation, and lack of clean water for many are sad realities of our world. This book will consider how the need for human-nature union could be realized through the atonement.

---

16. Roy and Sarikwal, *Marxian Sociology*, 407–8.

Fourthly, we are aware that sometimes we live in a state of alienation from ourselves. This is often noted as self-alienation. We will call this one-oneself alienation. This book will briefly point out that our model of atonement can address this problem as well.

Scope of the Proposed Atonement Model

We do not aim to be exhaustive in this work, suggesting a final theory of the atonement. No, not at all. This book will identify a direction in which comparative doctrinal theology can be formulated, using the concept of means to salvation,[17] as found in Visistadvaitic Hindu thought and atonement theology in Christian scripture and tradition. Precisely, this book will use the Visistadvaitic Hindu concept of the means to salvation in the construction of an atonement model before going on to formulating the potentialities and problems involved in constructing an atonement model using the Visistadvaitic strand within Hinduism. Within the scope of this book it is impossible to give attention to religious doctrines other than the atonement and religious traditions other than Christianity and Visistadvaitic Hinduism even though there can be interesting and inspiring outcomes.

The first objective of this book is to formulate the concept of means to salvation in Visistadvaitic Hindu thought, with special reference to Ramanuja. This will enable us to understand why the traditional understandings of the atonement are being criticized within that Hindu tradition. The second objective is to outline an atonement model, using the Visistadvaitic Hindu religious system. In chapter 4, we will attempt this. It is our hope that our model of the atonement will be plausible and fruitful in a world of alienation, emphasizing a four-fold union. Moreover, our atonement model will call for a union between different times, between different religious persuasions and between different theological doctrines.

Thirdly, another objective of this book is to contribute to, and promote, the ongoing conversation between the different religious and theological traditions. This book is presented as a literature that will fill part of the gap, in relation to the enormous work necessary, of comparative doctrinal theology with particular reference to the atonement concept. It is also our hope that this work will motivate Christian and other theologians worldwide to engage in conversation with the different religious traditions, using other theological concepts as well.

---

17. Hindus understand salvation in terms of liberation from ignorance. We will return to this subject later.

Background Analysis for the Construction of an *"Atonement Creating Unions"* Model

In this book, we will be dealing with theories or models of the atonement in Christian tradition. Traditional and modern theories of the atonement are more or less constructed in light of a background theme within the New Testament. Here, we shall briefly analyze the New Testament motifs that underlie the construction of various atonement theories in Christian tradition. There are five predominant themes that have provided ground for the construction of the various atonement models. Here, we look at them very briefly.

Five Subject Matters in the New Testament on the Atonement

A casual reading of the New Testament itself will reveal the fact that a number of images and metaphors were used to convey the meaning of Christ's work on the cross. Most images, in addition to explaining the atonement, seek meaning for human life caught up in sin. The different images and metaphors employed in the New Testament, to elucidate the atoning work of Christ, have paved the way to the construction of various models of the atonement in Christian tradition and modern theology. We will analyze the inadequacy of traditional theories and selected modern theories of the atonement in the Visistadvaitic Hindu contexts in chapter 3, and we will outline our comparative doctrinal theology of the atonement in chapter 4. Our aim in this chapter is only to provide a brief background analysis of the different New Testament subject matters that led to the formulation of the various atonement models.

Five New Testament themes that play enormous roles in the creation of various atonement theories are: 1) the wrath of God, 2) reconciliation, 3) redemption, 4) propitiation/expiation (placed in legal setting), and 5) atoning sacrifice.

1) The Wrath of God

Atonement theories like the penal substitution and the juridical are based on the notion of the wrath of God. The wrath of God is understood as being active in history as well as being an active part in eschatology. Wrath, of course, cannot be understood as an attribute of God, but God's reaction to human sin manifested in his wrath.

In the Old Testament we read about God building nations as well as tearing them apart when they turn to evil ways. We see his anger arising against injustices. For example, in Jeremiah 5 we read,

> For scoundrels are found among my people; they take over the goods of others. Like fowlers they set a trap; they catch human beings. Like a cage full of birds, their houses are full of treachery; therefore they have become great and rich, they have grown fat and sleek. They know no limits in deeds of wickedness; they do not judge with justice the cause of the orphan, to make it prosper, and they do not defend the rights of the needy. Shall I not punish them for these things? says the Lord, and shall I not bring retribution on a nation such as this?[18]

In the New Testament, we see Jesus getting angry against evil forces and people who go against God. For instance, Mark 3:5 says that Jesus got angry due to the multitudes that were hard-hearted, and John 11:33 and 38 tell us that he was angry with those who did not believe that he was the resurrection and the life. In fact, the nature of God's wrath was found in Jesus' wrath because it stood in close relation with his love, mercy, and compassion for people. Significantly, Jesus once said, "Do not fear those who kill the body but cannot kill the soul; rather fear him who can destroy both soul and body in hell."[19]

Paul says, "For the wrath of God is revealed from heaven against all ungodliness and wickedness of those who by their wickedness suppress the truth."[20] According to Dodd, Paul is of the view that everyone has sinned, and in Romans 6:23, he says that sin brings forth more sin and they inevitably lead to spiritual catastrophe.[21] We ask God to let us free, as it happened at the Garden of Eden, and when God gives us that freedom, that itself is our punishment. God's wrath can also be expressed in the form of abandoning us to the natural consequences of our sinfulness.

For Karl Barth, the infinite weight of the wrath of God is only revealed in its full depth, and in a positive way, on the cross. In the light of the cross all other catastrophes that have come upon humanity are just shades of the wrath of God, not the real wrath itself.[22] Thus it is clear that the Bible speaks of God's wrath in history and it may not be wrong to understand that the

---

18. Jer 5:26–29, NRSV.
19. Matt 10:28, NRSV. Also, see Luke 12:5.
20. Rom 1:18, NRSV
21. Dodd, *Epistle of Paul*, 118. Also, see Eph 2:3 and 5:6, NRSV.
22. Barth, *Church Dogmatics*, Vol. II, 394–96.

cross is the ultimate revelation of God's wrath. Now we turn to see the eschatological dimension of God's wrath.

Jesus over and again insists on the coming of the judgment day and the coming of his kingdom. He says that the sheep and the goats will be divided on that day.[23] He also portrays this idea in other parables. For example, he says, "The Son of Man will send his angels, and they will collect out of his kingdom all causes of sin and all evil-doers, and they will throw them into the furnace of fire, where there will be weeping and gnashing of teeth."[24]

Similarly, he says,

> Then you will begin to say, 'We ate and drank with you, and you taught in our streets.' But he will say, 'I do not know where you come from; go away from me, all you evildoers!' There will be weeping and gnashing of teeth when you see Abraham and Isaac and Jacob and all the prophets in the kingdom of God, and you yourselves thrown out.[25]

This teaching is consistent throughout the gospels. Moreover, the book of Revelation says that the Lamb who was slain will be the wrathful Judge.[26] This means that Jesus himself will be the judge on the day of judgment.

Paul too talks about the eschatological wrath of God, but finds hope in the death and resurrection of Jesus. For Paul, the entire humanity had sinned and had fallen short of the glory of God.[27] He also sees that human condition itself as enmity to God[28] and as slavery to sin.[29] Commenting on Paul, Howard Marshall says that God "does not ignore sin."[30] However, Paul is hopeful that although the wages of sin is death, the free gift of God is eternal life in Jesus.[31] He maintains this idea throughout his writing. Thus, the Bible indisputably emphasizes the theme of wrath of God. We will not go beyond this here, and our aim is only to very briefly point out that this is a theme on which atonement theories have been built. We will analyze the theories later in this book. Here, it is worth mentioning that the wrath of God is ultimately not as negative a theme as it may sound. More positively,

---

23. Matt 25:31–46, NRSV.
24. Matt 13:41–42, NRSV.
25. Luke 13:26–28, NRSV.
26. Rev 19:11, NRSV.
27. Rom 3:23, NRSV.
28. Rom 5:1, NRSV.
29. Rom 6:17–19, NRSV.
30. Marshall, Travis, and Paul, *Exploring the New Testament*, 111.
31. Rom 6:23, NRSV.

it gives us the confidence to know that God is *moved* by what happens to humanity and it also calls people to turn toward him.

2) Reconciliation

The second theme we need to look at is reconciliation. C. H. Dodd says that reconciliation is "the initial act of a process; but it carries with it the assurance that the process will be completed."[32] The word reconciliation is derived from the Greek word, *katallasso*, which is a verb. With a variant of spelling, *katallage* is the noun in the Greek language.[33] Other related Greek words are *apollasso*, meaning "to forgive," "to set free," "to release," or "to send away," and *apokatallasso* meaning "to reconcile."[34] Using the terms *katallasso* and *katallage*, Paul explains his understanding of the atonement in Romans 5:10–11 and 2 Corinthians 5:18–21.[35] Paul writes, "For if while we were enemies, we were reconciled to God through the death of His Son, much more surely, having been reconciled, will we be saved by His life. But more than that, we even boast in God through our Lord Jesus Christ, through whom we have now received reconciliation."[36]

In another instance, Paul says,

> All this is from God, who reconciled us to himself through Christ, and has given us the ministry of reconciliation; that is, in Christ God was reconciling the world to himself, not counting their trespasses against them, and entrusting the message of reconciliation to us. So we are ambassadors for Christ, since God is making his appeal through us; we entreat you on behalf of Christ, be reconciled to God. For our sake he made him to be sin who knew no sin, so that in him we might become the righteousness of God.[37]

In the words of Marshall, "It is not human estimates that matter, for believers live in a new creation, stemming from the reconciling act of God."[38] Firstly, we need to be clear that Paul holds that the subject of reconciliation is God and not humanity. Precisely God has done the atoning

---

32. Dodd, *Epistle of Paul*, 98.
33. Aland, et al., *The Greek New Testament*, 94.
34. Aland, et al., *The Greek New Testament*, 21–22.
35. Morris, *Apostolic Preaching*, 214.
36. Rom 5:10–11, NRSV.
37. 2 Cor 5:18–21, NRSV.
38. Marshall, Travis, and Paul, *Exploring the New Testament*, 98.

work in Christ to reconcile us to himself even while we were sinners.[39] The reconciling work of Christ goes before all that humans can do. In fact, God not only initiates it but also completes it. However, humanity is expected to receive it.

Secondly, Paul elucidates how the atonement achieves reconciliation. For him, reconciliation is closely related to justification.[40] In 2 Corinthians 5:19, he says that in Christ, God was reconciling the world to himself, not counting their trespasses against them. The guilt caused by humanity's sins is not counted against them. Howard Marshall says, "It is not human estimates that matter, for believers live in a new creation, stemming from the reconciling act of God."[41] The Greek word, *logizomai,* is commonly translated as "counted" or "calculated."[42] However, it also has the meanings of imputed (as in the Latin Vulgate) and reckoned (as found in some English translations). The thought that underlies in Paul's mind is that something is given to our benefit instead of what we really deserve. On the one hand, sin and its consequences are not charged to us. On the other hand, as Paul says in 2 Corinthians 5:21, "He made Him who knew no sin to be sin on our behalf that we might become the righteousness of God in Him." In theological terms, this is called the imputation of Christ's righteousness to us.[43] For Paul, Christ's righteousness is credited to us and thus we are made to be righteous in Christ. A great exchange or transfer has occurred. Christ is made a sin offering[44] and in Christ's sacrificial death, God was reconciling humanity unto himself. Thus, the atonement is the ground of human justification. Humanity is set free from sins and is given the righteousness of Christ.

Thirdly, humanity has made themselves as enemies of God and not the other way around.[45] According to Paul, in Christ, our enmity with God is removed and peace prevails in the place of enmity.[46] C. H. Dodd writes, "This standing, or status, which is the effect of justification, is one of peace with God, in place of the state of hostility between Him and us in which our

---

39. Dunn, *The Cambridge Companion to St Paul*, 181.
40. Dunn, *The Cambridge Companion to St Paul*.
41. Marshall, Travis and Paul, *Exploring the New Testament*, 98.
42. The dictionary gives further meanings. See, Aland, et al., *The Greek New Testament*, 108.
43. Aland, et al., *The Greek New Testament*, 281.
44. Rom 8:3, NRSV.
45. Morris, *Apostolic Preaching*, 220.
46. Rom 5:1, NRSV.

sin had placed us."[47] Significantly, the object of reconciliation is not just a few people, but the entire human race.

Fourthly, as Leon Morris states, Paul holds that humanity has a responsibility even though reconciliation has been fully achieved in the atoning work of Christ.[48] Although reconciliation is an accomplished phenomenon and nothing needs to be added to it, if it is not inherited, we go on to live as those who are enemies of God. We continue to live as those who do not believe that God has reconciled us to him through the cross of Christ. The problem with a performance-based understanding of reconciliation is that it creates the false impression that if we are good, then we belong to God. If we think along these lines, we would treat the reconciliation achieved on the cross as though it is not fully adequate. Hence, Paul is careful in saying that along with the unbeliever, the believer should also be reconciled to God.

Finally, in relation to the theme of reconciliation, Paul also says that Christ set aside the power of the law to accuse us, having made peace with God.[49] The implication that Paul draws from this is that there is no Jew or Greek in Christ (Gal 3:28). Reconciliation with God carries with it reconciliation and equality amongst humanity. As we will see later, for Paul, peace with nature is also accomplished through Christ's atoning work on the cross.

The theme of reconciliation is at the root of some atonement models in Christian tradition and modern theology either directly or indirectly. This will become apparent in chapter 3. Of course, there cannot be a model of the atonement which doesn't revolve on the theme of reconciliation. The next theme we will highlight is redemption.

3) Redemption

What is redemption? Tom Wright says, "Redemption is . . . neither a status that Christians possess nor an element of the life that they live, but the accomplishment of God on their behalf, the great new Exod through which they have been set free from the slavery of sin."[50] It should be affirmed that the Old Testament idea of redemption leads directly into the New Testament. The Greek word, *lutron,* is translated as redemption or release.[51] In

---

47. Dodd, *Epistle of Paul*, 94.
48. Morris, *Apostolic Preaching*, 233.
49. Morris, *Apostolic Preaching*, 237–39.
50. Wright, *Justification*, 133.
51. Aland, et al., *The Greek New Testament*, 109.

the Septuagint, the *lutron* group is used to translate the Hebrew words, *goel, padah,* and *kopher.*[52]

Significantly, all these words are used to denote buying back by the payment of a price. The word, *goel,* is used within the context of family law. If a price is paid by someone to preserve a family's honor, *goel* would be the word used. *Goel* (or *ga'al* in the verb form) also has a general sense of vindication. It was a practice that if someone were killed unjustly, a member of that family might kill the murderer. The debt was taken from the offender in this way.[53] The Old Testament talks of buying a slave who has fallen into debt[54] and buying a family property which was lost on account of accumulated debts.[55] In fact, the Old Testament understanding also denotes the price paid in compensation for a forfeited life. The Septuagint either uses *goel* or one other *lutron* group of words to translate a debt paid, especially when a price is paid.

The word, *padah,* is generally used in the context of commercial transactions and not in a family context.[56] In this case, anyone could pay the price and hence an act of graciousness would be involved in the payment. Nevertheless, both *goel* and *padah* denote the thought of deliverance and buying back, either through some act of labor or a payment of price.

Now, the word, *kopher. Kopher* is used in instances when law demands a person's life and when the life can still be "saved" by paying a particular price.[57] The ransom is paid in the place of a person's life and thus the idea of substitution is prevalent. The *kopher* is accepted in place of a life that otherwise would have been lost.

Paul's idea of redemption is this. He writes, "Christ redeemed us from the curse of the Law, by becoming a curse for us."[58] Paul writes about the curse of the law as well. In his words,

---

52. Morris, *Apostolic Preaching*, 19.

53. Gemeren says that Israelite law expects the close blood relatives to redeem their relatives when they are sold or in trouble. The word *goel* is used in this situation. In Exod 6:6 and Isa 40–66, YHWH is seen as divine *goel* who helps those who have fallen into need. Van Gemeren, et al., *Dictionary of Old Testament Theology*, 790–792.

54. Deut 19:11–13, Lev 25:48, and Num 35:21 are a few examples of this usage.

55. Ruth 4:4–6.

56. Morris, *Apostolic Preaching*, 22.

57. Morris, *Apostolic Preaching*, 25. For example, the word *kopher* plays an important role in Exod 21:28. It was the practice that if an ox has been in the habit of goring people and if the owner is already being warned and he did not do anything about it, and the ox continued to gore people, the owner's life can be forfeited. But he can still buy back his life by paying a ransom. In this instance, the word used will be *kopher*.

58. Gal 3:13, NRSV.

> For all who rely on the works of the Law are under a curse, for it is written, 'Cursed is everyone who does not observe and obey all the things written in the book of the Law.' Now it is evident that no one is justified before God by the law. . .[59]

None of us in practice manage to keep the whole law, and hence, to seek redemption through the law is a curse since it results in failure. For Paul, Christ took the curse upon himself and redeemed us from the curse of the law. Obviously, it is the idea of substitution that dominates here. As Veeramoni says, "A judge cannot pardon offenses because he is subject to the will of another. But God can pardon because he is the judge and arbitrator of his own law."[60] Christ died in our place but, in fact, it is we who are to be put to death for not keeping the law. Through his death on the cross, Christ redeemed us from sin, the guilt which accrues from it and from the death which is the effect of sin. Interestingly, Sanders points out that it is not clear whether the Jews expected national redemption or individual redemption.[61]

However, in his letter to Colossians, Paul develops a parallel thought. Interpreting Paul, Tom Wright says, "He (Jesus) has become 'redemption' for us; that is , in him God has accomplished the great new Exodus, the crossing of the Rea Sea of death, leaving behind the hordes of Pharoah who had enslaved God's people, so that those who are 'in Christ' are now the people already rescued from that slavery."[62] In Colossians 2:13–14, we read,

> And when you were dead in trespasses and the uncircumcision of your flesh, God made you alive together with Him, when he forgave us all our trespasses, erasing the record that stood against us with its legal demands. He set this aside, nailing it to the cross.[63]

In the sayings of Jesus the word, *lutron,* is found in Matthew 20:28 and Mark 10:45.[64] In both instances the wording is identical. Jesus says, "The Son of Man did not come to be served but to serve, and to give His life a ransom for many." Referring to this passage, David Hill, a New Testament scholar writes,

---

59. Gal 3:10–11, NRSV.
60. Veeramoni, "Redemption in Paul's Epistles," 56.
61. Sanders, *The Historical Figure*, 34.
62. Wright, *Justification*, 135.
63. Another possible parallel to Paul's words in Gal 3:13 is 2 Cor 5:21, where Paul says, "He made Him who knew no sin to be sin on our behalf, which we might become the righteousness of God in Him."
64. Morris, *Apostolic Preaching*, 29.

> The genuineness of the saying has been much discussed ... but no argument has yet been advanced which is so strong as to make it impossible for us to believe that Jesus could have spoken of his death in the kind of terms reproduced here—of vicarious and representative suffering for his people, in terms of the old Jewish martyr theology.[65]

Obviously, Hill writes this in the context of a debate on the authenticity of this saying by Jesus. But the New Testament definitely has other passages too which use the word, *lutron*. For instance, in Titus 2:14 and 1 Peter 1:18–19, the word *lutron* is used. First Peter 1:18–19 makes clear the idea of the price of redemption: "the precious blood, as of a lamb without blemish and without spot, even the blood of Christ." Commenting on 1 Peter 1:18, Stephen Travis says, "the work of Christ in past, present and future reverses the Christian's past life of ignorance and futility, provides a secure hope in their present suffering and brings the promise of future glory."[66]

Another word with the idea of redemption or release, used in the New Testament, is *apolutrosis*.[67] Although this word is used ten times in the entire New Testament, the LXX uses this word only once. Hence, any thought of making the Old Testament usage determinative is hard for consistency. In three occasions where this word is used, the simple idea of deliverance is ruled out because a price is paid.[68] In Ephesians 1:14 and Colossians 1:14, where this word is used a price being paid is definitely implied. In Luke 21:28, Romans 8:23, and Ephesians 4:30, this word is used but no attention is given to how redemption becomes possible because they are directed toward teaching the eschatological redemption that is forthcoming. The other places where *apolutrosis* is used are 1 Corinthians 1:30 and Hebrews 11:35. In these passages, too, the idea of a price being paid is not excluded.[69]

To conclude, we need to note that in most places the idea of a price being paid is prevalent. It is stated directly, or suggested indirectly, and the price is the shedding of blood by Christ on the cross. We also need to be clear that the ransom idea is used not only for explaining the atoning work of Christ, but also the liberating aspect of it. The idea of redemption employed has a wider aspect and not just redemption from guilt or sin. Redemption is also

---

65. Hill, *The Gospel of Matthew*, 289.
66. Marshall, Travis, and Paul, *Exploring the New Testament*, 266.
67. Aland, et.al., *The Greek New Testament*, 22.
68. Rom 3:24, Eph 1:17, and Heb 9:15. A detailed discussion on the use of the word *apolutrosis* can be found in Morris, *Apostolic Preaching*, 40–42.
69. Morris gives details of other forms of *lutron* being used. However, we will not be able to go into details within the scope of this chapter. See Morris, *Apostolic Preaching*, 29–38.

from all sin's consequences. Finally, as we noted, the person to whom the ransom is paid is really not very clear. This has been a problem for scholars for many centuries now. Preachers in churches too struggle to come up with a rational solution to this dilemma. As we will later see, many theologians who are in favor of the classical theory, particularly Gustaf Aulen, imply that ransom is paid to the devil. But there are also theologians who support the view that ransom is paid to God himself.

4) Propitiation/Expiation

The idea of propitiation/expiation is another dominant theme in the New Testament, in relation to the atonement. We begin by saying that there is an ongoing discussion on the accurate translation of Romans 3:25.[70] The Greek word, *hilasterion*, used in this verse, is translated as propitiation in traditional translations (e.g., KJV). However, in the RSV, it is translated as expiation, and in the NRSV, it is translated as atonement.

C. H. Dodd observes that the word, *hislasterion*, is derived from the verb *hilaskomai* or *exhilaskomai*, which in pagan writing has two meanings.[71] In ancient Greek tradition, the enmity of gods can be easily aroused, but they can also be easily purchased by an appropriate gift. It is simply to say that gods can be bribed. This word is also used to denote the function of expiation—i.e. in Dodd's words, "to perform an act (such as the payment of a fine or the offering of a sacrifice) by which guilt is annulled."[72]

According to Dodd, it is the second meaning that is more apt in the New Testament writings. The meaning of the word, *hilasterion*, in Romans 3:25, according to Dodd, is a means by which guilt is annulled and hence the appropriate translation should be "expiation" and not "propitiation." Furthermore, Dodd's point is that if we use the word "propitiation," then God would be the object and not the subject. For him, God is the subject and hence the apt translation should be "expiation." In his words, "Our versions in such cases use the phrase 'to make propitiation'; but the more proper translation would be 'to make expiation.' This meaning holds good wherever the subject of the verb is a man."[73] Thus it is clear that the change in translation that occurred in the RSV, in comparison with older translations, is due to the influence of Dodd. However, if atonement should be understood in a more in-depth sense, God should be seen as both object and subject.

70. Morris, *Apostolic Preaching*, 159.
71. Dodd, *Epistle of Paul*, 47.
72. Dodd, *Epistle of Paul*, 54.
73. Dodd, *Epistle of Paul*, 78.

C. K. Barrett, the New Testament scholar, translates the word *hilasterion* as expiation but in his view, expiation has the effect of propitiation as well.[74] He writes, "It would be wrong to neglect the fact that expiation has, as it were, the effect of propitiation: the sin that might have excited God's wrath is expiated and therefore no longer does so."[75] Although Barrett's words give a clear direction for doctrinal theology the word *hilasterion* still has a problem because it is only the problem of sin that is being solved. But the penalty for our previous sins still exists. Paul is probably trying to show God as just even when he overlooks the sins of our past and the penalty for them. In fact, when the anger of God prevails, we need to say that propitiation might be the right translation.

Nevertheless, *hilasmos* is a word closely related to *hilasterion*,[76] and this word is used in First John 2:1–2.

> *My little children, I am writing these things to you so that you may not sin. But if anyone does sin, we have an advocate with the Father, Jesus Christ the righteous; and He is the hilasmos for our sins; and not for ours only but also for the sins of the whole world.*[77]

The word, *hilasmos* is translated as both propitiation and expiation in different translations. But another notable fact is the concept of "advocate with the Father."

This concept makes it apparent that we are condemned before God's Law. Significantly, it is the blood of Christ[78] that provides the ground of Christ's advocacy for us. Here, propitiation should be the normal translation because the object is God. It may be pointed out that the idea of propitiation can be liberated from the pagan ideology, as Dodd had understood, if God is seen as both the subject and object of the atoning work. God will not do anything that is inconsistent with his own moral laws.

Prior to ending the problem with the translation of the word *hilasterion*, we will briefly portray how it is done by Luther. The word *hilasterion* is often used in the place of the Hebrew word *kapporeth*—the lid on the ark of the covenant upon which the blood of the sacrifice was sprinkled on the Day of Atonement.[79] Following William Tyndale's translation in 1536, this

---

74. We can argue that this idea has the support of the book of Hebrews too. Jesus is seen as the High Priest who is the Son of God (and thereby God himself) and he offers himself to God the Father.

75. Barrett, *The Epistle to the Romans*, 74.

76. Morris, *Apostolic Preaching*, 159.

77. 1 John 2:1–2, NRSV.

78. 1 John 1:7.

79. Exod 25:17–20.

term has sometimes been translated as "mercy seat." This is what Luther adopts in translating Romans 3:25—whom God set forth to be mercy-seat through faith in his blood. If it is translated this way it would be similar to saying, " . . . we have confidence to enter the sanctuary by the blood of Jesus, by the new and living way that he opened for us through the curtain."[80] As we will see later, Luther's view on the atonement, on which German Lutherans have depended for centuries, is essentially developed on the basis of this translation.

However, one problem with this translation is the reduction of the juridical setting which Paul constructs in Romans 3. The atonement is given as a solution to a legal problem and it should satisfy God's just wrath. It is in this context that the "mercy-seat" translation becomes problematic.

Thus, it may be proper to understand that whilst using *hilasterion* in Romans 3, Paul must have had the idea of propitiation and expiation together, as C. K. Barrett puts it. Before we end this section, we need to also mention that the New Testament has other ways to speak of the atoning work of Christ as the basis of our salvation. The final theme with which we will deal here briefly is the language of sacrifice.

5) Atoning Sacrifice

Within the scope of this section it is impossible to do full justice to this interesting theme. In fact, there are scholars who have written an entire book on this theme alone. Here, we will only look at some passages of the New Testament which bear this theme and had a role in the formulation of an atonement theory in the tradition. Although the notion of sacrifice faded away in the church as centuries passed by, it has its origin and place in a cultic context.[81] According to Mike Highton, "Sacrifices could mean many things in the ancient Jewish and Roman worlds, but the most relevant idea seems to be of sacrifice as a response to impurity, dishonor and transgression."[82] Similarly, Sanders points out, "The readers of the gospels knew that animals were sacrificed at festivals, and they also knew that

---

80. Heb 10:19–20, NRSV.

81. Although Morris says, "It is not easy to find out exactly how the sacrifices were thought to make atonement . . .," he is of the view that the cultic context is important here. The technical Hebrew word used here is *kipper*. See, Morris, *Apostolic Preaching*, 167.

82. Higton, *Christian Doctrine*, 276.

festivals and sacrifice involved purification."[83] This gives us a basic idea of what sacrifice meant.

However, unlike the passages which we came across in the previous sections that presumed a "judicial" setting, these passages speak of the atonement in a quite different way. The author of the book of Hebrews provides one such case of understanding the atonement in an explicitly cultic setting. The book of Hebrews establishes the relationship of Jesus' priestly ministry to the priesthood writings of the Old Testament. Elliott says, "Aaron, at best a shadowy figure even in Old Testament, is only mentioned in New Testament here, 7:11 and in 9:4."[84] Hebrews 5:10 says that Jesus is a priest according to the order of Melchizadek. Hebrews 7:1–3 explains this:

> This King Melchizedek of Salem, priest of the Most High God, met Abraham as he was returning from defeating the kings and blessed him. . . . His name, in the first place means 'king of righteousness'; next he is also king of Salem, that is, 'king of peace.' Without father, without mother, without genealogy, having neither beginning of days nor end of life, but resembling the Son of God, he remains a priest forever.[85]

Although there are no precise details of whoever or whatever Melchizedek may have been, the author of Hebrews, by placing Jesus in this line, wants to say that Jesus' priesthood too is without beginning and without end. Perhaps the author of Hebrews wants to show that the priesthood of Christ supersedes the Levitical priesthood.[86] Stephen Travis writes, "Remember that Melchizedek is not one of the standard levitical high priests; the author uses this mysterious figure . . . as a picture of the superior kind of priesthood embodied in Jesus."[87] Further in Hebrews 7:22 and 8:6, we read that, unlike the other high priests who had to offer a sacrifice for themselves before being qualified to offer sacrifices on behalf of others before God in the holy of holies, Jesus did not have to offer sacrifice for himself because he is sinless. The lamb without spot or blemish which Jesus offers is none other than he himself. Unlike the way it happened according to tradition, the priest and the victim are one and the same. The sacrifice is also given once and for all. The author also goes on to speak of the effect of Jesus' sacrifice.

---

83. Sanders, *The Historical Figure*, 251. However, Sanders is keen to say that it is not generally considered that sacrificial thinking is at the heart of Paul's thought. See Sanders, *Paul*, 93.

84. Elliott, *Hebrews*, 40.

85. Hebrews 7:1–3, NRSV.

86. Kee and Young, *The Living World of New Testament*, 425.

87. Marshall, Travis, and Paul, *Exploring the New Testament*, 238.

> Therefore, my friends, since we have confidence to enter the sanctuary by the blood of Jesus, by the new and living way that he opened for us through the curtain (that is, through his flesh), and since we have a great priest over the house of God, let us approach with a true heart in full assurance of faith, with our hearts sprinkled clean from an evil conscience and our bodies washed with pure water.[88]

Unlike the situation in Paul's writing in Romans 1:3, there is no judicial setting that takes over here. One could argue that Christ offering himself as a sacrifice is clearly to deliver us from the judgment to come. But the point is that the author does not put the offering of Jesus himself with the setting of a courtroom in mind. Christ's sacrifice is also unique in the sense that it cannot and need not be repeated.

The Greek word, used by the author of Hebrews to denote the atonement is *hilaskethai* (a verb related to *hilaskomai*—to expiate or propitiate—that we have already seen). This is translated as follows: "Therefore he had to become like his brothers and sisters in every respect, so that he might be a merciful and faithful high priest in the service of God, to make a sacrifice of atonement for the sins of the people."[89] Thus, obviously the context is not judicial but cultic. Morris says that the words, *hilaskomai* and *hilaskethai* "retain the idea of putting away the divine anger, since it means that in the cult itself there is the thought of ransom being paid."[90]

Precisely, in Hebrews 2:17, the word *hilaskethai* is used to reveal the idea of removal of sins. Commenting on Hebrews 2, Stephen Travis emphasizes the "fully human" nature of Jesus in his act of removal of sins.[91] C. K. Barrett's explanation for Romans 3:25 is suitable here as well. We have an expiation which has the effect of being propitiation. Hence, the conclusion could be the same with or without a judicial setting with reference to Romans 3 and Hebrews 2. Karl Barth writes,

> When we spoke of Jesus Christ as Judge and judged, and of His judgment and justice, we were adopting a definite standpoint and terminology as the framework within which to present our view of the pro nobis. In order to speak with dogmatic clarity and distinctness we had to decide on a framework of this kind.[92]

---

88. Heb 10:19–22, NRSV.
89. Heb 2:17, NRSV.
90. Morris, *Apostolic Preaching*, 174.
91. Marshall, Travis, and Paul, *Exploring the New Testament*, 238.
92. Barth, *Church Dogmatics*, 273.

According to Karl Barth, although the New Testament has many starting points to enable one to look at the atonement, the most significant one is cultic. In his words,

> What we have tried to say in another way, if it is said correctly, cannot be anything other than that which could and can be said in the images and categories of cultic language. It would therefore bode ill for our results if we could not recognize them in the mirror of this other language which was so important to the men of the NT to think and speak.[93]

The cultic setting had led later theologians to formulate the sacrificial theory against the judicial theory. We will outline these theories later in this book. In sum, in the light of this very brief background analysis of New Testament themes that provide the major grounds for the construction of atonement models, we discern that theologians have understood the atonement in various ways. This will become apparent in chapter 3.

"Union": A Neglected Theme in the Construction of Atonement Theology

The New Testament, however, has another theme of "union," both in the gospels and in other writings relating to the atonement. This theme has not been greatly used in understanding the atonement. The word, union, and related words are used in Ephesians 1:10, Colossians 1:17, Romans 6:5, John 17:21, John 15:1, and in many other instances as we will see in chapter 4. In fact, this theme, as we will see later, is much more amenable to the Visistadvaitic Hindu concept of means to salvation. Precisely, the atonement model, which we will outline in this work, will support the need of a fourfold union. Thus our model of the atonement will be based on New Testament teaching and it will be readily applicable and intelligible in the Indian Visistadvaitic Hindu context as well.

Structure of This Book

This book presumes that theology of the atonement needs to be intelligible in every context, and in this work, we attempt to make it intelligible to those who belong to the Visistadvaitic Hindu tradition, in effect taking a

---

93. Barth, *Church Dogmatics*, 275. In chapter 3, whilst we analyze the different atonement theories in an Indian context, we will outline how Barth precisely understands the concept of the atonement.

comparative doctrinal perspective. This is in conformity with a traditional Christian way of thinking because, as we saw, the New Testament writings use many insights from the Graeco-Roman and Jewish religious traditions to express its own meaning and to serve its own purpose. Hence, in a way, our work is going back to the New Testament in attempting to formulate a doctrinal theology with contextual relevance. Thus, methodologically, this book is in the nature of finding a direction toward formulating Christian theology in the Visistadvaitic Hindu context.[94]

It should also be affirmed that we are devising a theology in comparative doctrinal perspective using theology of the atonement as an exemplar. Using the doctrine of atonement, this work will make explicit the connections between Christian and Visistadvaitic Hindu thinking. It is anticipated that this is a creative way forward for pursuing the doctrine of the atonement in a new direction. This line of thought will retain the particularity and historicity of the work of Christ, whilst linking clearly to the universal considerations that are encountered within Visistadvaitic Hinduism, and they, in themselves, could contribute to a new way of seeing the Christian revelation.

It is fitting for us to end this chapter with the structure that we have created to pursue the goal of formulating a model of the atonement in an Indian context, and of highlighting its usefulness. In what follows, we set out the basic structure of what we are attempting to do in this book.

This chapter began by identifying the problem of theology of the atonement in an Indian context. On this topic we pointed out the writings of Mahatma Gandhi, Swami Vivekananda, and Raja Ram Mohan Roy which are fairly typical. Further, the problem of alienation was identified, and we noted that any theology of the atonement needed to address this problem in today's world. Then we moved on to illustrate a background analysis for this work dealing with theology of the atonement. We observed that there are five New Testament motifs that provide the substantive tone of most current atonement models: the wrath of God, reconciliation, redemption, propitiation/expiation, and atoning sacrifice. In this context, we also became aware that the New Testament theme of "union" has been noticeably neglected in the interpretation of the atonement. We also indicated the intention of outlining a "comparative" and inter-religious theory of the atonement in this book.

The next chapter will give the necessary background to the formulation of a new model of the atonement by analyzing the liberating concept of Brahman as construed in the Visistadvaitic Hindu theological tradition.

---

94. Similar work can be done using other religious traditions and other doctrines. For example, Singh tries to seek ways in which the theology of the cross can be used for a Christian-Islam relationship. See, Singh, "Rethinking Jesus," 239–60.

Specifically, the theological/philosophical understanding of Ramanuja, the most renowned of the Vaishnava Hindu theologians, will be described and explored. Ramanuja's perception is that the problem of ignorance is that which brings about the divine-human, human-human, human-nature, and one-oneself alienations. In fact, we need to realize that the world is in union with Brahman like the body is in union with the self. Brahman alone can bestow this knowledge of union and it is this that is the means to salvation. Ramanuja is careful to comprehend that this knowledge bestowed by Brahman is not merely an abstract and theoretical knowledge, but it is an intuitive and practical knowledge which in turn presumes a mastery of the will. It is also interesting to note that the means to salvation, in Ramanuja's thought, has objective as well as subjective dimensions. The objective dimension is Brahman's gracious offering of the knowledge and the subjective dimension is our careful devotion toward the divine and good action. This will be confirmed by an outline of the beliefs of *tengalai* and *vadagalai* Hindus, the two sects that emerged after a split within the followers of Ramanuja. Further, the nature of Brahman's liberating function as ongoing, as transcending religious barriers, and as providing a union between the various theological doctrines within Visistadvaitic Hinduism, will be exploited. This chapter will be constructed in a way that will help us to understand why the existing Christian theories of the atonement in an Indian context are deemed to be inadequate and enable us constructively to formulate a fresh atonement model using the concept of means to salvation provided in Ramanuja's thought.

Chapter 3 will move from a descriptive enumeration of aspects of Brahman's liberating role in Hinduism to interpretive analyses of the inadequacy of theories of the atonement in a Hindu-Christian Indian context. Brahman liberates the soul by providing the knowledge of the necessity of a divine-human union, human-human union, human-nature union, and one's union with oneself. The knowledge provided by Brahman includes the capacity to destroy the selfish will and to be one with the divine will. It is in this context that the Christian atonement theology will be analyzed. Regarding theories of the atonement, one may usefully differentiate the existing theories of the atonement by categorizing them as subjective and objective theories. The Penal Substitutionary and the Representative theories will be dealt with in detail in this chapter. They will be used as representatives of the atonement theories in tradition and in modern theology respectively. However, we will also examine briefly the other traditional theories as well as a few modern theories of the atonement questioning whether any of those could incorporate the concerns raised by the concept of the means to salvation in Ramanuja's Visistadvaitic Hinduism. The inadequacy of existing atonement theories in an Indian context will become evident. It is a fact that none of the existing theories of the atonement revolve around the four-fold union. Moreover, hardly any existing atonement model raises the issues of the universal significance of the atonement, the relevance of Christ's atonement to people of other religious persuasions and the place of atonement theology amongst the different doctrines of the atonement. The need for a fresh model of the atonement will be made evident in the light of the limitations of existing atonement models in an Indian context.

In chapter 4, we will outline a fresh model of the atonement in a comparative doctrinal perspective. The concept of sin will be reinterpreted as consisting of a four-fold alienation, and the concept of salvation will be enumerated in terms of a four-fold union. The atonement will be pictured as creating the intuitive and practical knowledge of the need of divine-human union, human-human union, human-nature union, and one's union with oneself. On the cross, Christ creates the knowledge of being one with the will of the divine even in suffering, death, and beyond. The importance of suffering in the atoning work of Christ will be seen as the ground for understanding reality in its fullness. Insights from Simone Weil and Karl Popper will be used at this point. We will call this understanding of the atonement as the *atonement creating unions*. In the light of Brahman's liberating concept, our model of the atonement will also interpret the atonement as having an ongoing implication and transcending history/chronology. Then we will move on to see that the atonement transcends religious barriers and provides a ground for theological interpretation of the various Christian doctrines. However, our model of the atonement is likely to present some problems and pitfalls. But we will address them with theological astuteness in the next chapter.

In chapter 5, we will delineate the potentialities and problems of our constructed comparative model of the atonement with contextual relevance. This chapter will be broadly divided into two sections. The first section will discuss contextual and interpretative concerns under the subtitles, metaphysics, intercontextual concerns, economics and politics, ecology, psychology, and belief and understanding. The second section will consider theological concerns with reference to the nature of union, particularity and universality, pluralism and unity, tradition and reformation, and finally we will briefly analyze the compatibility of our fresh atonement model with the central biblical concepts of the Torah and the new covenant. This, eventually, will lead into illustrating the nature and usefulness of our atonement model in the next chapter.

The concluding chapter will deal with the nature and use of the outlined model of the atonement. We will make it clear that our model of the atonement is presented as a contribution to filling a gap in the literature of comparative and inter-religious doctrinal theology, with theology of the atonement at its core. Precisely, our work evolves in a comparative study between Christianity and Visistadvaitic Hinduism with particular relevance to the Hindu-Christian Indian context. As Berkey and Edwards claim, "Christologies, be they ancient or modern, are evoked first and always by dialog."[95] Different features and understandings of Christ's atonement will continue to emerge in dialog, through theologians present and future, keeping the theology of the atonement fruitful and always fresh. Now, we move on to analyze the Visistadvaitic Hindu conception of the means to salvation with special reference to Ramanuja.

---

95. Berkey and Edwards, *Christology*, 24–25.

2

Visistadvaitic Hindu Conception of the Means to Liberation (Salvation)

With Special Reference to Ramanuja

As mentioned in the previous chapter, our main objective in this project is to elucidate a fresh model of the atonement in a comparative doctrinal perspective, using the Visistadvaitic Hindu concept of means to liberation (salvation). It is our hope that the Hindus of the Visistadvaitic tradition will more readily understand our new model of the atonement. Moreover, we hope that our model of the atonement will help Christians perceive the atonement in a new dimension. In fact, prior to articulating our theology using the theological system of others we need to understand the others' religio-theological system, of which, as yet, we have no thorough knowledge.

Admittedly, appropriating the means to salvation[1] is a core concern of most, if not all, major religions. However, it would not be right to think that traditionally "means to salvation" is understood in precisely the same way in religions such as Hinduism[2] and Christianity. In Hinduism, in general, it is understood that God provides the necessary knowledge for

---

1. Here, there is a problem with replacing the word liberation with salvation, but we do it with caution. For consistency, we will use the word, salvation. However, we need to be aware that in Hindu system, salvation is largely understood in terms of liberation. The concept of liberation in Hinduism is similar to, and most nearly equivalent to, the concept of salvation in Christianity. Further, it could also be noted that the word "liberation" is emphasized more by the *advaitins* than the people of the *Visistadvaitic* strand within Hinduism. More importantly, one should be aware that the similarities in terms like "sin and ignorance" and "salvation and liberation" exist in the mind of the inter-religious scholar. No doubt, this should be seen as an unavoidable pitfall of inter-religious theology.

2. In this book, wherever we use the word Hinduism, we refer to Hinduism in general, and Visistadvaitic Hinduism in particular.

salvation. This understanding is known as the *Jnana marga* or the path of knowledge. There are also the paths of *karma* (action-effect) and *bhakti* (devotion). In Christianity, it is the atoning work of Christ that is considered to be the means to salvation.

Anyone who seeks to exploit a particular Hindu theological concept is expected to state which strand of the tradition and which philosopher/theologian one has selected for one's analysis and study. In this chapter, we will draw attention to the thought of Ramanuja, the Visistadvaitic-Hindu theologian, for the understanding of the means to salvation in Hinduism. Ramanuja is the most important theologian of Visistadvaitic Hinduism just as Sankara is the most important theologian of the Advaitic Hinduism. The followers of Ramanuja and Visistadvaitic Hinduism are called Vaishnava Hindus.

Ramanuja holds that all three paths to salvation are valid. Eric Lott writes, "His [Ramanuja's] system is inclusive, for example, of all three principal methods—*karma, bhakt,* and *jnana*."[3] Although we will refer to the *bhakti* and *karma margas*, we will be more concerned to analyze the "path of knowledge" understanding of salvation because the other two are easily comprehensible. As we shall see, the path of knowledge, along with the paths of *karma* and *bhakti*, pay due attention to the objective and subjective sides of the means to salvation.[4]

We also need to mention the overriding reason for selecting Ramanuja for our analysis rather than Sankara or Madhava. We noted in the previous chapter that a crucial problem in our world, to which theologians need to attend, is the problem of alienation. More than any other theologian of Hinduism, Ramanuja emphasizes the need for the realization of God-World union/relationship with the help of a self-body analogy. This union, on which Ramanuja ponders, as we will see, has implications for a four-fold union: God-human, human-human, human-nature and one-oneself. Also, Ramanuja's thought on the means to salvation can be best grasped by analyzing it in terms of the aforesaid four-fold union. It is because Ramanuja's thought has the interesting analogy of self-body union for understanding God-World union, in its four-fold dimension, that we have chosen Ramanuja for our study.[5]

3. Lott, *God and the Universe*, 3.

4. In this book we will refer to the importance of *Bhakti yoga* and *Karma yoga*, whilst dealing with the objective and subjective sides of salvation. For a brief understanding of Ramanuja's thought on *yogas* (paths). See, Aiyengar, *The Life and Teachings of Sri Ramanujacarya*, 292–93.

5. Ramanuja could be called the Thomas Aquinas of India just as Thomas Aquinas could be described as the Ramanuja of Italy.

In the context of dealing with Ramanuja, some scholars prefer to use the word, union, whilst others prefer the word relationship. However, we will deliberately use the word, "union' to show the intimacy of the relationship, which is critically important. But we need to be aware that Ramanuja's conception of union is not that of a simple merger, as found in Sankara's thought. Ramanuja is very keen to observe that even in its united state, our atman (soul) is distinctly different from Brahman, like body and self, respectively. As Ramanuja's system is effectively a "unity in diversity," it is known as Visistadvaita (qualified monism).[6]

Ramanuja's thinking on the means to salvation should be understood within the Hindu tradition as well as with other related Hindu theological concepts. Hence, methodologically, we will first examine the central concept of Hinduism, namely Brahman, with reference to Ramanuja's interpretation of that concept. Secondly, Ramanuja believes in a personal God as distinct from Sankara. We will provide a brief exposition of Ramanuja's understanding of God, using the relationship between Brahman and God. Thirdly, we will analyze Ramanuja's thought on "sin" and "salvation." This will pave the way for us to construe Ramanuja's theology of the Means to Salvation. We will end this chapter by pointing out some of the possibilities that Ramanuja's understanding of the means to salvation has for the construction of a fresh model of the atonement.

The Purpose of This Chapter

In this chapter we will not go into the details of the life and career of Ramanuja but only a brief history of Hinduism, where Ramanuja's place within it will be explored. Our primary objective in this book is to outline a fresh model of the atonement in a comparative doctrinal perspective, using Ramanuja's Visistadvaitic thought, and not to provide an analytical study of Hinduism or Ramanuja. Hence, in this chapter, our purpose is to concentrate mostly on the concept of means to salvation in Ramanuja's thought. We will also examine briefly the most closely related concepts, namely the concepts of "Brahman," "God," "Sin" (ignorance), and "Salvation" (liberation).

In the introductory chapter, we observed that the problem of alienation is all too evident in our world. Interestingly, the concept of the means to salvation, in Ramanuja's thought, will address this problem in its manifold dimensions.

---

6. Srinivasachari says, "The central idea of *Visistadvaita* as a philosophy of religion is the integration and harmonization of all knowledge obtained through sense-perception, inference, and revelation. See, Srinivasachari, *The Philosophy of Visistadvaita*, 21.

Since we do not only aim at Visistadvaitic Hindu readers but also those of other religions, particularly of Christianity, and because we aim at readers not only of the East but also of the West, we will portray Ramanuja within the larger framework of Vaishnava Hinduism. It will help even those who are not familiar with Hinduism to understand Ramanuja within the broader Vaishnava Hindu tradition.[7] On the few occasions when Sanskrit or Tamil words will be used, they will be provided with a translation.

The Concept of Brahman and Ramanuja's Interpretation

We begin by analyzing the concept of Brahman because the understanding of the concept of means to salvation is not possible without gaining a brief knowledge of the concept of Brahman. Understanding the concept of means to salvation involves obtaining a modest knowledge of the concept of Brahman; and therefore a good grasp of this concept is a prerequisite.

Brahman is the ultimate concept of Hinduism. We will soon see that it is fundamentally equivalent to the concept of God within Christianity. The *Rigveda* considers Brahman as the supreme person.[8] The *Upanishads*[9] teach every concept other than Brahman always in its wider relationship with the concept of Brahman. The *Sruti* texts as well as the *Smriti* texts (the two varieties of scriptures in Hinduism) are dominated by their portrayal of the concept of Brahman. In *Bhagavad Gita*, we read that we are bound to Brahman.[10] The most celebrated Hindu scholars, Sankara and Ramanuja, have made attempts to interpret the concept of Brahman as their central ambition. And as we may expect, modern Hinduism too, along the lines of the earlier tradition, holds Brahman to be the fundamental concept of the religion.

The concept of Brahman is like the web of a spider that holds many components together. Brahman is the ultimate principle that can be imagined by us. In this sense, it is similar to Anselm's argument for the existence of God in looking to a being greater than that beyond which nothing can be conceived. Often, it is said that a full understanding of the concept of Brahman is beyond human comprehension.[11]

---

7. However, as noted earlier, Ramanuja is the most important theologian amongst the Vaishnava theologians and his system is called the Visistadvaitic Hindu way of life.
8. Bowen, *Themes and Issues in Hinduism*, 161.
9. The *Upanishads* are the most important part of Hindu scriptures.
10. Vyasa, *Bhagavad Gita*, 6:27–29.
11. Vyasa, *Bhagavad Gita*, 6:27–29.

The reason for the sophistication of the concept of Brahman is remarkable. Almost all attributes that can be ascribed to the Absolute are assigned to Brahman. For example, H. Nakamura writes,

> Brahman has unlimited extension (ayama) in terms of space; it is omnipresent (sarvagata, III 2, 37). It is endless (anata, III, 2, 26), and is called plenitude (bhuman, 1, 3, 8). It is without parts (niravayana, 11, 1, 26) and without form (arupavad, III 2, 33). It is eternal, and is called imperishable (aksara I, 3, 10; III 3, 1). Brahman in itself is undifferentiated (III, 2, 11). There occurs no increase or diminution of its qualities (III 3, 12). It is difficult to describe it positively in terms of words; it can be expressed only negatively (III, 2, 12). . . . Brahman is at the same time the world cause, and it is said that all the attributes (sarvadharma) of the world-cause can be applied to Brahman (II, 1, 37). The characteristics of the world-cause can be applied only to Brahman (I, 1, 15)[12]

It is evident that we are dealing with the central concept of Hinduism. The *Vedantic* conviction is also that Brahman is the one, the supremely perfect universal cause and transcendent goal of all existence.[13] In this respect, Brahman closely matches the Western concept of God.

Sankara and Ramanuja give their own interpretation of the concept of Brahman. Sankara understands that Brahman is without any qualities (*Nirguna*)[14] reflecting the *via negativa* of Western theology. On the contrary, Ramanuja says that Brahman is with all good qualities (*Saguna*), reflecting the *via eminentia* of Western theology. Interestingly, Hindu scriptures have space for both these interpretations as they do in Christian theology. As we shall soon see, it is interesting to note Ramanuja's exposition of the scriptural passages that refer to Brahman as *nirguna*.

Nirguna and *Saguna* Brahman

Nirguna and *Saguna* are different ways with which the concept of Brahman is approached.[15] This all-pervading concept with enormous ramifications,

---

12. Nakamura, *A History of Early Vedanta Philosophy*, 485. The citations in this quote are from the *Brahmasutra*—teachings based on the *Upanishads*.

13. Lott, *Vedantic Approaches to God*, 12. According to Eric Lott, the concept of Brahman marks the Hindu system off from all others.

14. For Sankara, to assign attributes to Brahman is to add phenomena to Brahman, something that is impossible. See Lott, *Vedantic Approaches to God*, 71–72.

15. *Nirguna* is emphasized by Sankara whilst other philosophers emphasize *Saguna*.

on the one hand, is understood as being beyond all qualities and, on the other hand, it is understood as possessing all good qualities. We need to be sure that it is the same Brahman that is understood as *Nirguna* and *Saguna*. In other words, though there are two different ways of discerning Brahman, Brahman is nevertheless one. Arvind Sharma explains *Nirguna* Brahman and *Saguna* Brahman with an example. He points out,

> There exists, according to the Constitution of the United States, the position of the president of the country, called 'the presidency of the Unites States.' Note that the presidency, per se, is impersonal; howsoever different the individual presidents may have been from one another, as presidents they all partook of the same presidency. However, each president was and is an individual with a distinct personality. One may compare the concept of Brahman as Nirguna or impersonal with the presidency of the United States and the Brahman as Saguna with the actual presidents of the United States.[16]

Thus, Brahman is *neti, neti* (not this, not this) at the same time it is the source of all because everything emanates from it, is sustained by it, and returns to it. In the Upanishadic thought both these aspects are retained and held in tension. These aspects are definitely different ways of describing Brahman.[17] The illustrious *neti, neti* understanding of Brahman was expounded by the eighth century philosopher, Sankara.[18] His intention was to show the highness, greatness, and the absoluteness of Brahman. But the problem with the *neti, neti* understanding of Brahman is that it reduces theology to silence, akin to apophatic theology in the West.

Interestingly, Ramanuja interprets that the scriptural passages, which talk of Brahman without qualities, point to the fact that Brahman is without any *bad* qualities, and that does not mean Brahman has no qualities at all.[19]

See, DeSmet, "Review Article," 800.

16. Sharma, *Classical Hindu Thought*, 2. Sharma also says that here we tend to regard the presidency as a mere abstraction and this is one of the criticisms levelled against the concept of *Nirguna* Brahman within Hinduism.

17. Some scholars understand these two aspects of Brahman as two sides of the same coin. For example, in the words of J. Fowler, "The unmanifest and manifest aspects of Brahman are not different, but simply two aspects of reality, two sides of the same coin—unity in diversity." See Fowler, *Perspectives of Reality*, 50.

18. Mahadevan, *Outlines of Hinduism*, 150.

19. Brockington says, "The statement that Brahman is *nirguna* means for Ramanuja that he is essentially beyond any qualification; it is to acknowledge that even scriptural descriptions do not exhaust the deity's perfections, while accepting that they are reliable so far as they go." See Brockington, *Hinduism and Christianity*, 11.

Ramanuja writes, for example, "When the *Brhadaranyaka Upanisad* says that Brahman is 'not this, not this,' it means that he is much more than the qualities described and not that he is mere being without attributes as the monists would have it."[20] Explicit scriptural support for the doctrine of a personal God is drawn by Ramanuja from the *Vishnu Purana* which abounds in such passages as these:

> Wisdom, might, strength, dominion, glory without any evil qualities are all denoted by the word Bhagavat . . . This great word Bhagavat is the name of Vasudeva, who is the highest Brahman and of no one else . . . All auspicious qualities constitute his nature . . . Glory, strength, dominion, wisdom, energy, power and all other attributes are collected in him . . . in whom no troubles abide . . . He who is the highest of the high, the Person, the highest self.[21]

Whilst for Sankara, Brahman is the absolute self, for Ramanuja, Brahman is the highest self. Thus, in relation to passages which are used by the monists [followers of Sankara] to claim there is nothing other than Brahman in the universe, or that Brahman cannot be known for the reason that there is ultimately no thinker or knower, Ramanuja adduced other scriptural passages to show that the characteristics of Brahman are so wonderful as to surpass the experience and knowledge of humanity.

Thus Ramanuja emphasizes that Brahman is *saguna*, i.e. with all good qualities, which helps him to the view that a personal union is possible with Brahman. In fact, Ramanuja construes the attributes of Brahman to be twofold. First, the essential attributes (*svarupa*) express the supreme self's essential nature without reference to his relation to any other entity.[22] The five defining attributes of Brahman are: true being, knowledge, bliss, purity, and infinity.[23] Obviously, these are well in tune with the Western metaphysical concepts of God such as aseity, simplicity, immutability, ubiquity, and omniscience. Second, there are other attributes that express Brahman's union with the world. Some relational attributes refer to Brahman's graciousness and saving love. God's gracious and loving nature is shown by his desire to

---

20. Ramanuja, *The Vedanta-Sutras*, 616–17.
21. *Vishnu Purana* VI. 5.72, 82–87, and I. 2. 10.
22. Lott, *Vedantic Approaches to God*, 33.
23. Ramanuja says that the term "true" expresses Brahman in so far as his possessing absolutely non-conditioned existence and distinguishing it from non-intelligence; the term "infinite" denotes that his nature is free from all limitations of place, time and particular substantial nature. See Thibaut, *The Vedanta Sutras*, 159–60. For Ramanuja, the quality of being free from evil is an attribute of the supreme self alone.

bring his devotees to a state of eternal communion with him.[24] Ramanuja spends most of his time talking about the relational attributes because his concern is with Brahman's relation to the world of persons and things.[25] We will briefly point out a few important attributes ascribed to Brahman and move to illustrate its relationship to the concept of God.

Significant Attributes of Brahman

Though there are numerous attributes ascribed to Brahman, within the limited scope of this chapter, we will limit ourselves to dealing with only the most important ones and with those that are directly related to the concept of the means to salvation.

The nature of Brahman can be best construed by viewing its attributes. First, in Hindu scriptures, Brahman is frequently referred to as *Sat-Cit-Ananda*.[26] *Sat* means being, *Cit* means consciousness and *Ananda* means bliss. Ramanuja says that consciousness can only be a quality of a person and hence Brahman is personal. To go further, the epithet *Sat* points to the positive character of Brahman distinguishing it from all non-beings. The epithet *Cit* shows that Brahman is spiritual, and the epithet *Ananda* stresses its unitary and all-embracing character in as much as asserting that variety is the source of all trouble and restlessness. We will deal with the unitary character of Brahman in detail whilst analyzing its function in relation to salvation. The Upanisad says that Brahman not only enjoys perfect bliss but also causes bliss in souls of different worlds.[27] It is true that the nature of *Sat, Cit,* and *Ananda* gives Brahman a personality and character. Interpreting *Sat-Cit-Ananda*, Radha Krishnan claims that Brahman is all-knowing and this knowledge is immediate, i.e. not dependent on senses.[28] No doubt the *Sat-Cit-Ananda* approach to Brahman shows the deep reflection concerning the ultimate reality by Visistadvaitic Hindu philosophers.

Secondly, Brahman is construed as righteousness. No other being can be perfect in righteousness. In Bhagavad Gita, righteousness is regarded

---

24. Carman, *The Theology of Ramanuja*, 72.

25. Carman, *The Theology of Ramanuja*, 97. Also, it may be noted that, for Ramanuja, Brahman has a real and personal bodily form, in addition to the paentheisitstic notion of his having the entire universe as his body. Carman, *The Theology of Ramanuja*, 168–69.

26. *Satyam jnanam anantam brahma*: Taittiriya Upanisad, II. 1, *vijnanamanandam brahma*: Brhadaranyaka Upanisad, III. 9, 28.

27. Taittiriya. Upanisad. II 8. 4.

28. Krishnan, *Indian Philosophy*, vol. II, 683

as Brahman's essential attribute. Arvind Sharma writes, "The thought that righteousness is as all important that the Deity considers even His infinitude of little account when righteousness needs to be established is a remarkable contribution which the Gita makes to the conception of the Divine."[29] It should be noted that the understanding of Brahman as righteousness indirectly acknowledges the existence of wickedness and the need of our liberation from it with the help of Brahman. Furthermore, Brahman understood, as righteousness reveals, the central significance of Visistadvaitic Hindu ethics most clearly.

Thirdly, another attribute given to Brahman is that it is unchanging. Hindus, in general, understand that reality does not undergo change and Brahman alone is real. Everything else is subject to change. Interpreting the Bhagavad Gita, Swami Chidbhavananda writes, "The Absolute Reality is Brahman. It is supremely above time, space and causation which are the characteristics of the universe . . . The changes that take place in the universe do not affect Brahman."[30] Brahman is unique in the sense that it is unchanging.

Fourthly, Brahman is called the truth. According to Pratima Bowes, the term "truth" has ontological as well as epistemological meanings. Brahman is true in its being and Brahman is also true in a full understanding of it expressed in language.[31] Brahman as truth is again qualified by the understanding that Brahman alone is real.

Fifthly, Brahman is one and there is no second. The Chandogya Upanishad tells us that Brahman is the one lump of clay from which a variety of vessels are made; the metal from which various instruments are made; the fire from which sparks fly off; the spider emitting and withdrawing its web; the waves of the sea from which foam is stirred up; the one who desiring a second, made himself into an embracing man and woman, from which all beings derived; the one egg, by the splitting of which heaven and earth emerged; the one self whose body this universe is.[32] Interpreting this picture of Brahman, Eric Lott says, "the general intention is to show how Brahman in the beginning was one only, one without a second, and from this one being all finite beings have derived."[33]

The other important attributes of Brahman, the details of which we will not investigate here, are power, the imperishable, infinity, the word,

29. Sharma, *Classical Hindu Thought*, 61.
30. Chidbhavananda, *Bhagavad Gita*, 453.
31. Bowes, *The Hindu Religious Tradition*, 269.
32. Chandogya Upanishad, 6, 2.
33. Lott, *Vedantic Approaches to God*, 16.

the perfect personality, the breath, the food, the transcendent reality, and the incompatible.

For Ramanuja, along with all these attributes there are also other numerous attributes. Significantly, as S. Tsoukalas says, "For Ramanuja, Brahman is above all personal and in the highest sense possesses an infinite amount of favorable attributes."[34] According to Ramanuja, Brahman is the really real (*satyasya satyam*) in the knowing of whom all else is known.[35] This is because of his view that all beings participate in one being. Ramanuja's is a relational view of reality and, regarding the interconnectedness of reality, Ramanuja writes, "everything participates in the nature of everything else."[36] Ramanuja's is a substance metaphysics with enduring substance and changing attributes.[37] In his thought, "being" and "becoming" together constitute reality.

Brahman-God Relationship

Obviously, Hindu theology cannot talk of God without talking about Brahman and vice versa. For instance, Sharada Sugirtharajah, before talking about God, tells us about Brahman,[38] which advocates the view that Hindu religiosity, in general, is grounded on in-depth metaphysics. Admittedly, having a grasp of the concept of God is necessary for understanding the concept of the means to salvation. This, we will do by analyzing the relationship between the concept of Brahman and the concept of God still further.

Nonetheless, there is no easy distinction between God and Brahman. Hinduism is generally conceived as both polytheistic and monotheistic at one and the same time.[39] The many gods are understood as having different

---

34. Tsoukalas, *The Krsnavatara doctrines*, 116.
35. Thibaut, *The Vedanta Sutras*, 132.
36. Thibaut, *The Vedanta Sutras*, 119.
37. The enduring substance has essential and accidental attributes.
38. Bowen, *Themes and Issues in Hinduism*, 161–200.
39. Though strange, in Hinduism, there are many gods and one God at the same time. In Brihadaranyaka Upanishad III 9.1. it is said, "Then Vidagdha, the son of Sakalya, asked him, How many gods are there, Yajnavalkya? . . . As many as are indicated in the Nivid (sacred verses) of the Visvadevas (hymns to the gods)—three hundred and three and three thousand and three.

Very well, said Sakalya, how many gods are there, Yajnavalkya?

Thirty three.

Very well, said the other, how many gods are there, Yajnavalkya?

Six.

functions. Some gods separately perform many functions as well. Sharada Sugirtharajah says, "The supreme is conceived of as having many attributes, functions, forms, manifestations and names but, at the same time, oneness is seen as the basis of all multiplicity."[40] In general terms, the emphasis of the word, Brahman, is on oneness and unity with creation and the emphasis of the word, God, is on the otherness.

Brahman, in relation to the world is called *Isvara*. M. Hiriyanna says that the qualified Brahman, if personified, becomes God or *Isvara*.[41] No doubt, Brahman is everything, including God. Brahman encompasses God, the all-powerful, the individual atman, unknowing and powerless and nature, made up of primeval matter. In Zaehner's words, "Brahman pervades the gods."[42]

Panikkar is among the very few who has dealt with the Brahman-God relationship. He says that the names Brahman and God are used to denote the same reality in different ways. In his words,

> Both names (Brahman and God) stand for the same ultimacy, yet they seem to connote distinct functions. Brahman stands at the end of philosophico-theological speculation, at the limits of the intellect, or just behind it, being essentially immanent. God, on the other hand, is the end and object of human adoration and love. The two different names refer ultimately to one unity, because our will and our intellect will not stop short of absolute oneness, but the God of Man's worship cannot be just the foundation of being, the mere condition of existence—it has also to be a person, a subject, an "I" . . . The one is abstract, general, all pervading from below as it were, common to everything and the presupposition of every being; the other is concentrate,

---

Very well, said the other, how many gods are there, Yajnavalkya?
   Three.
Very well, said the other, how many gods are there, Yajnavalkya?
   Two.
Very well, said the other, how many gods are there, Yajnavalkya?
   One and a half.
Very well, said Sakalya, how many gods are there, Yajnavalkya?
   One . . . " See, Brhadaranyaka Upanishad III 9.1.

40. Bowen, *Themes and Issues in Hinduism*, 162.
41. Hiriyanna, *The Essentials of Indian Philosophy*, 164.
42. Zaehner, *Hinduism*, 48.

personal, all embracing, from above, as it were, calling to union, but yet transcendent, the end and goal of every being.[43]

Panikkar again claims that Brahman and God are *materialiter* the same reality, but *formaliter* different.[44] Thus, Brahman and God on the one hand are the same and on the other they are different.

Ramanuja does not deal with the relationship between Brahman and God very explicitly.[45] Nonetheless, Ramanuja indicated that the incarnate forms are two steps removed from Vasudeva, the highest Brahman. He says that from the worship of the incarnations one can attain the vyuhas (emanations), and from the worship of these vyuhas one can attain Brahman.[46] To go deeper, Ramanuja understands that the different gods and goddesses are the manifestations of Brahman. For him, Vishnu, Vasudeva, Narayana, Krishna, the vyuhas, and the avatars of Vishnu are all mere bodily forms, which the highest Brahman voluntarily assumes.[47] In this sense, for Ramanuja, Brahman and God are one and the same.

The Concept of Sin (Ignorance) in Ramanuja's Thought

With our objective to explain as lucidly as possible the concept of means to salvation in Visistadvaitic Hinduism, with special reference to Ramanuja, we have outlined the most fundamental concept of Hinduism, which is Brahman in the light of Ramanuja's interpretation of the concept. We have also noted the relationship between the concept of Brahman and the concept of God. Here we will briefly examine the concept of ignorance in Ramanuja's Vedantic thought.

The concept of ignorance is the closest equivalent and the most similar to the concept of sin in Christianity. In Visistadvaitic Hinduism, there is no concept of sin as such. However, it is understood that all mistakes and errors that we do are due to *avidya* (ignorance). For coherence and clarity, we will use the word sin but we always need to remember that

---

43. Pannikkar, *The Unknown Christ of Hinduism*, 136.

44. Pannikkar, *The Unknown Christ of Hinduism*, 143.

45. Although Ramanuja is not explicit about God-Brahman relationship, his writings show that when he wants to speak of God in relation to his theory of knowledge, he uses the word Brahman. Hence, it is not wrong to say that, for Ramanuja, God and Brahman are one and the same, and with whom a personal union, in terms of association, is possible.

46. Ramanuja, *The Vedanta-Sutras*, 266–67.

47. Aiyangar, et al., *Sri Ramanujacharya*, 92–93.

it is the undesirable ignorance that we are dealing with here using the Christian vocabulary of sin.[48]

The familiar way of understanding sin (ignorance) in Hinduism is through the concept of bondage (*pasam*). The Sanskrit word *pasam* literally means "a snare, trap, noose, tie, bond, cord, chain and fetter."[49] Visistadvaitic Hindus believe that we are not able to enjoy union with Brahman because the essential self in us is in bondage. This bondage is due to *avidya*, or the lack of the intuitive and practical knowledge of Brahman. More precisely, it is not knowing that we are in union with Brahman. In other words, it is living and acting with the false knowledge that we are alienated beings from Brahman.

For Ramanuja, the entire universe constitutes the body of Brahman. Brahman is the self and the entire universe is the body. This does not mean that Ramanuja is a pantheist because his writings again and again claim that the world, as the body of Brahman, is dependent on Brahman, but Brahman is in no way dependent on the world. As Brockington says, Ramanuja adopts "a broad definition of a body as anything that can be controlled by and is subordinate to a conscious atman."[50] However, not realizing Brahman as the self, and the world as the body of Brahman is exactly what ignorance is. Lott says, "the universe and the *jivas* (lives) have Brahman and just in so far as all this comprises the body of Brahman, is Brahman."[51] Here, sin is well understood in terms of a four-fold alienation. The first alienation is caused by not realizing that we ought to be one with the will of Brahman because we (our souls) constitute Brahman's body. Spiritual pride and self-righteousness happen because of the ignorance of our union with Brahman.[52] Secondly, human-human alienation is also sin because it is we who together constitute the body of Brahman. In other words, the entire humanity is part of the same body of Brahman. Thirdly, the other *jivas* (lives) which are present in the world are also understood as constituting

---

48. It should be acknowledged that in the construction of a inter-religious theology, such as ours, the similarities in the words sin and ignorance/*avidya*, or salvation and liberation, should be used as a point of contact. One might argue that this is a pitfall of inter-religious theology. But if one overemphasizes this pitfall there cannot be a dialog at all, especially in relation to atonement theology. This is one of the reasons why atonement theology remains more alien in the Indian context compared to most other theological doctrines.

49. Williams, *A Sanskrit-English Dictionary*, 623.

50. Brockington, *Hinduism and Christianity*, 9.

51. Lott, *God and the Universe*, 22.

52. Desire, anger, and greed are root causes of sins of pride and self-righteousness. In his commentary of Bhagavad Gita, Ramanuja deals with these aspects of sin. See Ramanuja, *Gita Bhasya*, 398–409. Also see Ramanuja, *The Vedanta Sutras*, 10.

the body of Brahman. This implies that acting from the assumption that we are completely different from nature is sin. Fourthly, as Lipner elucidates, in Ramanuja's thought, there are two different selves. One is the contingent self and the other is the essential self.[53] Whilst the contingent self is selfish and shallow, the essential self is deeper and of the divine. For this reason, we ought to live in union with the essential self in us. One-oneself alienation, which is living with a knowledge that we are alien to our essential self, is also undesirable and is sin.

There are three factors that amount to *avidya* (ignorance) and the consequent alienations. They are *anavam* (selfishness), *karma* (action-result), and *maya* (matter). The essential self in us is infinite but becomes finite, limited, and ignorant because of the three factors that constitute the bondage.[54]

The first cause of sin is *anavam*, also known as selfishness. And the selfishness we possess is due to ignorance. Again ignorance is part of the original impurity and its nature is darkness. It leads us to delusion and the source of the wrong knowledge in us. Specifically, atman (soul) seems to be mortal through a basic misconception that the atman is identical with the body in which it resides. This evil leads to sin.[55] This deceiving character of ignorance is at the root of alienation. This is overcome by the right knowledge given by the grace of Brahman.

The second cause of sin is *karma*. All Vedantins agree that atman is subject to *karma*.[56] M. Hiriyanna explains this cause of bondage. He says that Hinduism, on the one hand, teaches that every event in the physical world is determined by its antecedents and, on the other hand, teaches that whatever we knowingly do will—sooner or later—bring us the result we merit and there is no way to escape from it.[57] The relevance of Brahman as the essence of the right knowledge of union can be noted here. It is also worthwhile to construe that even in pre-determined matters, we are judged by how we react to them. Here too, it is ignorance which prevents us from working against the bondage of *karma*.

The third cause of sin is *maya*, or matter. *Maya* gives to the essential self the location, the instruments and the objects of experience. *Maya*, in fact, is a trick played on the universe. The absolutistic school of thought is interesting. It teaches that the trick lies in the way the world's materiality

---

53. Lipner, *The Face of Truth*, 49–79.
54. Karmakar, *Sri Bashya of Ramanuja*, para. 11–12.
55. Buitenen, *Ramanuja on the Bhagavadgita*, 1–2.
56. Neelamkavil, "Reconstructing the Foundations," 345.
57. Hiriyanna, *The Essentials of Indian Philosophy*, 46–48. Also see, Carman, *The Theology of Ramanuja*, 56.

and multiplicity pass themselves off as being independently real—real apart from the stance from which we see them—whereas, in reality, it is undifferentiated Brahman throughout.[58] However, in the theistic thought of Ramanuja, *maya* is that quality of the world which distracts us from God: "seductive in the attractiveness in which it presents the world, trapping us within it and leaving us with no desire to journey on."[59] It is considered that we are ignorant of this *maya* as well.

Notably, these three factors affect us due to the ignorance of our being in union with Brahman. Certainly, Ramanuja understands that human beings do wrong because of ignorance or due to the lack of right knowledge. In this context, one is expected to seek the right knowledge offered by Brahman. Right knowledge is necessary for realizing that we are united to Brahman as the body is united to the self. It is also said that one should do one's duties as well as possible, and doing the duty of others, even in the best way, doesn't deserve appreciation. Brahman is the one that gives the knowledge of one's duties. In Hinduism, the duty of everyone is specified on the basis of caste. Visistadvaitic Hinduism too endorses the caste system.

Theodicy is an issue related to the concept of sin. The problem of justifying belief in an omnipotent and good personal God in the face of evil and suffering in the world is a special problem for anyone who holds a theistic worldview. Ramanuja asserts that God is just and is not responsible for evil. He defines Brahman as the one who is "free from all evil, devoid of all imperfections, all knowing, all powerful and all its wishes and purposes realize themselves."[60] If so, why is there evil and suffering in the world? Why would God not create and rule the world in such a way as to prevent all evil and sufferings? Ramanuja's answer is that evil is due to the freedom of individual selves (free will) to do good and evil and the resultant *karman*.[61]

To the question whether Brahman, who dwells in the body like that of individual souls, experiences pain and pleasure due to connection with the body, Ramanuja's answer is that the cause of pleasure and pain is not dwelling within the body, but the subjection to the influence of good and evil deeds, and such subjection is impossible in the case of the highest self to whom all evil is alien.[62] Thus, according to Ramanuja, Brahman, although abiding

---

58. Smith, *The World's Religions*, 71.
59. Smith, *The World's Religions*, 71.
60. Thibaut, *The Vedanta Sutras*, 218.

61. Thibaut, *The Vedanta Sutras*, 609. For Ramanuja, the supreme Person causes pain to one and pleasure to another, according to the law of *karma*.

62. Thibaut, *The Vedanta Sutras*, 265. That a soul experiences pleasures and pains caused by the various states of the body is not due to the fact that it is being joined to a body, but due to its *karma* in the form of good and evil deeds. To illustrate his

within all things, is free from all evil and imperfection.[63] Connection with the world/body does not make Brahman imperfect. A question that we may ask Ramanuja is that if both Brahman and the world are real, and are really united, then how can Brahman remain unaffected by the imperfections and the sufferings of the world? In his enthusiasm, to avoid implicating Brahman in the changes and sufferings of the world, Ramanuja stresses the impassivity of Brahman in relation to the world. Ramanuja, incidentally, also brings out Brahman as knowing the *karma* of individual selves in affecting creation, and speaks of giving *anumati* (free will), checking sin and the tendency to do evil, as well as influencing and acting to "save" the world.

We will conclude here by asserting that being ignorant of our union with Brahman is sin. Ignorance leads us to live an alienated life not only with Brahman, but also with others, nature, and ourselves, which is sin. If ignorance of the four-fold union (God-human, human-human, human-nature and one-oneself) is sin, then obviously realizing that union is salvation. We will now outline the concept of salvation in Ramanuja's thought.

The Concept of Liberation (Salvation) in Ramanuja's Thought

Here again we use the word salvation with care. As noted in the introduction to this chapter, in Hinduism, salvation is generally understood in terms of liberation. It is liberation from ignorance relating to a knowledge of Brahman.[64] No doubt the closest equivalent in Christian theology to the concept of liberation in Hinduism is the concept of salvation. For coherence and clarity throughout this project, we will use the Christian vocabulary salvation, but bearing in mind that salvation in Hinduism is fundamentally construed in terms of liberation.

Visistadvaitic Hindu tradition repeatedly emphasizes the inability of the self (soul) to save itself by its own efforts. Brahman alone can save the self from its *avidya* (ignorance) and consequent alienations. The stress on "the function of Brahman" as necessary for our liberation (salvation) is well documented in the Bhagavad Gita. In Bhagavad Gita 18.66 the Lord says,

---

view, Ramanuja even uses the analogy of a coercive ruler who does not experience the pain and the pleasures of subjects. See, Thibaut, *The Vedanta Sutras*, 427–28. Ramanuja refutes the bhedabheda view which holds that Brahman is perfect and this world of suffering and change are dangerous.

63. Thibaut, *The Vedanta Sutras*, 611.

64. Here, it may be worth noting that the liberation is not construed in terms of economics, in particular, but it refers to the liberation from living in ignorance of Brahman toward union with Brahman. Referring to Hinduism, Donald R. Davis calls this spiritual liberation. See Davis, "Being Hindu or Being Human," 19.

"Abandon all other dharma (duties) and come unto Me alone for refuge. I will free you from all sin."

Salvation/*moksha* (heaven) is the highest end of life. For Sankara, the realization of atman as Brahman is salvation. One's self, understanding itself of its transcendent oneness with Brahman is the only means to such a realization. Sankara is keen on insisting that the ultimate identity of self with Brahman is all that matters. As soon as this oneness is realized, all further expectations come to an end, and no further effort is required.

In contrast to Sankara's thought, for Ramanuja, there is a more personal union in the sense of an intimate relationship with the divine in the saved state.[65] The significance of Brahman in the theistic thought of Ramanuja is that it can be in union with atman and yet be distinctly different.[66] It is interesting that salvation is construed in terms of our union with God as perceived in the Christian tradition. In Visistadvaitic Hinduism, God, matter, and the essential self in us are eternal. Salvation for the individual self occurs by the salvific knowledge of a union between them. The knowledge necessary for the realization of this union can be given by Brahman alone and is a matter of grace.

As we noted, Ramanuja understands that the entire world/universe comprises the body of Brahman and we are ignorant of this fact. Realizing that we ought to live in union with Brahman is precisely what salvation is.[67] This realization also includes knowing that the whole of humanity is connected because it constitutes the same body of Brahman. In other words, all individual souls present in each person are part of the body of Brahman. The divine knowledge of the human-human union is thus essential for salvation. In the saved state, our union needs to be extended to other beings of the natural world because they too constitute the body of Brahman. Eric Lott rightly says that all spiritual and non-spiritual entities constitute Brahman's body and

---

65. As mentioned earlier, we use the word union in the sense that the word is used in students' union or a workers' union or as used in United Kingdom, and not in the sense of merging. It is here clear that the word union is used in the sense of merging as described by Sankara. For Ramanuja, as S. Tsoukalas writes, "the *jiva* does not reach ontological equality with Brahman in 'co-existence,' but instead enjoys bliss in 'communion' with Brahman and retains its personality." See Tsoukalas, *The Krsnavatara Doctrines*, 130.

66. In fact, the union between Brahman and atman, as well as between Brahman and all jivas (lives), is possible because all jivas, though distinct from each other and from Brahman, are pure *cit* and are of the same substance as Brahman. See Zaehner, *Hinduism*, 99.

67. When atman realizes its union with Brahman, it lives in bliss. In Lipner's words, "For Ramanuja the perfect state of this bliss is in *moksha*, when the atman in the union of Brahman comes in the self's perfect realization of union with its source and goal." See Lipner, *The Face of Truth*, 61.

in this way Brahman is embodied and modified by all.[68] Finally, as there is the empirical self and the essential self in us, we need to know that the essential self in us is the important one. Living a life in union with the essential self, which we call one-oneself union also amounts to salvation.

Ramanuja's system has three kinds of souls. First are the eternal (*nitya*) souls, i.e. those lives which have never been in bondage; second are the freed (*mukta*) souls, i.e. the souls which have already reached salvation; and third are the souls that are bound (*baddha*) souls, i.e. those which are caught up in the vortex of *samsara* (bondage).[69] We ourselves and everything around us belong to the third category.

Prior to complete salvation, there is the stage called *mukti*. The conscious self persists even in its *mukti* state.[70] That is, the individual self's self-identity is retained. In Ramanuja's opinion even in *mukti* the continuing reality of the relational mode of existence is assured. The ultimate saved stage is *moksha* and it is definitely not a negation of life but is eternal communion with God.[71] Further, the tension between "the already now and not yet" is also present in Ramanuja's theology. Lipner says,

> Ramanuja is not saying that the liberated soul ceases to perceive the evil and suffering of the world, which indeed continue; on the contrary, he is saying not only that the liberated soul continues to keep in touch with the world for what it is essentially—an expression of Brahman in the relation of identity-in-difference Ramanuja has sought to articulate—the liberated soul has overcome the world; it is no longer under the world's karmic sway.[72]

When we are released from the state of bondage that is caused by ignorance, the individual selves are in inseparable relation and communion with the supreme self. It is an everlasting and constant union with God. The saved souls enjoy Brahman. The released souls abide within Brahman and are conscious of Brahman.[73] Salvation is not cessation or annihilation of self. In fact, the four-fold union can be discerned in the saved life and each union is closely related to the others.

68. Lott, *God and the Universe*, 147.
69. Mahadevan, *Outlines of Hinduism*, 153.
70. Mahadevan, *Outlines of Hinduism*, 69.
71. Carman, *The Theology of Ramanuja*, 187. Unlike Sankara, Ramanuja holds that there is no ontological union between Brahman and atman in *moksha*. An I-Thou distinction exists even the liberated and united state. But, definitely, the atman enjoys bliss in union with Brahman. See Lipner, *The Face of Truth*, 60.
72. Lipner, *The Face of Truth*, 119.
73. Thibaut, *The Vedanta Sutras*, 759.

Moreover, for Ramanuja, "Brahman is the only one reality; but this Brahman is qualified by individual selves and matter, which are also real, but not independent."[74] Ramanuja holds that the soul is not identical with Brahman. He explains the union between Brahman and atman with a self-body analogy. He understands that our atman is united with Brahman in the way that our body is united with our self. For Ramanuja, by grace, God seeks to lead people to a life of perfection and complete devotion to himself and once they have attained it, he will never allow them to be separated from him again.[75] With this concise exposition of Ramanuja's concept of salvation, we will move on to analyze his self-body union analogy.

Brief Exposition of Self-Body Union Analogy

It is now clear that realizing our union with Brahman, which is related to realizing our union with others, nature, and ourselves, is salvation. Ramanuja understands that we are united with Brahman in the same way as our body is united with our self. This analogy is found to be of immense significance for scholars like Lott and Lipner, whose works we have referred to. Nevertheless, a brief exposition of Ramanuja's self-body union analogy is essential here.

For Ramanuja, atman (soul) is atomic substance[76] (*dravya*). Self is a permanent conscious subject with changing consciousness. It is the consciousness of atman that experiences its body.

Ramanuja frequently says that the body is an entity and has a being only by virtue of it being the mode of the soul. However, by using the term, world, Ramanuja means the collection of all finite individual substantial entities. Lipner says, "Ramanuja is as prone to refer separately to such individuals/aggregates as Brahman's body as he is to the world."[77]

Thus, for Ramanuja, there is inseparable union between self and body.[78] The body's union to self is one of inseparable dependence. A radical distinction is present between self and body. The self is the one which uses the body for its purpose. The body has a subordinate instrumental role under the control of self and fulfills the self's purposes. Though an

---

74. Thottakara, "A Vedantic Perspective of Ecology," 13.

75. Kumrappa, *Hindu Conception of the Deity*, 327.

76. Thibaut, *The Vedanta Sutras*, 560.

77. Lipner, *The Face of Truth*, 123.

78. Lott observes that there is real communication between self and body, meaning that there is real communication between God and the universe. See Lott, *God and the Universe*, 148.

individual's body is made up of many parts, the sum of these parts alone does not make a body. That is, the body is ruled by a single intelligent principle. It is by consciousness that the self rules the body and effects changes in the body. Changes in the bodily states affect only the consciousness of atman and not atman itself.

Significantly, Ramanuja considers sense perception of body as faulty, and holds body as the conglomeration of elements of *prakrthi*. Further, Ramanuja considers body as *desa*[79] or (one) place, bringing out that body is the field in and through which the self comes to expression. Other analogical relations—supporter-supported, controller-controlled and principal-accessory—are specifically applicable in considering the relation between God and sentient selves, as they bring out the social or interpersonal union between self and the world. These corollary analogies enable Ramanuja to interpret the organic self-body union in interpersonal terms in the case of God-world union. We will soon see how self-body union analogy has implications in understanding the means to salvation.[80]

Function of Brahman in Relation to Salvation/Liberation

An analysis of the concept of Brahman in Hindu thought, together with Ramanuja's interpretation of the concept (the concepts of sin and salvation in Ramanuja's thought, and a brief exposition of the self-body union analogy), have set the stage for examining the saving role of Brahman. In fact, understanding the function of Brahman/God in Ramanuja's thought in relation to salvation is a central concern in this chapter. Whilst we deal with the functions of Brahman, we need to be careful not to personalize Brahman because it is a concept like that of God in Christianity.

As *the* foundational concept, Brahman plays a significant role in making salvation possible. The primary work of Brahman is granting the necessary knowledge for salvation.[81] As we noted, salvation is realizing that the world is the body of Brahman and Brahman is the self. In Lipner's

---

79. Lipner, *The Face of Truth*, 563.

80. Lott deals with the criticisms against using self-body analogy and counterargues, which we will not deal with within the scope of this project. For details, see Lott, *God and the Universe*, 165–67.

81. It should be noted that although there are the *bhakti* and *yoga margas*, in addition to *jnana marga* for attaining salvation, without the grace of God salvation is not possible, no matter what the path is. Carman observes that the goal of salvation is attained entirely by God's grace in "the acknowledgement that there is no human means to salvation without divine grace." Carman, *The Theology of Ramanuja*, 222.

words, Brahman is the "ensouler."[82] There are four distinct dimensions of the role played by Brahman in this regard. Firstly, it is Brahman who provides the ground for a four-fold union (relationship), namely God-human, human-human, human-world, and one-oneself. We noted that the realization or attainment of this union is salvation in Ramanuja's thought. Secondly, Brahman as the one causing salvation, functions continuously transcending any particular period of history and transcending any geographical arena. In other words, the role of Brahman in relation to salvation is ongoing. Thirdly, Brahman, as it dwells in the souls of everyone, causes salvation for all, transcending religious barriers. Fourthly, the uniting principle of Brahman provides a union between the different doctrines within Visistadvaitic Hinduism.

The saving/liberating function of Brahman denotes his supremacy. Brahman is also gracious to prepare the world for communion with it/him. This is well said by Carman. He writes,

> God's most intimate control of the finite self is . . . both an expression of His supremacy over that self and of His will to prepare that self for a state of uninterrupted communion with Him, a communion of which there may be some foretaste in this life for one whose devotion is animated or encouraged by the indwelling Ruler. Here supremacy and accessibility meet without paradox.[83]

Thus, along with affirming the role of Brahman for salvation, Carman rightly states that supremacy and accessibility is of the nature of Brahman. At this point, we will move on to analyze Ramanuja's understanding of Brahman's role in providing saving knowledge.

Brahman as the Provider of Saving/Liberating Knowledge

The supreme function of Brahman in relation to salvation is to provide the knowledge for salvation. According to Ramanuja, the knowledge given by Brahman is not to distinguish between good and evil, but to know our union with Brahman. In reality, we are one with Brahman. We are ignorant of this fact. Brahman grants the knowledge to realize our oneness with him. In fact, this enlightening knowledge that proceeds from Brahman enables us to experience our oneness with the divine. Moreover, the saving knowledge of Brahman is that which enables us to know Brahman. Knowing Brahman

---

82. Lipner, *The Face of Truth*, 37.
83. Carman, *The Theology of Ramanuja*, 186.

is to be one in will with Brahman. Selfishness vanishes and we adhere to the qualities of the divine. It is this knowledge which also leads us to live in union with others, nature, and ourselves. Lipner says that the chief goal of human living is Brahman himself.[84]

Sankara says that Brahman in us, in the form of soul, gives us the knowledge to realize that we are one with Brahman. Ramanuja differs from Sankara and says that Brahman, who is distinctly different from us, gives the knowledge that we are united with Brahman like the body is united with the self. Thus, whilst Sankara holds an auto-centric view of salvation, Ramanuja has a theo-centric view. Ramanuja says, "What has been stated [by you] that the cessation of *avidya* alone [is] salvation and that cessation too results from the special knowledge of Brahman—alone is accepted by us."[85] Brahman offers the redeeming knowledge by means of which the soul can get rid of *avidya* regarding the true nature of union and obtain release.

Thus the function of Brahman is crucial in providing salvation. Kumarappa says that the self chooses and reveals its being to the one who is chosen.[86] There is a common misunderstanding that the idea of grace is unique to Christianity. In reality, Visistadvaitic Hinduism too finds a significant place for the grace of God, especially in relation to salvation. For example, elucidating Ramanuja, Bede Griffiths says that Hinduism has "a personal God, who is Being, Knowledge and Bliss in the fullness of self-consciousness, eternal, infinite and unchanging and who yet reveals himself as a God of *grace* and *love*, delivering souls from sin, drawing them to himself, perfecting them by his *grace*."[87] To quote from the scriptures, the *Katha Upanishad* teaches that it is by the grace of the supreme self (Brahman) that atman can be realized.[88] However, still the Brahman should be understood as a concept and not as a person, in strict terms. Brahman provides the grace of intuitive knowledge not directly but *through gurus (teachers), scripture, consciousness, or through the combination of all of these.*

Now the question which arises is whether knowledge alone is sufficient for salvation. The answer to this is that it is not an abstract and theoretical knowledge which Brahman offers to its devotees, but it is an intuitive and practical knowledge that *inter-alia* presumes a mastery of the will. We will move on to deal with this briefly.

---

84. Lipner, *The Face of Truth*, 32.
85. Karmakar, *Sri Bhasya of Ramanuja*, para. 12. Emphasis in original.
86. Kumarappa, *Hindu Conception of Diety*, 295.
87. Griffiths, *Vedanta and Christian Faith*, 41.
88. *Katha* in *Upanishad*, 1–2, 23.

Abstract and Theoretical Knowledge vs. Intuitive and Practical Knowledge

All knowledge that we acquire is not used in our practical life. Most of the knowledge that we get stays at the intellectual level for some time and then disappears. We often tend to forget what we know if it is not practice. The knowledge of the unions given by Brahman is not such an abstract or even a mere intellectual knowledge.

On the contrary, the knowledge of Brahman is a knowledge of unions that must be lived. It is a complete way of understanding oneself, God, and the rest of the cosmos. Specifically, it is in intuitively[89] discerning the knowledge that we are united with others, nature, and ourselves in and through Brahman. Once this knowledge is received from Brahman within us, any further obstacle for salvation is removed. It is expressed in every action and thought in *samsara*. Ramanuja invites one to a practiced knowledge.[90] In fact, an abstract theoretical knowledge of what the atman basically is, is not, however, enough to shatter the bonds that tie the atman to its body.[91] It should be practice in our daily life. Van Buitenen says, "The knowledge of the proper nature of the atman as an entity distinct from the body is followed by buddhiyoga, the practical application of this knowledge to every-day life."[92]

The means of the intuitive knowledge of union is Brahman himself and it is never through the initiative of humans. However, Brahman can grant this knowledge either through scripture, a guru, reason, perception, inference, or through a combination of them all.

---

89. Radhakrishnan says that in Hinduism, intellect is subordinated to intuition. He also claims that experience is superior to abstractions. In his words, "Intellect is subordinated to intuition, dogma to experience, outer expression to inward realization. Religion is not the acceptance of academic abstractions or the celebration of ceremonies, but a kind of life or experience . . . This experience is not an emotional thrill, or a subjective fancy, but is the response of the whole personality, the integrated self to the central reality [Brahman]." See, Radhakrishnan, *The Hindu view of Life*, 13.

90. Ramanuja, *The Vedanta Sutras*, vol. I, 17.

91. Buitenen, *Ramanuja on the Bhagavadgita*, 20.

92. Buitenen, *Ramanuja on the Bhagavadgita*, 20. Further, Radhakrishnan calls the abstract knowledge as erroneous and the practical knowledge as true knowledge. See Radhakrishnan, *The Vedanta According to Samkara*, 242.

Objective and Subjective Sides of the Means to Salvation:

We have made it clear that it is Brahman alone who can provide the specific required knowledge for salvation. However, Brahman offers this knowledge through consciousness, scriptures, or gurus (teachers); hence we need to be careful not to personalize the concept of Brahman. Further as Lipner says, "Though reason on its own was a treacherous guide in matters theological, directed and illuminated by scripture it had a very important part to play in the systematic inquiry into Brahman."[93] No matter what the means is, the ignorance which our soul bears is overcome by the knowledge offered by Brahman alone. This is the objective side of the means to salvation.

For Ramanuja, there is a subjective side in the means to salvation as well. Here, the role of *yogas* (paths) gains importance. The subjective side of Brahman's saving knowledge can be construed through the paths of knowledge, *bhakti* (devotion), and *karma*. Although it is by the knowledge of Brahman alone that salvation is possible, we also have to play a subjective role. Our response to Brahman's grace should be revealed in anticipation of right knowledge, right actions, and sincere devotion.

As stated earlier, though we will be concerned more with the path of knowledge, a very brief idea of other paths will help us to understand Ramanuja more thoroughly. Ramanuja holds that *bhakti* is important for salvation. He declared *bhakti* to be the most suitable means to achieve purity, sinlessness, and selflessness in life; hence this same *bhakti* was, according to him, the truest and the most unfailing means for the attainment of salvation or *moksha*.[94] For him,

> The atman's relation to God is marked by religious worship and pious representation and animated by the spirit of love for these very religious acts which have such an exalted object. These acts performed in the spirit of love ultimately result in the closest possible individual union of the atman with God.[95]

Karma is also an important theme in Ramanuja's thought. It deals with the concept of action-result. The guidance that the soul gets in doing good and turning away from evil is also *karma*. Through *karma*, Brahman can work in us. Ramanuja says that God voluntarily acts with *karma*. It is within the bounds of *karma* that God equips us to lead a righteous life and we are morally free to do so. An appropriate righteous life culminates in

---

93. Lipner, *The Face of Truth*, 4.
94. Ramanuja, *The Vedanta-Sutras*, vol. II, 525.
95. Buitenen, *Ramanuja on the Bhagavagita*, 1–2.

salvation. We are expected to perform our duties faithfully so as to receive the grace of God.

Carman clarifies that Ramanuja's thought includes the objective and subjective sides of salvation. In his words,

> Once it is recognized that it is fundamentally God who accomplishes man's salvation, the joys of mystical communion and humble service, which might previously have been considered part of the human path to reach God, are understood to be part of the divine estate into which the devotee enters by the grace of God.[96]

A question that arises is whether Ramanuja claims that any one path is sufficient for salvation or not. There are a few interpreters who consider that one path can be chosen. However, there is no evidence for this in Ramanuja's thought. What Ramanuja intended is that Brahman's knowledge and God-centered actions of devotees together bring salvation to the devotees. Carman's aforesaid words imply that Ramanuja holds all paths together. We had already noted in the introduction to this chapter that Ramanuja's is an inclusive system.

It is significant to construe that the paths of knowledge, *karma*, and devotion are related and compatible. It is ignorance, concerning the true nature and interrelation of *cit*, *acit* and Brahman (souls, matter and God), that binds us to the cycle of birth-life-death-rebirth. Therefore, it is necessarily a knowledge or intuition of the unions which frees souls from this bondage, and it is universally accepted in Vaishnava Hinduism that *bhakti* is the path in which one must walk in order to receive God's *bhakti* saving gift of new vision. Thus knowledge, *karma*, and *bhakti* are related, hence the objective and subjective sides are complementary.

Ramanuja's followers are now divided into *tengalai* and *vadagalai* Hindus. An observation of the belief of both these groups is relevant for us, because whilst one group emphasizes the subjective side of salvation, the other sect stresses the objective side of salvation.

---

96. Carman, *The Theology of Ramanuja*, 217. Also, Bharatan explains the objective and subjective sides of salvation with the help of a story. He says that a son who gets lost is filled with supreme joy to find his father to be still alive and as the king ruling the nation. Similarly, the king will also be happy to know that his son who was lost years ago is fine and in good health. The son takes steps to meet his father and the father takes steps to recover his son as well. The son is equated with a human being and the father is equated with Brahman. See Kumarappa, *Hindu Conception of Deity*, 295–96.

Tengalai and Vadagalai Hindus.

A brief portrayal of the *tengalai* (southern school) and *vadagalai* (northern school) sects will enable us to reassert that Ramanuja's thought included both the objective and subjective understanding of salvation. After the time of Ramanuja, his followers split among themselves and they came to be known as the *tengalai* and *vadagalai* Hindus.[97] Whilst the *tengalai* sect considers the Sanskrit and Tamil texts as sacred, the *vadagalai* sect considers Sanskrit alone as the sacred language.[98] In relation to means of salvation, which is more important to us, the *tengalai* sect emphasizes the objective side in Ramanuja's thought, whilst the *vadagalai* group emphasizes the subjective side of his thought. Following this they are called the cat school of thought and the monkey school of thought respectively. This is because the *tengalai* Hindus believe that God saves us like the mother cat carries its kittens away in case of fire, whereas the *vadagalai* Hindus believe that we need to cling to God like the young of a monkey clings to its mother to save itself from fire.[99] However, the presence of both these interpretations by the two groups along with our earlier analysis asserts the presence of both objective and subjective sides of the means to salvation in Ramanuja's thought.

Our discussion has focused on significant themes in Hinduism with relation to the means to salvation, and with special reference to Ramanuja. It is in this context that the four dimensions of Brahman's function in relation to salvation must be construed.

Four Dimensions of Brahman's Function in Relation to Salvation

There are four important dimensions of Brahman's salvific function. Firstly, it is useful in the creation of the true knowledge of the four-fold union. Secondly, Brahman offers this knowledge continuously and not in a particular historical period of time. Thirdly, as Brahman is present in our souls, its function transcends religious persuasions. Fourthly, the saving concept of Brahman provides a union between different doctrines within Visistadvaitic Hinduism.

---

97. Lipner refers to this split in his work. See, Lipner, *The Face of Truth*, 2. It is said that this split arouse in the fourteenth century. Rudolf Otto too writes of this in his book, *India's Religion of Grace and Christianity*, 56.

98. Klostermaier, *A Concise Encyclopedia of Hinduism*, 183, 194.

99. Klostermaier, *A Concise Encyclopedia of Hinduism*, 183, 194. For details on Vadagalai and Tengalai Hindus, see also, Kumarappa, *Hindu Conception of Deity*, 310–12.

1) The Saving Knowledge of Brahman and the Four-Fold Union

It is interesting that the saving knowledge of Brahman expounded by Ramanuja can be readily comprehended in terms of the four-fold union. It is an axiom that the four unions are necessary for peace and harmony. In Vaishnava Hinduism, the saving knowledge of Brahman is that we ought to lead a life recognizing the four-fold union overcoming our alienations from God, others, nature, and also from ourselves. We now focus on the four aspects of Brahman's functions in the process of establishing the unions.

a) God-Human Union

Firstly, the saving knowledge of Brahman created in us includes the knowledge of God-human union often obscured by *avidya*. The role of Brahman's function is significant for God-human union. Brahman establishes the ideal relationship between God and human beings by taking away the ignorance of the self. According to Ramanuja, various scriptural passages assert that the knowledge of oneness of the self with the Brahman is essential for the destruction of ignorance.[100]

In the general anthropology of Hinduism, as well as for Ramanuja, it is the atman (soul) within human beings that is of prime importance. Lott observes that atman is transcendent over the body in Ramanuja's system.[101] Again one shouldn't misunderstand the atman to which we commonly refer to as self. There are "two" selves in us: the essential self and the empirical self (soul). R. N. Dandekar claims that the essential self is indeed of the nature of pure self-consciousness, which is beyond all bodily and mental conditions. The empirical self, the self which experiences this changing world of the senses, comes into being, according to the Hindu view, when through the operation of original ignorance (*avidya*) the essential self falls from its serene aloofness, thereby forgetting, so to speak, its identity with the Supreme Being.[102] In fact, the essential self is beyond and deeper than the empirical self.

The physical body doesn't get enough attention in Hindu anthropology because it is considered as mortal and of no use after death. For Ramanuja, body is "a conglomeration of elements of *prakrti* that has developed into a certain nature and structure, it is essentially non-spiritual or non-conscient and essentially transient . . . Entirely different from this non-conscient

---

100. Ramanuja, *The Vedanta Sutras*, vol. I, 32–33.

101. Lott, *God and the Universe*, 38.

102. Morgan, *The Basic Beliefs of Hinduism*, 117–20.

prakrti is the atman, an essentially spiritual and conscient principle whose essential attribute is knowledge."[103] The essential self or atman in us is in union with God. However, only the wise are aware of this union.

To say that I am part of the body of Brahman is not wrong. Referring to atman the Kaivalyopanishad says, "I am the Lord. I am golden. I am the auspicious form."[104] The real "I" or the essential self in us is atman. We may understand that the spiritual essence in us is atman. The eternal, which dwells in the soul, has to be known as the ultimate. This helps us to understand that Brahman lives in us. In the words of Zaehner, "Man is the city of Brahman."[105] Ramanuja says that the relation between atman and God is a unity and our body is the means for atman to know and be united with God.[106] Thus it is clear that when we speak of the union between God and humans, we, in fact, speak of the union between Brahman and atman.

Salvation, according to Ramanuja, is a life with the right knowledge of our union with God. Certain knowledge of the desire to know God given to us is grace or a gift. A desire to know Brahman, however, is very different from the real knowledge of Brahman. This desire is a means to union with Brahman. R. Panikkar points out, "It [The desire] is, as it were, a thin thread that already unites us with Brahman, an ignition-point, a kind of identity or at least a communication, not to say communion, which grows and develops from *Brahmajijnasa* to *Brahmajnana*, from the desire to the knowledge."[107] Lott says, "to be joined with God is the end of all yogic self discipline in the Gita."[108]

Ramanuja illustrates that the devotee and the beloved, "enjoys a more or less continuous imageful contemplative (but not inactive) union with the Lord and offers up all his actions as expressions of divine worship, his spiritual ascent becomes ever more sure, unitive and grace-laden."[109] In Ramanuja's understanding, for salvation, "the recognition of similarity of God and atman is essential."[110]

Ramanuja repeatedly says that the world is the body of Brahman. For him, God is united to the world as the self is united to the body. Realizing this union is salvation. Precisely, the real self within us is of Brahman.

---

103. Buitenen, *Ramanuja on the Bhagavadgita*, 19.
104. Kaivalyo, *Upanishad*, 20.
105. Zaehner, *Hinduism*, 48.
106. Zaehner, *Hinduism*, 2.
107. Panikkar, *The Unknown Christ of Hinduism*, 117.
108. Lott, *God and the Universe*, 39.
109. Lipner, *The Face of Truth*, 100.
110. Buitenen, *Ramanuja on the Bhagavadgita*, 22.

Salvation and *moksha* is the state of realizing this union of ourselves with Brahman. The ultimate goal of life is realizing this union and living practically one with the will of the divine. Further, it is a relational union, which is attained between Brahman and atman. Lipner writes, "the consciousness of enlightenment too, in which an 'I-Thou' union between the knowing subject, viz. the liberated individual and the object known, viz. the Lord himself, is established and eminently relational."[111]

The various avatars for Ramanuja portray the union between God and us. God also creates the knowledge of union in us only because he is united with us. Without freedom from our separateness from God, salvation is impossible. In the saved state we will lead a life with the intuitive knowledge of our union with God like the body's union with the self.

b) Human-Human Union

Secondly, the saving knowledge of Brahman includes the knowledge of a human-human union. Again, it is the function of Brahman that makes human union with one another intimate. It is the same Brahman who lives in all and helps all overcome the differences between one another caused by ignorance. Certainly, the God-human union implies that it is the same divine self that is shared with the entire humanity. Kumarappa says, "When Brahman was thus identified with the self of the individual, it was only natural that the usual distinctions of father, mother, husband, wife, Brahman, Sudra, thief, and sage should cease for ultimately all individuals are Brahman, 'a unity without duality.'"[112] Since the essential self is the same with all, to think in terms of "I am you" or "you are me," is not incorrect. For Ramanuja, whether it is *jnana yoga* or *karma yoga* or *bhakti yoga* they should culminate in the recognition of atman in oneself and all others, which is Brahman. Carman says that the intuition of Brahman as the self of all comes through the study of Vedic rituals.[113] The highest state, however, is acting upon the recognition of not distinguishing between one's own atman and the atman of others.

The intensity of the relationship expected of humanity is present in the Rigveda itself. The Rigveda says, "Common be your end, common be your purpose, common be your deliberations, common be your desires, united be your hearts, united be your intentions, perfect be the union amongst

---

111. Lipner, *The Face of Truth*, 60.
112. Kumarappa, *Hindu Conception of Deity*, 36.
113. Carman, *The Theology of Ramanuja*, 56.

you."[114] In the Upanishads, we read, "Lo, verily not love for all is dear, but for love of the soul all is dear."[115] This verse claims that we ought to love one another because the soul is dear. Brown says, "The presence of the Lord in our husband or wife, parents, siblings and children makes them dear to us."[116] It is possible to move further and say that the presence of the Lord (Brahman) in all should bring a union between one another. In the words of Brown, "The world is one family. The entire universe is a manifestation of the divine which is found in the heart of each and every human being."[117] Apparently, "To bring prosperity to family, nation and humanity as a whole, we need to have a unity of purpose. We need to see the interests of others apart from our conflicting desires."[118] Brahman's role is significant here because it is Brahman, by the granting of right knowledge, who helps us realize that we are grounded in the same being.

The human-human union caused by the function of Brahman is in agreement with science, says Swami Rama Tirtha. He claims, "Science has proved that if a body is to act upon another body, there must be continuity between the two. It is because of this law of continuity that we are all united to one another psychologically."[119]

Though human beings are of diverse natures, and though the plane of existence varies from person to person, a oneness can be discerned at the very core of being a human. Visistadvaitic Hinduism claims that Brahman brings the knowledge of this oneness that promotes the union. This union should help one fulfill one's role in society though renunciation is a way one searches for the ultimate goal. Humans are not only responsible for themselves but also for others. This is expressed by the word *dharma* in relation to humans.[120]

Now how does Ramanuja's self-body analogy portray a human-human union? St. Paul understands that Christ is the head of humanity. Though not in the same way, in a similar way, Ramanuja views that Brahman is the self of humanity. John Carman says that, for Ramanuja, the intuition of Brahman as the self of all comes from Vedic studies.[121] Ramanuja again and

---

114. *Rigveda* X, 191, 3–4.
115. *Brhadaranyaka Upanishad*, 11.4.5
116. Brown, *The Essential Teachings of Hinduism*, 144.
117. Brown, *The Essential Teachings of Hinduism*, 144.
118. Brown, *The Essential Teachings of Hinduism*, 149.
119. Swami Rama Tirtha, "Universal Unity," quoted in Brown, *The Essential Teachings of Hinduism*, 149.
120. Morgan, *The Basic Beliefs of Hinduism*, 132.
121. Carman, *The Theology of Ramanuja*, 56.

again insists that it is the entire humanity that forms the body of Brahman. In this sense, we all constitute the one body of Brahman. In other words, we are different parts of the same body of Brahman.

Significantly, for Ramanuja, all souls are equal in their essential nature. He writes, "All selves are alike in so far as having knowledge as their essential nature."[122] The equality between all souls is useful in the practical application of the intuitive knowledge given by Brahman, which is essential for our salvation. For Ramanuja, the presence of the same Brahman in us, as ourself, brings a unity between the whole of humanity.

It is believed that when Ramanuja learned from his guru a secret mantra, he proclaimed it to many from a tower because he was clear that it is the same Brahman which resides in all and all must be saved.[123]

c) Human-Nature Union

Thirdly, the saving knowledge of Brahman includes the knowledge of a human-nature union. Visistadvaitic Hinduism teaches that Brahman is one with the universe, the natural world of multiplicity and differentiations, believing that Brahman transforms itself into the ever-blossoming and developing form of the world. Radha Krishnan interprets Svetavatara Upanishad to say, "Is he (Brahman) from whom this compounded world proceeds. Righteousness (dharma) he brings, rejecting evil, he, the Lord of good fortune."[124] Thus, Brahman is affirmed not only as transcendent but also as immanent. In the immanent form, Brahman is present with every creation.

Although a human is nearer to the Supreme Spirit than an animal is, and an animal is nearer to him than a plant is,[125] every being has its purposes in its union with Brahman. Brahman is common to all lives including the flora and fauna. Nature is thought of possessing divine quality because nature too is the manifestation of Brahman. *Rta*, a concept in the Vedas, affirms that humanity is in harmony with nature.[126] Hence, human beings are expected to be in union with nature. Many gods have different creatures as their vehicle, and in Hindu festivals different creatures play significant roles.

Lipner says that because Vedanta lacks a concept of the eschaton, Ramanuja, like Paul, cannot say that the entire creation is waiting eagerly for

---

122. Thibaut, *The Vedantic Sutras*, 562.
123. Lott, *God and the Universe*, 14.
124. Radhakrishnan, *Indian Philosophy*, vol. II, 686.
125. Morgan, *The Basic Beliefs of Hinduism*, 14.
126. Robertson, "Hindu Spirituality," 5.

liberation.¹²⁷ However, why should there be a concept of the eschaton for perceiving that the entire creation needs salvation? In fact, for Ramanuja, all creation will receive salvation but in a different way. Ramanuja, like any other Hindu theologian, believes in reincarnation. Salvation comes to all beings in this process of reincarnation. In fact, it is the same Brahman, which is present as atman in us, that is present in the wider creation.¹²⁸ This very presence of the same Brahman in all beings is what brings human-nature union.

The concept of human-nature union in Visistadvaitic Hinduism makes ecology important to Vaishnava Hindus.¹²⁹ Human beings are responsible to respect and maintain the universe. Even in day-to-day practices, the Hindus are expected to be tolerant to other beings, and they are. They are very keen on feeding the creatures at temples and homes.

In Ramanuja's thought the recognition of similar atman in all beings is vital.¹³⁰ The self-body union analogy plays a crucial role in human-nature union too. Ramanuja understands that the self of entire creation is that of Brahman's. For him, the entire universe is Brahman's body. We are united with nature because it is our self and the self of all creation in nature that together constitutes God's body. Realization of this union is within the realm of salvation. Analyzing Ramanuja, Eric Lott observes,

> God's Being penetrates his whole creation, so that creation participates in Him, though is not identical with, his perfect Being. In an organically dependent relation with his supreme Reality, substantial character is imparted to every 'part' included in this

---

127. Lipner, *The Face of Truth*, 131.

128. According to Hindu scripture, "Everything different from that highest self, whether conscious or non-conscious, constitutes its body, while the self alone is the unconditioned embodied self." See Radhakrishnan, *The Vedanta According to Sankara*, 280–81.

129. It could also be thought that unlike the modern people of the West, the people of countries like India, were largely dependent on nature for their survival. Anil Agarwal says, "in 1974 I came across an extremely evocative movement called the Chipko movement in the high Himalayan ranges of Uttar Pradesh. The village women there were threatening to hug the trees if the government allowed them to be cut . . . It showed how important the environment was for the poor of India: it was their source of daily survival, the foundation of their economy and culture . . . I began to see the people living in those diverse habitats—the fisher folk dependent on the vast grasslands of the Thar Desert and the upper Himalayan pastures, and the forest-dwelling people dependent on the diverse forest types of India. This could have helped them to see divinity in nature and consequently formulate a theology of human-nature union." See Agarwal, "Can Hindu Beliefs and Values Help India Meet its Ecological Crisis?" in Chapple and Tucker, *Hinduism and Ecology*, 165–66.

130. Buitenen, *Ramanuja on the Bhagavadgita*, 21.

divine 'body.' Thus there is real communication between Infinite Being and finite being—similar to that between self and body.[131]

The saving knowledge of Brahman, however, embraces the ability to see that there is a oneness about the world and God and yet that creation is real and distinct, standing as the attributes of God, in a dependent union to him.[132] God, along with humanity and nature, is seen as a whole. For Ramanuja, there is a unity of composition.[133]

Human beings are expected to act responsibly, respecting and maintaining the universe. We see that there is hostility and killings among animals and birds themselves. However, Hinduism, in general, overlooks this "necessary evil" and teaches that we need to be in union with nature because it is the body of Brahman.[134] We now move on to see the final aspect of the four-fold union.

d) One-Oneself Union

Fourth, the saving knowledge helps one to overcome the split within oneself. In Visistadvaitic Hindu thought, when the true knowledge of ourselves is attained from Brahman, one becomes free from selfishness. The selfish "I" is dissolved, which is a product of ignorance. One will not be in conflict with oneself but will realize that they are one with the Brahman (atman) in themselves.

In Ramanuja's system, the essential self in us is forgotten by us due to *avidya*. In fact, the self forgets its divine origin and destiny, and lapses into the private particular self of *prakrti* (matter). The real "I," which is of the divine, is forgotten in the empirical me. This makes one selfish and one lives for the empirical self. Often there occurs a separation between the real self and the selfish self in us. In general terms, there is a struggle between the divine spark and the evil spark within us. The divine spark in us can be called atman, which is essentially of the nature of Brahman. The knowledge of Brahman helps us triumph over selfish desires, and thus, helps us to be in

---

131. Lott, *God and the Universe*, 160.
132. Lott, *God and the Universe*, 41.
133. Srinivasachari, *Ramanuja's Idea of the Finite Self*, 14, 17.
134. Hinduism doesn't move further to reflect on the concept of one species depending on another for its food. Also, the complex questions of our world today (in animal testing and so on) are not analyzed. Most works limit their analysis with the use of Cow and Bull. For example, Prime, *Hinduism and Ecology*, 99–102.

union with our real selves, our atman. Ramanuja urges that one should see the self and not the self in oneself.[135]

An inner conflict in us is also caused by feelings of guilt, fear, and depression. The saving knowledge of Brahman frees us from the wrong notion of the selfish "me" in us, and provides us with the knowledge that we do not belong to us, but to Brahman. Hence, one-oneself union, in fact, is the realization that it is the divine who lives in us. Srinivasachari says, "In the ecstasy of union the devotee's feeling of self melts away and he sees everything with the eye of God and summons the world to share in the ineffable joy of immortal nectar."[136] When one relies on Brahman he becomes the self-ruler.[137] Nothing else rules him.

For Ramanuja, the contingent self is unimportant and the significant one is the essential self. The essential self is of the divine. We ought to realize our union with the essential self. This essential self is in the form of atman. Lipner says, for Ramanuja, self-knowledge is essential for the ultimate communion with the Lord. Also, the "self-knowledge implies an intuitive realization of the nature of the atman."[138] Perhaps this union stresses our union with the immanence of Brahman, whilst divine-human union stresses our union with the transcendence of Brahman.

It is when the four-fold union is realized that we attain *mukti*. When we practically live with the intuitive and practical knowledge of Brahman, the fullness of *moksha* is experienced. It is after our life in this body. However, a foretaste of salvation is known in this life itself. It is now clear that the God-world union, which is central in Ramanuja's thought, can be construed clearly in this four-fold union perspective.

2) "The Saving/Liberating Function of Brahman" as an Ongoing Process

Salvation is not a static event but a work in progress. Hence, the function of Brahman should be construed as continuous in its nature. Ramanuja says that Brahman provides the knowledge of salvation till one acquires it to the necessary extent, provided one surrenders oneself to God. In fact, Brahman is continuously at work in any person.

Further, as the knowledge of Brahman is for a practical purpose, it logically should not be gained on one occasion alone. Rather, in reality, it

---

135. Ramanuja, *The Vedanta Sutras*, vol. I, 13.
136. Srinivasachari, *Ramanuja's Idea of the Finite Self*, 72.
137. Karmarkar, *Sri Bhasya of Ramanuja*, para. 5.
138. Lipner, *The Face of Truth*, 108.

should be acquired through a lifelong course involving the preservation of an attitude of contemplative *bhakti*.[139]

"The saving function of Brahman" is continuous also in another sense. Brahman has enabled salvation for every person who lived in the past and has "attained" salvation, and will continue to enable salvation to all forever. In other words, there is no beginning or end to the salvific work of Brahman. It is an ongoing process. Thus the saving function of Brahman is beyond history and beyond the limits of time; it is of eternity. Interestingly, as we noted earlier, there is no doctrine of eschatology in Visistadvaitic Hinduism, as there is in Christianity. Vaishnava Hindus, along with other Hindus, believe that our universe will exist forever.

It is also noteworthy that the saving function of Brahman not only transcends history, but also transcends geographical boundaries. Brahman is the one who causes salvation to all in spite of where one lives. Also, salvation/*moksha* is not circumscribed by a geographical place. It is a state of mind.[140] In John Milton's famous words, "The mind is its own place. It can make a heaven out of hell and a hell out of heaven."

To all people from time, immemorial Brahman has brought about salvation and will continue to do so forever. Now we move on to see how Brahman's saving function goes beyond boundaries of religion.

3) The Saving/Liberating Function of Brahman as Transcending Religious Barriers

When Hinduism originated there could have been hardly any contact with the religions of the West. As we have pointed out earlier, it is a very ancient religion. Even other Indian religions like Sikhism, Buddhism, and Jainism were not in existence. Hence, the numerous founders of Hinduism must have had the idea that all who live will embrace Hinduism. Moreover, Hinduism was not understood as a religion but as a practical philosophy or as a way of life.

It is in this context that the vision of Brahman's "saving function" emerged. Obviously, in this context, the cause of salvation for all should come from the same being, which was interpreted as Brahman. Being one with Brahman formed the basis of salvation and not the religion, Hinduism as such. Hindus, in general, understand that the knowledge of Brahman is available to all irrespective of their religious affiliations. It is the desire for knowledge and a devoted life that brings us the grace of Brahman. This

---

139. Peery, *A Christian Understanding*, 194–95.
140. Brown, *The Essential Teachings of Hinduism*, 58.

philosophy or belief is prevalent even to this day. To be saved one need not be a Hindu. Evidently, the emphasis which Christianity or Islam lays on faith in the religion is not found in Hinduism, including the Visistadvaitic strand of it. One should remain in one's own religion and probably need to reform one's own religion. Salvation is far beyond religion. The function of Brahman in relation to salvation remains the same with all alike, no matter to which religion one belongs.

This leads Hindus to say that religious conversion is "twaddle." For instance, Swami Dyananda Saraswathi says,

> Religions that are committed by their theologies to convert are necessarily aggressive, since conversion implies a conscious intrusion into religious life of a person, in fact, into the religious person. Religious conversion is violence and it breeds violence. In converting you are also converting the non-violent to violent ... I request you to put a freeze on conversion ... You cannot ask me to respond to conversion by converting others to my religion because it is not part of my tradition.[141]

What matters for salvation in Visistadvaitic Hinduism is whether we are ready to proceed with the knowledge given by the grace of Brahman or not. One need not necessarily be a follower of Visistadvaitic Hindu religious tradition to attain the grace of Brahman.

There is sufficient support for the view that Ramanuja's theological vision is universal in aspect.[142] For example, referring to Ramanuja, Lipner writes, "He speaks time and again of the Lord as the inner controller of all embodied selves and of the whole world as the Lord's body.... There are recorded episodes in his life in which he showed a burning concern for the salvation of people outside the Sri Vaisnava pale."[143] However, according to Ramanuja, taken for granted his belief in rebirth, the grace of Brahman will allow anyone to be born into the Vaisnavite Hindu faith. It is only after being born in that faith that one can attain salvation.[144]

It should also be pointed out that if Ramanuja were to live today, in a world which is becoming more and more cross-cultural everyday, he would probably have accommodated all human beings directly in the divine plan of salvation in this life itself, without having to be reborn in Vaishnava

---

141. Saraswathi, "An Open Letter." (Saraswathi is the head of *Arsha Vidya Gurukulam*, a Hindu educational institute in India.)

142. Ramanuja, *Gita Bhasya*, 29, 32, 270–73.

143. Lipner, *The Face of Truth*, 102.

144. Lipner, *The Face of Truth*, 102.

Hinduism.[145] Nevertheless, what is crucial to note is that our salvation is based on being a *jivatma* (soul) and not based on being a Vaishnava Hindu. Also, his openness in accommodating all in the divine salvific plan, in spite of anyone's religious affiliation, should be appreciated.

4) The Saving/Liberating Function of Brahman as Providing a Union between Visistadvaitic Hindu Doctrines

As we expect, Ramanuja's Hindu system has several theological doctrines that constitute the religion. Ramanuja's writings reveal that all theological doctrines revolve around the concept of the saving function of Brahman. In other words, the saving function of Brahman is that which provides the particular meaning to the other doctrines. In fact, we have briefly dealt with the relationship of the Brahman concept with other important theological concepts namely those of God, Sin and Salvation.

Precisely, the concept of Brahman's saving function brings a particular meaning to the doctrines of creation, revelation, worship and the like in Ramanuja's thought.

Though we need not go into details here, we will point out how a union between theological doctrines is established by the saving concept of Brahman. Ramanuja understands that the purpose of creation is a voluntary game of Brahman and a means for attaining salvation. Thus the purpose of creation is related to salvation. With regard to revelation, it is a means of providing the saving grace to the devotee. Specifically, the revelations by avatars are to save God's creation from the dangers of *karma* and ignorance. Further, understandably, worship and *bhakti* are part of the means to salvation in Ramanuja's thought. Thus there is continuity amongst the central theological doctrines in Ramanuja's Visistadvaitic theological thinking.

Possibilities of Constructing an Atonement Model Using Ramanuja's Thought

Evidently, the means to salvation in the Hindu thought of Ramanuja has profound implications in the construction of an atonement model. The concept of ignorance (sin) understood in Visistadvaitic Hindu thought as four-fold alienation will help us to interpret the concept of sin in Christianity in a new dimension. Similarly, the concept of liberation (salvation)

---

145. Lipner, *The Face of Truth*, 102. Also See Carman, *The Theology of Ramanuja*, 39–40.

construed as four-fold union in Visistadvaitic Hindu thought will enlighten us in interpreting the concept of salvation in Christianity in that dimension. This will enable us to construct a new model of the atonement saying that the atoning work of Christ creates the intuitive and practical knowledge of the four-fold union. We will draw support from the Bible as well as from theologians who have ventured to understand the work of Christ in this direction. Nevertheless, we will be careful to retain the particularity and historicity of the atoning work of Christ in this work because that is central to Christianity. Further, it is the reality of particularity and historicity which makes each human being unique before God. However, our model, along the lines of Ramanuja, will affirm that the atonement has both objective as well as subjective roles. Again, Ramanuja's interpretation of the concept of means to salvation will enable us to analyze the prevailing state of affairs to see if the atonement has implications for salvation before and after the time of historical Jesus, whether the atonement brings a unity between different religious traditions and whether the doctrine of atonement provides a unity between the different doctrines of Christian theology. Our new model of the atonement can be called "the atonement creating unions." We will develop this in chapter 4.

Prior to attempting to outline our comparative model of the atonement, we will proceed to analyze the inadequacy of existing traditional and selected modern theories of the atonement in a Hindu-Christian context, in the next chapter.

3

An Analysis of Existing Theories of the Atonement in a Hindu-Christian Indian Context

OBVIOUSLY, FOR MOST CHRISTIANS, the atoning work of Christ is perceived to be crucial in making salvation possible. We have already noted the dominant themes of the New Testament, in the introductory chapter, on which the different atonement theories are being developed. Throughout the tradition, the theology of the atonement has been a central concern of Christian theologians and in many respects may be taken to be at the heart of Christian theology. The emergence of various theories or models of the atonement and the discussion this represents testify to this fact. The detailed discussions explicate the religious depth of the atonement and its implications for other theological claims made e.g., in the doctrines of God, Christology or Christian anthropology.

However, the theology of the atonement, as currently understood through the existing theories remains inadequate in an Indian context, where Hinduism predominates, by failing to address their key conceptions and concerns. We have already briefly highlighted a few criticisms from selected and influential Indian thinkers including Gandhi. As A. Wessels puts it succinctly,

> Gandhi rejected the notion of 'divine atonement and forgiveness through Jesus Christ . . . His reason [was that he] was not ready 'to believe literally that Jesus by his death and by his blood redeemed the sins of the world' and his heart refused to accept 'that there was anything like a mysterious or miraculous virtue in Jesus' death on the Cross.[1]

1. Wessels, *Images of Jesus*, 138.

It is not only Gandhi, but the majority of Hindus[2] today share the same opinion. We have noted the criticism of Ram Mohan Roy as well. He goes on to describe the supposed blessings of pardon so dependent on the atonement of Christ as childish.[3] Why does the idea of atonement, as understood in Christian tradition, remain inadequate in an Indian Visistadvaitic Hindu context? The simple answer is, as we have seen, Visistadvaitic Hindus believe that Brahman serves the saving function by creating an intuitive and practical knowledge of the divine-human, human-human, human-nature and one-oneself unions, which is salvation without the need for or reference to a particular and essentially brutal event. Also, they believe that the "saving function of Brahman" is ongoing, transcends the barrier of religious affiliation and provides greater coherence with other Visistadvaitic Hindu theological doctrines. And admittedly, none of the existing theories endeavor to elucidate the atonement as having a role in creating an intuitive and practical knowledge of the four-fold union. Nor do any of the existing theories venture to see the full significance of an atonement that creates the four-fold union in itself. Further, most theories do not refer to a truly ongoing function in the atonement, its universal scope nor to the need for a unifying function through the theology of the atonement with other theological doctrines.

Indian Christian theologians are well aware of the fact that, in an Indian context, the theology of the atonement should be interpreted from a unifying perspective. For example, Samartha, an Indian Christian theologian writes, "Salvation today has to be understood as personal healing, social healing, and cosmic healing within the larger unity of nature, humanity and God . . ."[4] Similarly, Kenneth Cragg commenting on the atonement in a pluralistic context writes, "The God, of whom we say that Jesus is the Son, unifies by his own unity the mystery of atonement . . . The inclusiveness of the cross belongs with the unity of God."[5] However, we will retain the historical particularity of the atoning work of Christ throughout this project as it has been seen to be crucial to Christianity. Precisely, our claim is that it is from the historical particularity of the cross—the entire humanity who lived and who will live in history attain their salvation. The atonement should be theologized as both an accomplished means and an ongoing method to this unity in an Indian context. We will proceed

---

2. Here the word Hindus refers to the followers of Ramanuja, in particular, as well as to all Hindus in general.

3. Das, *Shadow of the Cross*, 28. Also see Sumithra, *Christian Theology*, 40.

4. Samartha, *One Christ*, 138.

5. Cragg, *Christ and Faiths*, 225.

to outline a fresh model of the atonement relevant to the Visistadvaitic Indian-Hindu context in the next chapter.

Prior to that, our task in this chapter is to analyze and highlight some of the inadequacies of the existing theories from an Indian perspective and their incompatibility with the existing insights grounded in Brahman's saving concept. The frame of reference for our analysis in this chapter is to draw on the insights of the "saving function of Brahman," as understood by Visistadvaitic Hindus who follow Ramanuja's theology. We will effectively test the theology of the atonement in the Christian tradition against the saving concept of Brahman in Visistadvaitic Hinduism and solely not on the basis of a set of internal Christian theological criteria. However, this attempt is not to reject the existing theories completely but to show why the existing theories remain and appear superficial and alien to the majority of the Indian population.

There are five dominant theories of the atonement in the Christian tradition. Scholars have helpfully classified them as either subjective or objective theories. A few modern theologians have also viewed the atonement somewhat differently or using multiple models. In this project, it would be too ambitious to analyze fully every possible atonement theory and its incompatibility with the Visistadvaitic Hindu philosophy. We will select two theories of the atonement as representative of existing theories and analyze these in some detail. The two theories that we have selected are the penal substitutionary and the representative models. The penal substitutionary model can reasonably be used to represent the other traditional theories and the representative model can justifiably be used to reflect modern theories. However, within the compass of this chapter we will also very briefly portray the inadequacy of the other dominant traditional and modern theories in the Indian context because our claim is that none of the existing theories are immediately plausible in the Visistadvaitic Hindu context. This will pave the way for us to outline a fresh model of the atonement in the next chapter. Regarding modern atonement theories, within the limited scope of this chapter, we shall very briefly examine the works of Karl Barth, Vernon White, J. Denny Weaver, Michael Winter and Vincent Brümmer.

Whilst testing the adequacy of existing theories of the atonement in a Hind-Christian Indian context, our concern in this chapter is specifically to seek to answer the following questions. Can the concerns (human) problems addressed by the saving concept of Brahman be adequately served by the traditional theories and any of the existing works of the selected theologians? Can any one of the atonement theories be truly meaningful to the people of India? Given the context should different aspects of the atonement be stressed? Can an atonement model, if formulated on the basis of a comparative doctrinal perspective, using the saving concept of Brahman, offer creative new possibilities for a meaningful and fruitful human existence today? And can elements of the traditional theories and selected recent works on the atonement collectively, along with a new model of the atonement, offer better opportunities for a genuinely global conversation about the concerns in the theology of the atonement?

Preliminary Considerations: Theories of the Atonement

To begin with, we need to be modest and bear in mind that the atonement cannot be fully comprehended by us because 1) it deals with divine action and 2) we are finite creations. Houts says, "There are only theories which try to assimilate a wide array of Biblical images, theories which try to explain a mystery, theories which fit some cultural milieus better than others, theories which all have their flaws and glitches"[6] No doubt, in the end times the divine will unveil the mystery of the atonement in its fullness to us, but in the mean time we have to rely on best efforts, stories, speculations, "beautiful sayings and pictured realizations." Now, we can know the divine mystery only to the extent to which the divine wants to unveil it to us. It may be a fact that theology is a divinely ordained discipline and therefore seeking to construe the atonement in a range of ways is part of an endeavor of obedience. It is precisely this effort of the many theologians that has resulted in the theories of the atonement, as we know them today.

Another initial comment on the traditional theories of the atonement will help us in our discussion. On the one hand, there are notable modern theologians who favor one particular theory over other theories. Moreover, different theologians have formulated different traditional theories of the atonement in different periods of time and in different cultural contexts. Certainly, each traditional theory, as we will see in this chapter, vehemently strives for an in-depth understanding of the atonement from a specific direction. For example, the classical theory explains some of the possible ways in which Christ overcame evil powers as objective realities through his atoning work. Nevertheless, the problem with this account is that only one aspect of the atonement is normally stressed at the cost of ignoring other aspects e.g., the impact on the human subject.

On the other hand, there are theologians who maintain that no one theory can expound the full magnificence of the atonement. For instance, Vernon White says, "It is commonplace to insist that no single atonement

---

6. Houts, "Classical Atonement Imagery," 5–6.

model will do justice to every Biblical image and theological concern."[7] In similar vein, Steve Holmes writes, " . . . each additional model or metaphor we are able to deploy enlarges our understanding of what was done for our salvation at Calvary."[8] However, this perception also is not without criticisms. As one would expect, at times it looks like we hold two completely different and incompatible elements together. Most would agree that it does not appear very coherent to think that the key focus of the action is that Christ satisfied God and that he overcame evil at one and the same time through his atoning activity.

Nevertheless, the strategy of holding as many different theories together as possible has some merit because in this way we are much less likely to lose some important aspect of the atonement that we would otherwise do by sticking to one view only. Alan Walker says, "The more angles from which we can view the Cross, the more adequately shall we penetrate the mystery of it."[9] In other words, following a comprehensive philosophy here rather than a strictly logical one is deemed to be the more fitting. Certainly, a presupposition in this project is that no one theory, including the theory which we will construct in the next chapter, is likely to comprehend fully the complete truth of the atonement. In short, the various theories of the atonement only remind us of the story of the five blind men describing an elephant. The person who touched the stomach said that it is like a pot, the one who touched a leg said that it is like a pillar and the one who touched the tail said that it is like a broom and so on. They are all true but there is much more to an elephant. Likewise, each theory definitely points to one aspect of the atonement. Holding all theories appropriately together can give us a better picture of the atonement.[10]

---

7 White, *Atonement and Incarnation*, 51.

8. Holmes, "Can Punishment Bring Peace?," 122. Along the same lines, Frances Young says, "In the New Testament and in Christian tradition, there is a tremendous wealth of different responses to the cross, both at the thinking and the feeling level. All this is not reducible to any one single theory, or even some kind of combination of all of them. None of the traditional theories has proved satisfactory; none is adequate on its own." See Young, *Can These Dry Bones Live?*, 42.

9. Walker, *The Many-Sided Cross of Jesus*, 13. It may be that there are diverse ways of finding meaning for our lives in the light of the atonement as viewed from different cultures. However, in this work, we will construct a model of the atonement using the means to salvation concept in Hinduism.

10. Spence argues that a unified theory is essential for understanding "the truth" with uniformity. However, in my opinion, he fails in his attempt because he bends the various traditional theories too much to fit into two theories of his liking—the Substitutionary and the Representation. As is evident, I am more inclined to Dillistone's view, when he says, "the sociological and psychological needs of a particular era will manifest themselves in such a way that a particular theory or explanation will commend itself as

Five Major Traditional Theories of the Atonement

Many theologians discuss various models of the atonement and some select and focus on one. For instance, John Macquarrie deals elaborately with the classical theory. Nevertheless, five theories are generally considered significant. They are: 1) the moral influence theory, 2) the penal substitutionary theory, 3) the classical theory, 4) the satisfaction/juridical theory, and 5) the sacrificial theory. The moral influence theory is *human-ward*, the penal substitutionary theory is *punishment-ward*, the classical theory is *devil-ward*, the satisfaction/juridical theory is *God-ward,* and the sacrificial theory is *sin-ward*.

Here, we move on to show the inadequacy of the models that we have selected to represent the traditional and modern atonement theories, using the saving function of Brahman in the Visistadvaitic-Hindu Indian context. Following this, as we have noted, we will outline very briefly the inadequacy of other traditional and predominant modern theories in the Indian context, before we move on to outlining our fresh model of the atonement in the next chapter.

An Analysis of the Penal Substitutionary Model and the Representation Model in the Indian Visistadvaitic Hindu Perspective

The Penal Substitutionary Model

Prior to viewing the criticism of this model, in the Visistadvaitic-Hindu context, we need to understand this theory in detail. To begin with we may note that Indian theologians have written very little on the atonement compared to other theological doctrines. The reason is that there is no very obvious point of contact between the concept of the means to salvation in Hindu tradition and the existing theories of the atonement in Christian tradition. We will soon point out that the penal substitutionary model and the Visitadavaitic concept of means to salvation revolve on two different axles.

The penal substitutionary theory is also known as the reformation model and the transactional model. It is generally accepted that the reformers are responsible for the turning of "the satisfaction theory" (which we will briefly

---

most relevant and meaningful at that particular time . . . it does mean that no absolute sanction can be accorded to any human formulation and that every Christian theologian must be constantly seeking to relate himself imaginatively to the particular needs of his own age." See, Dillistone, *Christian Understanding*, 25–26. Spence's work mentioned is Spence, *The Promise of Peace*, 1–18.

analyze later) into a theory of "penal substitution." Before we turn to Luther and Calvin let us look at some fundamental aspects of this theory.

Precisely, in this section, we will first examine the words penal and substitution. Second, we will emphasize that, according to this theory, Christ underwent identical punishment as our substitute. Hence, the atonement is not only appropriate but also adequate. Third, if sin is the cause and death is the effect, we will analyze how the phrase, "Jesus came to the world to take away our sins," fits in with this theory. Fourth, we will examine some of the reflections of Luther and Calvin on this theory. Fifth, we will outline the positive and negative criticisms of this theory. Finally, we will move on to point out the inadequacy of this theory from the Visistadvaitic-Hindu perspective.

First, the terms "substitution" and "penal." The term, substitution is commonly used in most aspects of our life. For example, in the context of football or cricket, it is used to describe a replacement of a player. The substitute is the one who replaces an injured member, who is incapable of playing any further. Another example of the use of the word, substitution could be in the context of business. Brick or cement, when not available, is sometimes substituted by other products like wood and iron, which are available. Thus a substitute, although different, is considered equivalent to that for whom or for which it is substituted. Obviously, this term has been used in the understanding of the atonement in a particular direction.

Now the words, "penal substitution." It is important for us to note that within the description "penal substitution" there is sufficient room for at least three propositions through which we could understand the atonement. Two quotations which will help us understand the three propositions are by W. G. T. Shedd and J. Owen. The term substitution in the context of penalty is found in the works of Shedd and Owen. Shedd says,

> In every instance of transgression the penalty of law must be inflicted, either personally or vicariously; either upon the transgressor or upon his substitute. The remission of penalty under the divine administration is not absolute but relative. It may be omitted in respect to the real criminal, but, if so, it must be inflicted upon someone in his place . . . Justice necessarily demands that sin be punished, but not necessarily in the person of the sinner.[11]

J. Owen has also written along the same lines. In his words,"God may give to everyone his own, or what is due to everyone, in the infliction of

---

11. Shedd, *Dogmatic Theology*, 373. This is later quoted in Stevens, *Christian Doctrine of Salvation*, 175–76.

punishment, although he does not inflict it on sinners themselves, but on their surety, substituted in their room and stead."[12]

This leads us to point out that the three basic propositions underlie the penal substitutionary model of the atonement. Firstly, in this view of the atonement, God is conceived as a just law-giver. As Shedd writes,

> All true scientific development of the doctrine of the atonement, it is very evident, must take its departure from the idea of divine justice. This conception is the primary one in the Biblical representation of this doctrine . . . we shall find that just in proportion as the mind of the Church obtained a distinct and philosophic conception of this great attribute, as an absolute and necessary principle in the divine nature, and in human nature, was it enabled to specify with distinctness the real meaning and purport of the Redeemer's Passion, and to exhibit the rational and necessary grounds for it.[13]

Second, if God is the just law-giver, punishment is the inevitable outcome of transgressing God's law. As Berkhof observes, punishment denotes,

> . . . pain or loss which is directly or indirectly inflicted by the Law-giver, in vindication of His justice outraged by the violation of the law. It originates in the righteousness or punitive justice of God, by which He maintains Himself as the Holy One and necessarily demands holiness and righteousness in all His rational creatures. Punishment . . . is, in fact, a debt that is due to the essential justice of God.[14]

Significantly, Shedd comments on the relationship between transgression and punishment. According to him, "Retributive justice is necessary in its operation. The claim of the law upon the transgressor for punishment is absolute and indefensible. The eternal Judge may or may not exercise mercy, but He must exercise justice."[15]

Third, God the most high is the most merciful and loving and in his love for humanity permits a substitution, so that due punishment falls not on the real sinners, but on their substitute, namely Christ. J. Owen explains this in the following way.

> Christ dying for us as a surety . . . being made a curse for us, was an undergoing of death, punishment, curse, wrath, not only for

12. Russell, *The Works of John Owen*, vol. 9, 473.
13. Shedd, *A History of Christian Doctrines*, 216–18.
14. Berkhof, *Systematic Theology*, 256.
15. Shedd, *Dogmatic Theology*, 436.

> our good, but directly in our stead; a commutation and subrogation of his person in the room and place of ours, being allowed and of God accepted.[16]

It is in this background we need to construe this theory. As John Owen would say if we accept that Christ's substitution consists in his receiving the punishment for our sins, then it is necessary that he suffers the identical punishment we would have got. Otherwise, a rational basis for the forgiveness of God will be abandoned and the believer's certainty of their deliverance from punishment will be removed.[17] In Owen's words,

> ... if God laid the punishment of our sins upon Christ, certainly it was the punishment that was due to them; mention is everywhere made of a commutation of persons, the just suffering for the unjust, the sponsor for the offender . . . but of a change of punishment there is no mention at all.[18]

It is also significant to see the two ways in which Owen pursues satisfaction that became effected through Christ's substitution. He writes,

> First, by a solution, or paying the very thing that is in the obligation, either by the party himself that is bound, or by some other in his stead: as, if I owe a man £20, and my friend goeth and payeth it, my creditor is fully satisfied. Secondly, by a solution, or a paying of so much, although in another kind, not the same that is in the obligation, which by the creditor's acceptation stands in the lieu of it; upon which also, freedom from the obligation followeth, not necessarily, but by virtue of an act of favor.[19]

However, although the idea of identical payment may be logical and consistent, it is not without difficulties. For example, the death penalty was made in different ways in different context and time. In this regard, A. H. Strong says, "a golden eagle is worth a thousand copper cents. The penalty paid by Christ is strictly and literally equivalent to that which the sinner would have borne, although it is not identical. The vicarious bearing of it excludes the latter."[20]

Second, how could we constitute Christ's suffering and death as equivalent? We might understand that the dignity of the divine-human Christ makes the sufferings and death as an equivalent to the sufferings

---

16. Russell, *The Works of John Owen*, vol. 5, 390.
17. Russell, *The Works of John Owen*, vol. 5, 247.
18. Russell, *The Works of John Owen*, vol. 5, 122.
19. Russell, *The Works of John Owen*, vol. 5, 261.
20. Strong, *Systematic Theology*, 770.

and death that was due to the entire humanity. Shedd is of the view that Christ's suffering,

> ... contains the element of infinitude, which is the element of value in the case, with even greater precision than the satisfaction of the creature does; because it is the suffering of a strictly infinite Person in a finite time, while the latter is only the suffering of a finite person in an endless, but not strictly infinite time.[21]

Now, it is clear that this model can hold that what Christ has accomplished is not only appropriate but also adequate for maintaining God's holiness and justice.[22] Another notable theologian who talks about the adequacy of the penal substitutionary character of the atonement is A. A. Hodge. He writes that Christ,

> ... did suffer the very penalty of the law—that is, sin was punished in him with strict rigour of justice. His sufferings were no substitute for a penalty, but those very penal evils which rigorous justice demanded of this exalted person, when he stood in our place, as a full equivalent of all that was demanded of us. The substitution of a divine for a human victim necessarily involved a change in the quality, though none whatsoever in the legal relations, of the suffering.[23]

C. Hodge is more explicit in speaking of the adequacy of Christ's suffering. For him, Christ's suffering and death were "adequate to accomplish all the ends designed by the punishment of the sins of men."[24] Specifically,

> it is not to be inferred from this, however, that either the kind or degree of our Lord's sufferings was a matter of indifference ... He would not have suffered as He did, not to the degree He did, unless there had been an adequate reason for it. ... There must be enough of self-sacrifice and suffering to give dignity and inherent value to the proffered atonement.[25]

It is apparent that A.A. Hodge and C. Hodge move between the idea of intrinsic value of Christ's sufferings as constituted by his dignity as a fully divine and fully human person, and the value of Christ's sufferings as

21. Stevens, *Christian Doctrine of Salvation*, 177.
22. Along with Shedd, this idea is also shared by David Hewlett. See Hewlett, "Substitution and Representation," 33.
23. Hodge, *Atonement*, 28–30.
24. Hodge, *Systematic Theology*, 471.
25. Hodge, *Systematic Theology*, 474–75.

determined by God's acceptance of them as an adequate and full satisfaction of his justice.

Third, how does the idea of "sin as cause" and "death as effect" fit in with this theory? Interestingly, the language of penalty can also be used in this conceptual framework. If the concept of penalty is associated with death rather than with suffering it will have at least two consequences. Firstly, if sin and death are understood in terms of cause and effect, as St. Paul says, Jesus' death must have a very direct reference to sin. Emil Brunner says that sin issues in death for that is the consequence of a Holy God.[26] In the words of Brunner,

> God, as the One who is separated personally from man, is the angry One: the necessary effect of this separation is the opposite of the effect of personal communion with God, absolute disaster, death in the pronounced human sense.[27]

Here, the words that Jesus came to die our death, for our sins, make perfect sense. In and through the death of Jesus, God's love breaks through his wrath and he may forgive us without denying his Holy and just nature.

Secondly, the association of death with penalty helps us to understand how Jesus' death is in tune with God's justice. Emil Brunner writes,

> The objective aspect of the Atonement, therefore, may be summed up thus: it consists in the combination of inflexible righteousness, with its penalties, and transcendent love; thus it means that the world-dualism caused by sin, which issues finally in death, is declared valid, and at the same time the overwhelming reality of the Divine Love is also justified.[28]

Again, as J. Denney more explicitly says,

> ... in His atoning work Christ is our Substitute ... He enters into all the responsibilities that sin has created for us, and He does justice to them in His death. . . . In perfect sinlessness He consents even to die, to submit to that awful experience in which the final reaction of God's holiness against sin is expressed. Death was not His due: it was something alien to One who did nothing amiss. But it was our due, and because it was ours He made it His. . . . He died, and in so doing acknowledged the sanctity of that order in which sin and death are indissolubly united ... for how could men be saved if there were not made in humanity an

---

26. Brunner, *Mediator*, 480. See also, Denney, *Atonement*, 479.
27. Brunner, *Mediator*, 484.
28. Brunner, *Mediator*, 520.

acknowledgement of all that sin is to God, and of the justice of all that is entailed by sin under God's constitution of the world.[29]

Thus, the term "substitution" helps in understanding the atonement in more than one way. Wolfhart Pannenberg also makes use of the term "substitution" whilst writing on the atonement. For him, Jesus' death is the revelation of "the punishment suffered in our place for the blasphemous existence of humanity."[30] He translates the penal element of Jesus' condemnation into the more general anthropological statement that man is subject to death "because of his being closed in upon himself, while his destiny to openness to the world still points beyond death."[31]

Fourth, we will turn to the insights of Luther and Calvin. As we have noted, Luther and Calvin not only favored this model but also elaborated it. In fact, they largely took over the already existing vocabulary revolving around the term satisfaction and changed it into a theory of penal substitution. Paul Althaus, a Lutheran himself, is one of the finest Lutheran scholars of our times who offers a brilliant exposition of Luther. For Althaus, Luther's primary emphasis fell on the relationship of Christ's work to God's wrath and on our guilt. God cannot react to human sin in any other way than with enmity and death. This is a necessity rooted in God's being. Althaus writes, "Since Luther finds all commandments included in the first, he can also see the real nature of sin as an attack on God as God and find a corresponding basis for God's wrath in His determination to remain God."[32] Furthermore, for Luther, Christ did not die the honorable and noble death of a righteous man. He was made sin for us, and although he himself committed no actual sins, He suffered a sinner's death. Christ suffered, died and took the punishment in our place. It was a punishment we deserved, but he took it upon himself. Unlike Anselm's satisfaction theory, which we will briefly outline later, Luther's is a true penal substitution theory.[33]

Along the same lines, according to Pannenberg, Luther recognizes the meaning of Jesus' death in the fact that the punishment for our sins happened to him.[34] And according to Aulen, the Latin doctrine involved the idea of law and justice as the typical expression of God's relation to humanity. Luther powerfully tears the Latin idea into pieces, raising God's claim to a higher level and therefore treating law as, in one aspect, a tyrant from which

29. Denney, *Death of Christ*, 193.
30. Pannenberg, *Jesus-God and Man*, 279.
31. Pannenberg, *Jesus-God and Man*, 62.
32. Althaus, *Theology of Martin Luther*, 169.
33. Althaus, *Theology of Martin Luther*, 169–70.
34. Pannenberg, *Jesus-God and Man*, 278.

humanity needs to be delivered.[35] In short, for Luther, the mystery of the cross requires a change of paradigm, away from Law to one Gospel in which a wonderful exchange occurs where our sins are not ours, but Christ's, and Christ's righteousness is not Christ's but ours, is possible.

Moltmann, a modern theologian is of the view that certainly such statements as God passes judgment on the sin of man upon himself, God takes the judgment on the sin of man upon himself; he assigns to himself the fate that humanity should by rights endure, make use of a penal framework of thought.[36] However, he does not appear to have expunged such ideas from his own theology, perhaps because a judgmental connotation is ineradicably part and parcel of the understanding of Christ's suffering within the framework of Luther's *theologia crucis*.[37]

Although not in a fully developed manner, Calvin too held that Christ substituted us in his atoning work. Calvin writes,

> To take away our condemnation, it was not enough for him to suffer any kind of death: to make satisfaction for our redemption a form of death had to be chosen in which he might free us both by transferring our condemnation to himself and by taking our guilt upon himself. If he had been murdered by thieves or slain in an insurrection by a raging mob, in such a death there would have been no evidence of satisfaction. But when he was arraigned before the judgment seat as a criminal, accused and pressed by testimony, and condemned by the mouth of the judge to die—we know by these proofs that he took the role of a guilty man and evil doer.[38]

It is clear that for Calvin, Christ suffered death not because of innocence but because of sin. Even Pilate had to say, "I find no case against him."[39] Nevertheless, Pilate placed him under the official sentence of death reserved for criminals and thereby reckoned him amongst the criminals. According to Calvin, the form of Christ's death is a significant symbol, which testifies to the fact that in his death, God reckons to the Son the guilt of the whole human race. For Calvin, "This is our acquittal: the guilt that held us liable for punishment has been transferred to the head of the Son of

---

35. Aulen, *Christus Victor*, 137.
36. Moltmann, *Crucified*, 193.
37. Moltmann, *Crucified*, 183.
38. Calvin, *Institutes of the Christian Religion*, vol. 2, chapter 16:5.
39. John 18:38, NRSV.

God."[40] Thus, there is no doubt that Calvin too held a penal substitutionary view in relation to the atonement.

For him, Christ had an unfallen human nature, unlike us, and Christ alone is worthy of substituting us.[41] Calvin's view of the atonement can be precisely construed from his writing given below. He says,

> Nothing had been done if Christ had only endured corporeal death. In order to interpose between us and God's anger, and satisfy his righteous judgment, it was necessary that he should feel the weight of divine vengeance . . . Like a sponsor and surety for the guilty, and, as it were, subjected to condemnation, he undertook and paid all the penalties which must have been exacted from them, the only exception being, that pains of death could not hold him. Hence there is nothing strange in its being said that he descended to Hell, seeing he endured the death which is inflicted on the wicked by an angry God . . . Not only was the body of Christ given up as the price of redemption, but . . . he bore in his soul the tortures of condemned and ruined man.[42]

The crux of this theory is the binding power of law that affects both body and soul. Christ has truly suffered (body and soul), been crucified, dead (physically and spiritually) and buried (the tomb and hell/God forsaken), that he might reconcile God, the Father to the creation. Again, according to Calvin, the idea of the transmissibility of merit led to the conception of the transfer of punishment, whilst growing practice of substituting humanity to do penance for payment instead of the guilty, led to the idea of the substitution of Christ for the sinful, in their guilt and punishment for sin.[43] It is true that the Law demands a penalty for human failure or contravention of the Law. The atonement is Christ's payment of this penalty on our behalf, or in our stead. It is a fact that this theory has deepened the dimension of guilt in sin over Anselm's definition of it as the failure to render God his due.

Thus the penal substitutionary theory turns on the idea that Christ substituted us and took our punishment for our sins onto him. The focus of this theory is on punishment exacted by the Law of God. It is generally understood that the person who does wrong is subject to punishment. All human beings commit sin, living in a sinful world, and hence deserve punishment. Here Christ gives himself to be punished in our place thereby setting us free.

---

40. Calvin gets this idea from Isa 53:12.
41. McCormack, "For Us and Our Salvation," 17–18.
42. Calvin, *Institutes of the Christian Religion*, vol. 20, 413.
43. Calvin analyzed in Hughes, *Atonement*, 67.

It is because Christ substitutes us and takes our punishment onto himself that this theory is known as penal substitutionary theory.

Fifth, as we may expect, this theory has merits and demerits. This theory has a strong biblical basis, firmly supported by Paul's teaching (Gal 3:13, 2 Cor 5:21, and Rom 8:3.) Yung Hwa argues that Jesus' self-understanding of his passion fits best with the "penal" type of the atonement—penal type in the sense that Jesus entered into the blight and judgment of a God who is holy love.[44] Boyd points out that this theory speaks of something which really happened—an action or transaction—on the cross which has resulted in forgiveness for me.[45] Steve Holmes favors this theory because a large part of the hymnody, liturgy and devotional writing of Reformed and Evangelical Christianity use penal language and more importantly, because, in his view, the penal metaphors take the reality of sin most seriously.[46] It should be also noted that this theory is the first to see Jesus' death as vicarious penal suffering.

Nonetheless, this theory is criticized for the idea of penal suffering as the expression of the wrath of God against Jesus. We can question the vicarious character of Jesus' suffering being replaced with Jesus' suffering as the highest fulfillment of his vocation in this theory. Albert Ritschl does not want to see any effect of divine wrath against sin in Jesus' death.[47] A. J. Appasamy, an Indian theologian, knowing the Indian context, is reluctant to think of the cross as Penal substitution.[48] M. M. Thomas, another Indian theologian, too rejects the idea of penal substitution because it isn't readily applicable to the Indian context.[49] Further, though Boyd has pointed out a merit in this theory he also raises the question as to whether it is ever just to punish the innocent (Christ) for the guilty; or to "impute" righteousness to the guilty?[50] We will later see the same criticism posed to the Juridical theory as well. Hughes criticizes the penal substitutionary theory by claiming that it emphasizes sin rather than the sinner and regards the punishment of sin as more important than the restoration of the sinner.[51] Wolf is another theologian who criticizes this theory. He asks whether Christ's bearing the punishment of sin is possible and reasonable.

44. Hwa, "Theories of Atonement," 550.
45. Boyd, *Khristadvaita*, 184.
46. Holmes, "Can Punishment Bring Peace?," 122.
47. See Ritschl, discussed in Pannenberg, *Jesus-God and Man*, 279.
48. Sumithra, *Christian Theology*, 104–05.
49. Sumithra, *Christian Theology*, 168.
50. Boyd, *Khristadvaita*, 185.
51. Hughes, *Atonement*, 69.

In his opinion, it is outrageous to think of God as inflicting punishment on Christ because He was angry with him, as a sort of substitution for being angry with sinners.[52] F. W. Camfield points out, "If there is one conclusion which had come almost to be taken for granted in enlightened Christian quarters it is that the idea of substitution has led theology on a wrong track; and that the word "substitution" must now be dropped from the doctrine of the atonement as it is too heavily laden with false and even misleading connotations."[53] Sydney Cave says, "Recent scholarship has shown that the attempt to find in St. Paul's Epistles a penal theory is based on a misunderstanding of his words due to a confusion of form and content, so that the Penal theory lacks support in the New Testament."[54] Notably, though the Indian thinker, Ram Mohan Roy is against seeing any significance in the atonement, he is particularly against the view that on the cross Jesus paid the penalty for the sins of mankind in their place.[55] Commenting on Calvinism, Chakkarai, a renowned Indian theologian says,

> the Indian with his Indian experience of the spiritual life is bound to recognize these elements (imputed righteousness, justification of faith and the election of Bhaktas), even though they may not appeal to those who have moved away from it or perhaps have never had the atmosphere of spiritual longings in which alone they can flourish.[56]

Finally, our concern now is to view this theory in the light of the saving concept of Brahman. Obviously, this theory portrays a dimension of the atonement. It argues that Christ brings us salvation by taking our punishment for our sins onto himself. It needs to be emphasized that the concerns raised in the saving concept of Brahman are very different from the concerns of the penal substitutionary theory. In the context of the

---

52. Wolf, *No Cross*, 111. Further, in recent years there has been attempt to see the value of penal atonement in relation to God's eschatological hospitality. See Boersma, "Penal substitution," 80–94. Hans claims that in the penal theory we could find the centrality of God's eschatological hospitality plan. In his words, " . . . I want to come to the defense of traditional atonement theology. In particular, I want to make the case that by including a penal aspect in our view of the atonement we adopt an element that plays a role in safeguarding God's eschatological hospitality." Hans' attempt to find a new interpretation for the penal aspect of atonement is inspiring. However, the overemphasis given to the "eschatological hospitality" concept leaves us with no relevance of the atonement for our lives here and now.

53. Camfield, "The Idea of Substitution," 282.

54. Cave, *Doctrine of Work of Christ*, 258.

55. Sumithra, *Christian Theology*, 41.

56. Thomas, *Vengal Chakkarai*, 327.

Reformation, Luther wanted to break the control which the leadership of the Roman Catholic Church had over the forgiveness of sins. He argued that Christ has already set us free by taking our punishment upon himself on the cross. On the other hand, the saving concept of Brahman is interested in portraying the intuitive and practical knowledge of the four-fold union, which is understood as salvation in the Indian context. Thus the Penal theory will not directly suit the Indian context. Nevertheless, our model of the atonement, as we will see in the next chapter, will also view that Christ substituted us, however not by paying penalty, but by creating a renewed union and the knowledge of that union between God and us.[57] Thus, our theory will be *alienation-ward*, thereby avoiding the perception of the Father as some angry monster.

The Representation Model

Obviously, representation is a complex word with a wide variety of meanings. G. Sartori provides seven possible meanings of the term: 1) The people freely and periodically elect a Body of Representatives—the electoral theory of representation; 2) The governors are accountable or responsible to the governed—the responsibility theory of representation; 3) The governors are agents or delegates who carry out the instructions received from their electors—the mandate theory of representation; 4) The people feel the same as the state—the *idem sentire*, or syntony, theory of representation; 5) The people consent to the decisions of their governors—the consent theory of representation; 6) The people share, in some significant way, in the making of relevant political decisions—the participation theory of representation; and 7) The governors are a representative sample of the governed—the resemblance, or mirroring theory of representation.[58]

These understandings of the term "representation" itself make it clear that the representation of Christ should be understood in a sophisticated manner. It is a fact that the atoning work of Christ can be understood in all these ways. Having noted the complexity of the term "representation," we shall move on to analyze how theologians have used it in relation to the atonement. Theologians who write on the representational model, generally, hold the view that Christ took the atoning work onto himself on our behalf.

---

57. Our theory will understand that only because a renewed God-human union is made possible in the atonement, human-human, human-nature, and one-oneself unions, too, become possible.

58. Sartori, "Representational Systems," 462.

Firstly, scholars have understood the obedience of Christ unto death in relation to the representation model. Christ was obedient because he was well aware that he was representing us. H. Smith, commenting on Irenaeus' understanding of "recapitulation," says, "here we have the effect of Christ's 'Active Obedience' as not only our example, but our Representative."[59] Similarly, the New Testament scholar, Vincent Taylor says,

> The obedience is also representative obedience . . . As representing men, Christ in His suffering offers that obedience, truly embodied in Himself, in their name and for their sake, not by way of barter or exchange, but with the intention that they should identify themselves with it and so offer it themselves.[60]

Vincent Taylor, having understood the obedience of Christ as representational, emphasizes the claim that human beings ought to identify themselves with Christ. He goes on to say,

> The truer view of the representative activity of Jesus is one which recognizes that in His suffering and death He has expressed and effected that which no individual man has the power or spirituality to achieve, but into which, in virtue of an ever-deepening fellowship with Him, man can progressively enter so that it becomes their offering to God.[61]

It is obvious that in understanding Christ as our representative there is a moral obligation on the part of humanity represented to repeat and appropriate in their own life the qualities that have been claimed as potentially theirs in the person of their representative. As we will see later, this point is emphasized by Solle as well. However, for Taylor, even when Christ represents us there is an imitative participation on our part to appropriate the atonement as our own. Precisely, Christ's representation does not "indicate one whose activity lies apart from ourselves, or serves instead of our own, but on whose service leaves in our hands the decisive word in the affirmation of faith."[62] In other words, with respect to Christ's offering himself in obedience and penitence it is in the name and for our sake "not by way or barter or exchange, but with the intention that they should identify themselves with it and so offer it themselves."[63]

---

59. Grensted, *Atonement in History*, 180.
60. Taylor, *Jesus and His Sacrifice*, 307.
61. Taylor, *Jesus and His Sacrifice*, 283.
62. Taylor, *Jesus and His Sacrifice*, 306.
63. Taylor, *Jesus and His Sacrifice*, 307.

Secondly, another aspect which comes to the fore in relation to Christ's representation is his intercession on our behalf. F. Schleiermacher says,

> Christ appears before the Father, first, to establish our fellowship with Him, and then, further, to support our prayer before the Father. . . . [I]n virtue, therefore, of that relation to us which is based upon His peculiar dignity He remains the representative of the whole human race, for like the High Priest, He brings our prayer before God and conveys to us the divine blessings.[64]

In his obedience and intercession, there can be no doubt that Christ represented us in his atoning work as well. Two questions that arise when we discuss the theme of representation are: 1) the significance of the personality of Christ, and 2) did anything happen to every human being because of the atoning work of Christ.

It should be held that Christ did the atoning work on the cross on our behalf as fully divine and fully human. B. Westcott helps us in this regard. He says,

> If Christ had been born as other men, he would have been one man of many, limited by an individual manhood, and not in very truth the Son of Man, the perfect representative of the whole race. . . . We can see that the Divine personality of the Son, the Son of God, the manhood and a universal manhood in Christ, and gives to this Humanity that absolute completeness in which each man to the end of time can find the fulfillment of his partial nature, and through which the will of God could be accomplished for all under the conditions of earthly existence.[65]

Thus, Westcott is careful to say that Christ died in solidarity and with a corporate nature with the entire human race not only as Son of God but also as Son of Man. Again, according to G. Lampe, the epistle of Hebrews claims,

> There lies the Hebraic idea of corporate personality, the notion which finds expression in the Old Testament tendency to think of the nation collectively as a single person, Israel; to mingle . . . the thought of the patriarchs as individuals as the corporate personae of the tribes which traced their descent from them, so that the ancestor can stand for the tribe as its Representative. . . . [L]ife is more than the life of the individual, . . . it extends to the group, bound together as a single entity, capable of being

---

64. Schleiermacher, *Christian Faith*, 464.
65. Westcott, *Victory of the Cross*, 44.

represented by, summed up in and almost personified by a single individual life.⁶⁶

Thus, in this model it is considered that Christ, as he represents entire humanity, is capable of including all as well as he is capable of acting on their behalf.

Our second question is what happened to all. The Body of Christ gets significance here. In L. Thornton's words,

> When Christ died something happened once and for all, not only to him who died, but to all for whom he died. They also died with him upon the cross. . . . The Messiah and his people together form one organism. It was this new organism which was nailed to the cross and which was afterwards triumphantly raised from the dead. To it, in principle, all mankind belongs; and therefore, in some sense, "they all died" upon the cross. They were identified with their representative in what he there did for them, just as in that same event he was identified with them in their sinful condition.⁶⁷

What are the motifs by which Christ can represent us? Three predominant motifs which illustrate Christ as representative are the motif of Adam, the motif of the High Priest and the motif of the Son of Man. First, according to C. H. Dodd,

> Adam is a name which stands to [Paul] for the 'corporate personality' of mankind, and a new 'corporate personality' is created in Christ. All that Christ did and suffered he did and suffered as "inclusive Representative" of the new humanity which emerges in him. This idea is very fundamental to Paul's thought about the person and work of Christ.⁶⁸

Similarly, A. A. Hodge says, "When we say that he (Christ) is the Representative, we affirm this to be true of him as the second Adam or federal Head, undertaking and discharging all the obligations of the broken law in our stead."⁶⁹ Karl Barth also has once said that Christ is our

---

66. Lampe, *Reconciliation in Christ*, 54–55.

67. Thornton, *Common Life in Body of Christ*, 46. For Thornton, the concept of the body of Christ has a double reference in that it points back to the physical constitution of Jesus and points forward to the reality of the Church. Precisely, for him, "Christ and the Church are one flesh . . . the mystical body was implicitly included in the mortal body from the first." Thornton, *Common Life in Body of Christ*, 316.

68. Dodd, *Epistle of Paul*, 80.

69. Hodge, *Atonement*, 152.

representative because he is the first born. In his words, "As He is man, the first-born Brother of all men, He is the Head and Representative of man ... In and with His life from death He manifests our life as it is saved in Him, as it is graciously ... posited afresh in the fellowship with God which had been forfeited."[70]

Second, Christ is also representative in the light of he being the High Priest. James B. Torrance writes,

> The covenant between YHWH and Israel was concentrated as it were, in the person of the High Priest. . . . [I]t is this thought that lies behind the New Testament and patristic understanding of the inclusive and representative humanity of Christ, the Mediator of the New Covenant, who represents God to man and man to God in his own Person as the One on behalf of Many.[71]

Third, in relation to the motif of the Son of Man, S. C. Gayford helps us. He says, "In the manhood of Jesus Christ is summed up the whole human race. He is not just one among many, a son of man, but One in whom all others are represented, the Son of Man."[72] These provide ground for making the claim for Christ's representation in the atonement.

In recent decades, the representation model is thoroughly analyzed and used by Dorothy Solle in her work, Christ the Representative, and now we move on to her work to analyze the representation model in detail. Solle is a German-born theologian who taught systematic theology at Union Theological Seminary in New York. The thesis of her book is that as Christ represents us in his atoning work it is for us to step in at any time and it is expected of all human beings.

Solle says that there are four characteristics that determine the criteria of representation. They are 1) it is a temporary expedient, 2) it is limited to specific areas, 3) it needs to be approved by person represented, and 4) it is only acting on behalf and never a replacement.[73] She goes on to provide the structure of Christ's representation, which is the basis of this model. For Solle,

> Christ represents us only for a time, conditionally and incompletely, ... he represents us for a time. And this must be maintained in opposition to all forms of christocratic perfectionism. We remain irreplaceable precisely because we need him as

---

70. Barth, *Church Dogmatics*, 300.
71. Torrance, *Incarnation*, 137.
72. Gayford, *Sacrifice and Priesthood*, 131.
73. Solle, *Christ the Representative*, 20.

representative. . . . Christ does not replace our life, making us superfluous, not counted on by anyone any longer.[74]

Thus Solle makes it plain that unlike the penal substitutionary theory, the representational model provides us with responsibility. We earlier noted that this idea is shared by Vincent Taylor. For them, Christ represents us only for a temporary period of time and hence we ought to replace Christ and take his place once we realize that he represents us.[75] Further, Christ's representation is not only the representation of man before God, but also the representation of God before man.

Solle explains the work of Christ with a teacher-pupil relationship. For her, the representative act of the teacher in identifying with the pupil in punishment abolishes the difference between the agent and the one acted upon.[76] The punishment, in fact, is viewed as the restoration of a broken personal relationship.[77] Representing us provisionally, Christ punishes us in such a way that he suffers himself.[78] Christ also identifies with humanity because we are the agents of our own punishment. Solle writes,

> Christ makes the prison wardens aware of the prison in which they themselves live, and he does so by showing that he himself is its prisoner. . . . Christ belongs to both parties at the same time; he punishes and is punished. He thereby excludes any idea of punishment as a predetermined fate. It ceases to take by surprise those on whom it falls, as if it were something meaningless, for the judge identifies himself with the condemned, the teacher shares the punishment alongside the pupil.[79]

Solle further clarifies her theme of representation by arguing that in Christ's representation of humanity before God he makes himself dependent on us, suffering for us by suffering because of us. She stresses that the representative cannot refuse to be involved or wish to withdraw because the representative is in identification with the represented, rather the forerunner is shown up in all his provisionality when no one follows him.[80] In short, Christ is provisional—if we add "to God" we emphasize the provisionality but

---

74. Solle, *Christ the Representative*, 103.

75. "Representation," so defined stands in opposition to the thought of substitution. In contrast to "representation," which is a temporal concept, "substitution" is a spatial concept.

76. Solle, *Christ the Representative*, 119.

77. Solle, *Christ the Representative*, 119.

78. Solle, *Christ the Representative*, 120.

79. Solle, *Christ the Representative*, 121, 122.

80. Solle, *Christ the Representative*, 125.

say nothing new. Christ makes himself dependent on us—if we say "dependent on God," this simply means that Christ is radically surrendered to men. Christ identifies himself with us—if we add "before God," it amounts to the same thing, for whenever this *identificatio* takes place, God is there.[81]

Before we point out the strengths and weaknesses of this model, we will briefly highlight aspects of Solle's argument for Christ as representative of God among humanity to comprehend this model more fully. Solle understands that Christ represents the absent God to the world. Her argument becomes clear when she says,

> The cipher "Christ" is the mode in which Jesus continues alive to the end of the world—as the consciousness of those who represent God and calls on him for each other. Where this representative claim on God is made, the implicit Christ is present. For it is not only Christ who represents God in the world. Christ's friends and brothers also represent God by allowing God—and this means necessarily those as well who need him—time.[82]

Solle portrays the representation of God among humanity using the phrase that Christ identifies with God and hence God is now identified in Christ. She says that in representing God, Christ put himself in the place of God and yet he also made himself dependent upon God, acting in the name of God, putting himself unreservedly in the hands of God who can accept or reject him.[83] Again, as we identify with Christ and so participate in suffering as the representative of God we wait for God's identity, a personalized world, the Kingdom of God. In Solle's words, "God wills to be represented. He has made himself representable. He has made himself conditional, provisional. He has become dependent; he has mediated himself into the world. He became man."[84]

Thus, Christ's representation of God before humanity is similar to his representation of humanity before God. Interpreting Solle, Hewlett says, "Because such characteristics constitute the conditions under which identity appears the language of representation functions to provide a 'theology after the death of God' which answers the longing for identity and which safeguards the future of God."[85]

The representational model, certainly, has its own strengths. This model not only allows Christ to be our representative, especially in his atoning work,

81. Solle, *Christ the Representative*, 129.
82. Solle, *Christ the Representative*, 136.
83. Solle, *Christ the Representative*, 143.
84. Solle, *Christ the Representative*, 149.
85. Hewlett, "Substitution and Representation Patterns," 197.

but also maintains a subjective aspect in the sense that it allows humanity to take the place of Christ at any time. Furthermore, the incarnation, the life of Christ and the death of Christ are held together. Alister McGrath says that this theory helps to view the atonement as a covenant. He writes,

> All that Christ has achieved through the cross is available on account of the covenant. Just as God entered into a covenant with his people, Israel, so he has entered into a covenant with his church. Christ, by his obedience upon the cross, represents his covenant people, winning benefits for them as their representative.[86]

However, Colin Gunton criticizes Solle saying that the representative model is only a replication of the subjective theory in different words. He claims, "If, with Solle, we understand Jesus as a temporary representative, one who stands in for us until we can, so to speak, stand upon our own feet, the outcome is again Pelagian and exemplarist."[87] Moreover, the representational model does not move forward to explain the logic of God punishing and being punished at the same time. It also fails to give adequate importance to the divinity of Christ. For example, Priests, in most traditions including Christianity, are understood as God's representatives in this world.

It is important for us to note that the representation model also cannot do justice to an Indian understanding of the means to salvation because representing someone can be only for a period of time. Understanding this problem, C. F. Andrews (1871–1940), a missionary in India says that the atonement must be widened out far beyond a single act of Christ, however representative.[88] Moreover, representation model does not in any way include the concern for a four-fold union and hence can remain only superficial in an Indian context.

Finally, whilst the representation model is complex and understands Christ as our representative, the saving concept of Brahman views the divine as the one who creates the intuitive and practical knowledge of the four-fold union necessary for our salvation. The two concepts turn on two very different axles. However, just like the personality of Christ (divine-human being) is central to this theory, the personality of Christ will be crucial in understanding our model of the atonement as well. We now move on to very briefly examine the other existing theories and their inadequacy in the Indian context.

---

86. McGrath, *Historical Theology*, 288.

87. Gunton, *Actuality of Atonement*, 162.

88. Chaturvedi and Sykes, *Charles Freer Andrews*. Also see Tinker, *The Ordeal of Love*, and Cragg, *Christ and Faiths*, 183.

The Inadequacy of Other Existing Theories in the Indian Visistadvaitic Hindu Context

Within the scope of this chapter we will not be too ambitious to go into details of the following theories but only highlight the inadequacy of them in the Indian context to say that none of the existing theories are immediately applicable to the Indian context.

The Moral Influence Theory

The Moral Influence theory is also known as the subjective, Abelardian, "modern" and exemplarist theory. This theory is called Abelardian because Peter Abelard (1079–1142) is the one who constructed an impressive paradigm of it. The truth expressed in Mark 12:29–31, John 13:34, 15:12, and 2 Corinthians 8:8 is emphasized in this theory. Why is it called the moral influence theory? Specifically, this theory claims that as Christ has loved us even unto death so we are called to live our lives out of gratitude, imitating Christ as well as loving God and our fellow human beings unto death in return. Since this theory expects a "subjective" change in the moral standpoint taken in our lives it is called the moral influence theory or the subjective theory. This theory is "subjective" because it claims that the atonement effects a change within the life of the human subject.

Abelard, who expounded this model, was a Frenchman who came from Brittany, near Nantes. He lectured in Paris for sometime before becoming a monk. He attracted many audiences, whenever and wherever he preached. The primary source for Abelard's understanding of the Atonement is an excerpt from his commentary on Rom, contained in Eugene Fairweather's edited book.[89] Whilst formulating his theory, Abelard also drew his attention to John 5:13, which reads, "Greater love has no man than this, that a man lay down his life for his friends." Abelard says, " . . . by the faith which we have concerning Christ, love is increased in us through the conviction that God in Christ has united our nature to Himself and that by suffering in that nature, He has demonstrated to us the supreme love of which He speaks."[90] Notably, Abelard uses the word "united" which we will expound in detail whilst outlining our model of the atonement in the next chapter. Here we need to note that the key word for understanding Abelard's position is "demonstrated." Abelard goes on to say,

---

89. Fairweather, *A Scholastic Miscellany*, 276–87. (It is the section on Rom 3:19–27.)
90. Fairweather, *A Scholastic Miscellany*, 283.

> Through this unique act of grace manifested to us—in that His Son has taken upon Himself our nature and persevered therein in teaching us by word and example even unto death—He has more fully bound us to Himself by love; with the result that our hearts should be enkindled by such a gift of divine grace, and true charity should not now shrink from enduring anything for him . . . Wherefore, our redemption through Christ's suffering is that deeper affection in us which not only frees us from slavery to sin, but also wins for us the true liberty of sons [and daughters] of God, so that we do all things out of love rather than fear—love to Him who has shown us such grace that no greater can be found, as He Himself asserts, saying 'Greater love has no man that this . . . etc.[91]

By this Abelard means that Christ is not only the teacher but also the example of the love of God toward us. Christ was faithful to God, the Father even unto death. The self-giving love of Christ is to awaken our hearts and that is the ground of forgiveness of sins. Again, in the words of Abelard,

> I think that the purpose and cause of the incarnation was that God might illumine the world by His wisdom and excite in us a love to Himself . . . our redemption is that supreme love shown to us in the passion which, not only frees us from the slavery of sin but acquires for us the true liberty of the sons of God . . . The son took our nature to instruct us alike by word and example even to death and so bind us to Himself in love, so that the love kindled by so great a benefit of divine grace, should not be afraid to endure anything for His sake.[92]

Bushnell is a key representative of the moral influence theory in that he concentrates on the subjective change of human beings. For him, Christ's persuasive approach to human beings tends to subsume God and humanity under the same moral law.[93] Yung Hwa summarizes this theory and says that the efficacy of Christ's death is now quite definitely and explicitly explained by its subjective influence upon the mind of the sinner. The voluntary death of the innocent son of God on behalf of humanity moves the sinner to gratitude and an answering love—and so to consciousness of sin, repentance and amendment.[94] Nonetheless, one might argue

---

91. Fairweather, *A Scholastic Miscellany,* 283–84.

92. Fairweather, *A Scholastic Miscellany,* 283–84. Also quoted in, Hughes, *Atonement,* 32.

93. Browning, *Atonement and Psychotherapy,* 83.

94. Hwa, "Theories of Atonement," 545.

that presumably if people are not changed there is no atonement, and probably we might change without the example since it is we humans who make the decisive change. However, Abelard's claim is that Christ's death on the cross is the supreme exhibition of God's love. This in turn creates a love for the divine in us, urging us that we should attempt anything in response for the divine love. Moreover, for him, it is through this example of the cross, that God in Christ brought us the message of forgiveness. Precisely, Abelard's is a subjective theory in the following sense. It is the love of God in us which provides the basis on which God forgives sins.

The moral influence theory definitely has effected change in many lives. It is true that people have been converted in their hearts by viewing the love of Christ on the cross. It is also noteworthy to see that Hindus of India like Gandhiji and Ram Mohan Roy are in favor of the moral influence theory amongst the various existing theories. Gandhi accepted the cross as a great example. He says,

> Though I cannot claim to be a Christian in the sectarian sense, the example of Jesus' suffering is a factor in the composition of my underlying faith in non-violence [ahimsa], which rules all my actions, worldly and temporal. Jesus lived and died in vain, if he did not teach us to regulate the whole of life by the eternal Law of Love.[95]

Thus, the central argument of this theory is vital and the moral influence implicit in the atonement is acknowledged by many in Christian as well as other traditions. Hence, this theory has to be given adequate significance and theologically this theory deserves great appreciation. The theory which we will outline in the next chapter too, will underscore that the atonement manifests God's grace and love[96] in the utmost sense. However, our new theory will also point out the logic of the atonement in creating the four-fold union.

The moral influence theory touches upon one important aspect of the atonement; that is the subjective aspect. It is a fact that the fullness of the atonement cannot be construed if one neglects the subjective side of the atonement. This theory is perceptibly Biblically based. It explains the intensity of the divine love toward humanity in an insightful way and stresses the need for our response to the divine love disclosed on the cross. In fact, Abelard's model has always had its admirers and it may not be wrong to

---

95. Gandhi quoted in Wessels, *Images of Jesus*, 138.

96. We already noted in the previous chapter that Brahman is a God of grace and love, in Ramanuja's thought, particularly in granting the intuitive and practical knowledge of the four-fold union and thus bringing salvation to all created beings.

say that Protestant reflections on the atonement in the late-nineteenth century in Germany belonged predominantly to the Moral Influence model. In general terms, there is no doubt that Abelard has pointed out an important aspect of New Testament teaching on soteriology. It is true that Christ's love manifested on the cross ought to awaken in us a response of love. Significantly, strands of the subjective dimension like repentance and sanctification through the atonement are found not only in Pauline letters, but also in the synoptic gospels and the fourth gospel. Theologians like D. M. Baillie and R. S. Franks amongst others have powerfully stressed the significance of the subjective side of the atonement in their works.[97]

However, this theory has defects as well. The common criticism against this theory is that it requires one to give up belief in the divinity of Christ; for if sin is a defect, from which humanity can save itself, then there is no necessity of Christ's suffering and a human Christ is as good as a divine Christ. Furthermore, the importance of the doctrine of justification is not highlighted in this theory. Wolf says that one obvious defect in this theory is that it does not allow the New Testament concept of love to shine forth in its full power because it lacks the objective side.[98] Moreover, the questions that arise here are—if the love which Jesus bore for his contemporaries exhibited in his life and death is fundamentally an illustration of God's love for us, then what can be its distinctive status? Is it not one illustration amongst others many of which could be equally good? Again, an Indian theologian, Chenchiah's pertinent question, "Why should my salvation be conditioned by my reaction to the atonement at all?" deserves our attention here. In sum, the objective side of the atonement is not emphasized in the subjective theory and hence it continues to be disparaged by theologians and others.

Is this theory compatible with the saving concept of Brahman in Visitadvaitic Hinduism? On the one hand, the moral influence theory emphasizes that Christ's atoning work is a disclosure of the divine love toward humanity and we need to follow in his footsteps for our salvation In Paul's words, we need to imitate Christ in our daily lives. On the other hand, the saving function of Brahman, by and large, emphasizes the creation of the intuitive and practical knowledge of our union with the divine, with others, with nature and with ourselves. The subjective side of the saving concept of Brahman is that once Brahman has created the intuitive and practical knowledge of the four-fold union within us, we begin to live in oneness with the will of the divine. This stage of life in the physical body is only the foretaste of salvation and its fullness is beyond this life. Further, the

97. Baillie, *God Was in Christ*, 201–02; Franks, *Atonement*, 2.
98. Wolf, *No Cross*, 117.

objective side of the saving concept of Brahman is that the divine Brahman alone can create in us the intuitive and practical knowledge through the scriptures and/or a guru. Thus the moral influence theory and the saving concept of Brahman obviously turn on two very different insights. It could be construed that they both look at the mystery of the means to salvation in two different perspectives. Hence it is clear that the concern of the saving concept of Brahman, which is four-fold union, cannot be adequately addressed by the moral influence theory.

Suitably, from an Indian perspective, Vengal Chakkarai, an Indian Christian theologian, commenting on moral influence theory, says that no doubt, the moral constitution has produced many conversions, especially in Anglo-Saxon lands. But it is not relevant to India. In his words, "the Indian does not respond so easily to such appeals; or rather the same effects are not forthcoming . . . it is a mere aesthetical repugnance and not a moral one that is . . . emphasized by the Indian view."[99] Thus it is clear that the supposed moral influence does not work in the same way in an Indian context.

In fact, the moral influence theory views salvation as something outside Christ. In the Indian context, several people are considered to be good examples inspiring a change of life and perhaps Gandhiji is one amongst them. Hence, salvation understood on the basis of the moral influence theory not only remains alien but also can be easily misunderstood in India. Salvation is not to be seen as something apart from Christ. In the Indian context it should be stressed, "He Himself is Salvation; salvation consists in the union and communion of the Savior and the saved."[100]

It is now apparent that an atonement theory to be meaningful and applicable in India should portray the intuitive and practical knowledge of the various unions for our salvation and expect a subjective change in us. The saving concept of Brahman helps Visistadvaitic Hindus realize the divine being—being in and around them and to experience the various unions. In the Indian context, people are well aware of the four-fold union. Our union with the divine and the other unions are part of everyday talk amongst religiously minded people of India. The moral influence theory will remain inadequate, in the Indian context, because it does not deal with all the aspects of the four-fold union.

As mentioned before, we will proceed to formulate an atonement theory in an Indian context, in the next chapter. Whilst Abelard emphasizes

99. Thomas, *Vengal Chakkarai*, 298–99. Chakkarai is convinced that something more has happened on the cross than mere moral influence. Perhaps, as an Indian, he would say that the cross is that which causes our union with the divine. See also, Boyd, *Introduction to Indian Christian Theology*, 177–78.

100. Boyd, *Manilal C. Parekh*, 254.

that the atonement expects a response from us for the divine love toward us our model will expect us to lead a life realizing our union with the divine, with others, with nature and with ourselves. The vision of this life is that it will be a life in harmony and peace. As Dillistone would say, the moral influence theory along with the fresh model of the atonement, that will be formulated using the saving concept of Brahman, in fact, will provide a better picture of the atonement not only for people in India, but also for the world-wide community. The remaining traditional theories which we will briefly review are generally known as objective theories.

The Satisfaction/Juridical Theory

The Satisfaction/Juridical theory is also known as the Anselmian, Western and Latin model. The epistle to the Hebrews, particularly the application of the priestly tradition to the ministry and death of Jesus found in Hebrews 7:28, 9:14, and 10:5–7, have been of crucial importance to the formulation of the satisfaction theory. This theory of the atonement first appears fully developed in the *Cur Deus Homo*? (Why God-man) of Anselm, which explains why this theory is called the Anselmian model.[101]

Anselm (1033–1109) was an Italian, born and brought up in the Italian Alps. He decided to take monastic vows in the 1050s. The monastery of Bec in Normandy attracted Anselm and he travelled north to get there.[102] Later Anselm became the Archbishop of Canterbury in 1093 and, as we noted, his famous work, *Cur Deus Homo*, was written around 1098/1099.

Interestingly, the word, "satisfaction" itself is not found in the New Testament. Probably, it was first introduced by the church father, Tertullian. In fact, the concept has been taken from Roman law, where paying off a debt had the sense of a punishment. Although Tertullian used this term, it was to interpret the doctrine of repentance and not the doctrine of the atonement. Anselm uses the word, satisfaction in great detail to formulate his atonement theory.

In his work, *Cur Deus Homo*, Anselm ventures to answer the question: Was it really necessary that God become a human being and suffer and die if the human race was to be redeemed from sin? For Anselm, God is impassible (i.e. he is not subject to passions and he is incapable of suffering or pain).

---

101. Anselm, *Cur Deus Homo?*, 1. In this work, Anselm provides a logical insight in understanding the doctrine of the atonement by means of a conversation with his friend, Boso.

102. Bec had been founded in the early eleventh century and had already become famous as a school under the direction of Lanfranc, another Italian.

Hence, the divine nature of Christ does not suffer and die but it is the human nature of Christ which bears the suffering and dies. Again, for Anslem, we should not attribute anything unseemly or unjust to God.

With this he moves to define sin. Sin is the failure to render God his due. And to give God his due is to obey him. Adam and Eve and the entire human race had not rendered to God the honor that is due to him by disobeying him. Thus, we have robbed the honor of God. Anselm obviously thinks of God-Human relationship in terms of the basic feudal social arrangement: that of a Lord and his vassals. It is in this context that Anselm defines satisfaction. In a situation where a person has dishonored his Lord, satisfaction must be brought or the Lord will punish. The crucial element is that the person need to pay further recompense beyond the restoration of what that person had taken to satisfy the affected honor of the Lord.[103] This principle when applied to human relationship with God implies that we cannot satisfy God just by beginning to obey him. There need to be further recompense paid. We do not have anymore in us to pay recompense and all what we have cannot satisfy God's honor.

Let us briefly look at the issue from God's point of view. One of the questions of Boso is why God can't simply forgive humanity without the atonement. For Anselm, God does not do anything that is not "fitting."[104] It is only "befitting" for God to act in accordance with the moral law of the universe that he created. Hence, if God leaves humanity unpunished for what they have done God will remain unjust before the moral law that he himself created. In Anselm's words if God allowed his own moral law to be flouted that would be a "violation of the beauty of order, in the very universe which God ought to regulate, and God would seem to fail in his direction of the world."[105] Hence, every sin must be followed either by punishment or satisfaction.

From the human point of view, since it is humanity that has injured the honor of God, they ought to satisfy God's honor. And humanity has nothing to offer to satisfy God's honor because everything already belongs to God. In that case, God only can make the offering for satisfaction.[106] Hence, it was necessary for God to become a God-Man to make the offer.

Anselm then moves on to show how exactly the atonement works. Christ was the God-Man and he did not sin. Therefore, he did not deserve any punishment. Christ voluntarily chose to die, offering his life to

---

103. Anselm, *Cur Deus Homo?*, 11.
104. Anselm, *Cur Deus Homo?*, 12.
105. Anselm, *Cur Deus Homo?*, 15.
106. Anselm, *Cur Deus Homo?*, 6.

the Father. The offering of Christ has infinite value not only because of the voluntary nature but also because of the infinite worth of the sinlessness of Christ. Now, the Father would be unjust if he did not honor the offering given by Christ. In other words, Christ deserved a reward for his offering. However, the Son already possessed everything and hence nothing extra could be offered. Thus, the reward should go to someone or something else. The reward of Christ was directed toward humanity's salvation for which Christ came into the world. It is really incredible to see the logic of Anselm within the medieval penitential system.

Precisely, the voluntary offering of Christ saved humanity from eternal death. According to Anselm, in Christ's sufferings and death, he did not only represent the perfect obedience that all men owe to God; his experience and sacrifice were so precious and potent that it did much more. It acquired superabundant merit, so much merit that it secured blessedness for every believer.[107] Pannenberg superbly explains the argument of Anselm. On this theory, Pannenberg says that human beings are obliged to God to offer satisfaction for their sins, for their offense through sin against God's right as Lord, his honor and holiness. The death of Jesus becomes the only conceivable work of supererogation that can be offered to God as satisfaction for humanity's sin. It could be noted that Anselm showed in the eleventh meditation of his work, *"de redemptione humana"* (human redemption) that humanity in the person of Jesus offers God this satisfaction.[108] Precisely, according to the satisfaction theory, Christ restores the dignity of the Father through his atoning work on the cross.

A key concept to Anselm's account is the honor of God and he also points out that the origin of this concept is variously ascribed by Dillistone[109] to the institution of feudalism, by R. S. Franks[110] to Roman law and by others to the influence of Germanic law. For Anselm, a price should be paid even for damaging a person's honor and dignity over and above putting right the material wrong. Thus if we wrongly kill our neighbor's sheep we need not only restore the sheep but pay an additional amount to restore his honor. The higher the status of the person dishonored the higher the price. So if God is dishonored as the highest of all beings the highest possible price is required. The price for dishonoring God by humanity can be paid by Christ alone because as human beings we already owe our all to God and so

---

107. Hughes, *Atonement*, 32.

108. Pannenberg, *Jesus-God and Man*, 42. Anselm's theory is Godward, not in the sense that God needs to be changed, but in the sense that God needs to restore his dignity and honor.

109. Dillistone, *Christian Understanding*, 190.

110. Franks, *Atonement*, 138.

have nothing to offer to restore God's honor. As Christ fulfilled this demand of the *law* this theory is also called as juridical theory.

Two points emerge in *Cur Deus Homo?* and they need to be made clear. On the one hand, Anselm constructs a soteriology, a particular interpretation of salvation and on the other hand, he provides a demonstration that incarnation and crucifixion, however unseemly they may appear, are both necessary. The necessity of Christ's life and work is because human beings are powerless to save themselves. This theory emphasizes that if human beings are to be saved an act of a human being is not enough even if it is a response to a divine example. In fact, human beings are not only powerless to restore the honor of God but also are powerless to restore themselves from the damaging situation.

Nevertheless, like the moral influence theory, the satisfaction theory also has both advantages and disadvantages. Robin Boyd claims that Anselm's theory has been very influential in theology because firstly, it takes man's sin seriously. Sin is not seen as a failure but a condition in which humanity lives. Secondly, it lays great stress on the majesty, holiness and honor of God, who is not to be mocked and thirdly, it makes an effort to be cogent and logical.[111] Aulen points out that Anselm strongly repudiates the idea of ransom paid to the devil.[112] In fact, this theory gives proper attention to the concepts of God's love and divine grace found in the gospels and Pauline writings. Anselm's theory also maintains the unique status of Christ, unlike the subjective theory. Further, this theory shows that forgiveness of sin comes at great cost.

The major defects of this theory are as follows. Wolf is of the view that the cross is not clearly shown to rest upon God's love. For him, Anselm's argument requires that God should proceed primarily by conforming to juridical law, which makes love a secondary attribute of God after justice.[113] Interpreting Hastings, Hughes says that God, for his satisfaction, claiming an innocent God-Man to suffer on the cross as a fit punishment in place of the punishment of millions, doesn't sound logical because it seems so unjust, punishing the innocent in place of the guilty.[114] In other words, injustice done by humanity against the honor of God cannot be overcome by God unjustly accepting the atoning work of Christ. Boyd too makes an important criticism on the Anselmian model. He asserts that in the account which this theory of the atonement provides of the work of Christ, one can

---

111. Boyd, *Khristadvaita*, 183.
112. Aulen, *Christus Victor*, 82–83.
113. Wolf, *No Cross*, 108.
114. Hughes, *Atonement*, 32, 36.

hardly be said to do justice to the unity between the persons of Trinity.[115] Moreover, this theory poses a discontinuity in divine action. In other words, Anselm finds difficulty in explaining how Christ dies freely yet obediently according to God's plan. It is also unclear in Anselm how the merits of one person may be attributed justly to another person. Most importantly, Anselm's theory puts Law above God than the other way. Even if God has established his own law, isn't God powerful enough to change the law rather than sending Christ to suffer and die on the cross?

The Juridical theory is vehemently criticized in the Indian context. The question raised is: Can a just God send Jesus to the cross? Chakkarai says that the arguments against juristic view of the Atonement are based upon a fuller understanding of the Scriptures. He writes, "In the face of this overwhelming richness of Christian experience and of vision entering into that which is within the veil, is it possible to say that the poor elements of our human legal systems were the determining factors in the Divine Tragedy?"[116] It is true that the cross biblically is not only the method of salvation, but also the means to it. Shri Vallabhacharya, an Indian leader says that God being portrayed as a Monster of Justice, who exacts his full pound of flesh even to the last atom from Jesus on the cross, is in sharp contrast to the Law of Grace of Indian thought. For him, the belief in the transmigration of souls is unique to the religious thought and life of the Hindus.[117] It is true that the idea of physically inherited sin as believed in traditional Christianity and the necessary Justice-logic stands in sharp contrast with the union theory of Visistadvaitic Hinduism. Further, Boyd identifies that Indian thought, like Greek, is alien to the Roman juridical conception.[118] In the light of Anselm's model, K. C. Sen's statement is worth noting. K. C. Sen says,

> you admit that the justice of God must be satisfied with the punishment of the sinner, and in the same breath you insist that His mercy must be satisfied by the remission of that punishment. A suicidal theory indeed. Why, this is tantamount to saying that the two great attributes of God, justice and mercy, combat and annihilate each other.[119]

It is a fact that, in India, salvation is not thought of as involving any juridical procedures in relation to restoring God's honor. Hence, the juridical

---

115. Boyd, *Khristadvaita*, 183.
116. Thomas, *Vengal Chakkarai*, 324–25.
117. Boyd, *Manilal C. Parekhi*, 81.
118. Boyd, *Introduction to Indian Christian Theology*, 246.
119. Das, *Shadow of the Cross*, 98.

theory is scarcely used in an Indian context. Here, we could also note that the objective theories are criticized more than the subjective ones are by Indian writers. K. C. Sen goes on to say that the objective theories are worthless because, for him, if the atonement has any meaning, it is the example, which Jesus made on the cross.[120]

Thus it is obvious that although in the medieval cultural context of feudalism, this theory might well be apt, without the key features of this cultural context [fealty, honor etc.] in India this theory remains inadequate and especially since it does not include in any way the concerns of the saving concept of Brahman. However, the logic with which Anselm formulates his theory is interesting and this theory has, undoubtedly, created much discussion on atonement theology throughout the centuries. The fresh theory, which we will construct in the next chapter, will be based on a similar logic, but we will view the atonement as creating the four-fold union and not as satisfying God's honor.

The Sacrificial Theory

The idea of sacrifice is prevalent both in the Old Testament as well as in the New Testament. We have briefly portrayed the idea of sacrifice, in the cultic context, in the introductory chapter. St. John understands that Christ is the Lamb of God who takes away the sin of the world. Paul also comments that Christ is our Passover, who has been sacrificed.[121] Thus the sacrificial theory is also biblically supported. Bishop Hick's *The Fullness of Sacrifice*, Oliver Chase Quick's *Interpretation of the Cross in Doctrines of the Creed*, Father Lionel Thornton's *The Doctrine of Atonement* and Vincent Taylor's work on the atonement all expound the sacrificial theory in detail.

The sacrificial theory revolves around the logic of love and forgiveness. Sacrifice evolves out of love and according to this theory God forgives us due to the sacrifice of Christ. Wolf analyses Vincent Taylor and points out that on the one hand, in Israel, sacrifice was understood as God's own gift to men of a rite by which sin could be "covered." Sacrifice was not propitiatory, but expiatory. It was not conceived as a method of changing God's mind but as his given method for realizing reconciliation. On the other hand, Jesus offers himself in his obedience, instead of offering an animal, sinless only by

---

120. Sumithra, *Christian Theology*, 47. Another Indian thinker, Mozoomdar also says that there seems to be little significance in objective understanding of the cross. See Sumithra, *Christian Theology*, 54.

121. First Cor 5:7.

default of any higher status. Jesus' sacrifice replaces and annuls the need for the Old Testament system of sacrifices.[122]

Paul shows that there are three necessary aspects to sacrifice which must find their place in any adequate exposition of the Eucharist—an ethical element (I will have mercy), an evangelical element (Christ was offered once for all), and a Catholic element (this our sacrifice of praise and thanksgiving for what Christ has done).[123] Thus Paul finds a relation between the atonement understood as a sacrifice and the sacrament of the Eucharist. Remarkably, Boyd explains a few theologians who have understood the atonement as a sacrifice of Christ. He says that according to Pope Paul VI, the sacrificial character of the Mass consists in the fact that in it Jesus' sacrifice on the cross is actualized or represented in such a way that the church is included in, and enters into, Christ's act of obedience to the Father. Boyd also speaks of the Indian theologians who have tried to construe the atonement as a sacrifice. V. Chakkarai interprets Christ's death as a sacrifice. K. M. Banerjee sees the atonement as a sacrifice and compares the sacrifice of Christ with the sacrifice of *Prajapati* (Lord of creation in the Hindu tradition.)[124] In short, this theory claims that we are saved through Jesus' sacrifice on the cross.

The sacrificial theory has its own strengths. Boyd points out that the idea of sacrifice as "self sacrifice" has become common and acceptable in many languages—a usage which probably stems originally from its Christian use in reference to the sacrifice of Christ.[125] Again, Wolf puts forward five important advantages to this theory. First, it gives a sense of continuity between the life and death of Christ. Second, it overcomes the unnatural separation between supposedly "objective" and "subjective" theories by emphasizing the "givenness" of the atoning act. Third, it adequately shows that the revelation of God's love is by means of a redemptive act of God. Fourth, it helps to stress the atoning act of God on the cross and preach the atonement as a historical accomplishment. By stressing that it is the perfect sacrifice it acknowledges that we must become implicated in its full attainment and consummation and fifth, it permits the official Christology of the church to be unified with a theory of the atonement.[126]

The weaknesses of this theory are as follows. It emphasizes only one of the many New Testament metaphors for expressing Christ's work. Precisely, this theory often tends to construe the sacrifice of Jesus as propitiation,

122. Wolf, *No Cross*, 122–23.
123. Paul, *Atonement and Sacraments*, 261.
124. Boyd, *Khristadvaita*, 186–87.
125. Boyd, *Khristadvaita*, 188.
126. Wolf, *No Cross*, 123.

which is just a strand of New Testament thought. The concept of sacrifice is different in many other religions and so it could be misleading. For example, in Visistadvaitic Hinduism, sacrifice is given only to appease God and it, in any way, does not take away our sins. Kaj Baago points out that the doctrine of atonement understood as redemptive sacrifice is the stumbling block for many Hindus to accepting Christianity.[127] Further, Stanley Jones, a missionary in India says that in the Indian context the atonement understood as sacrifice through expiation by blood is irrelevant. Rather, the cross if interpreted for at-one-ment and harmony is meaningful.[128] Similarly, Boyd rightly observes that Indian thought is unfamiliar with the Hebrew sacrificial tradition.[129] Thus, the sacrificial theory remains inappropriate and misleading in the Indian context.

Moreover, it is obvious that modern humanity finds the background of the sacrificial theory completely uncongenial. Hans Kung writes, "Since in modern man's environment cultic sacrifices are no longer offered, and there is no need to point to a Christian sacrifice in defending the faith against pagans . . . the concept of sacrifice is not related to any experience and has thus become largely misleading and unintelligible."[130] Wolf points out that one cannot rest the preaching of the cross upon the sacrificial theory that the preaching must always be preceded by a series of archaeological addresses on the background of sacrifice.[131]

In our objective of analyzing the existing theories, the sacrificial theory definitely turns on a unique idea. It stresses that forgiveness of sins comes through the sacrifice of Christ. This theory helps us to view the atonement in one particular direction. However, whilst the sacrificial theory emphasizes the cross as the sacrifice of Christ, the saving concept of Brahman holds that the divine offers grace for the re-establishment of the four-fold union. Nevertheless, as we will soon see, it is not wrong to understand that Christ sacrifices his life by substituting himself for us to create the four-fold union.

The Classical Theory

This theory is also known as Greek, patristic, dramatic, *Christus Victor*, ransom and Eastern model. The biblical sources for this theory are abundant.

---

127. Baago, *Pioneers of Indigenous Christianity*, 106.

128. Martin, *Missionary of the Indian Road*, 188. Roy also precisely rejects the view that atonement is a sacrifice. See Boyd, *Introduction to Indian Christian Theology*, 23.

129. Boyd, *Introduction to Indian Christian Theology*, 246.

130. Kung, *On Being a Christian*, 425.

131. Kung supports this idea. See Kung, *On Being a Christian*, 124–25.

This theory explains that the forces of evil are defeated by the sacrificial self-giving of the servant Messiah (Mark 8:31.) Interpreting St. Paul, Macquarie says that God has delivered us from the state of darkness and let us into the kingdom of his beloved son (Col 1:13) and God has abolished the claim of dark powers over us.[132] It is interesting that often Jesus' healing miracles were accomplished through the expulsion of demons (Matt 17:14, 15:21; Mark 5:1; and Luke 8:26).

The classical theory necessarily presupposes the existence of an evil force. This theory expounds that that evil force caught hold of humanity as its slaves. It was possible for the evil force to put humanity into bondage because they have given themselves over to it through sinning. Christ in his atoning work frees humanity from this bondage by defeating the evil power. Aulen, in his book *Christus Victor* expounds this theory in detail. He says, "the patristic theology is dualistic, but is not an absolute dualism. The deliverance of man from the power of death and the devil is at the same time his deliverance from God's judgment. God is reconciled by His own act in reconciling the world to Himself."[133] Precisely, for him,

> God is at once the all-ruler and engaged in conflict with the powers of evil. These powers are evil powers, and at the same time executants of God's judgment on sin. God is at the same time the Reconciler and the Reconciled. His is the Love and His the Wrath. The Love prevails over the Wrath, and yet Love's condemnation of sin is absolute.[134]

Though Aulen tries to avoid dualism, the use of the phrase "power of death and the devil" well portrays the dualistic nature of this theory. Macquarie is another theologian who interprets the classical theory. According to him, the work of Christ finished on the cross is a victory over all the powers that enslave man and so a deliverance from them. This victory is always to be understood as God's victory over evil.[135] The central thrust of this theory is that Christ fights against and triumphs over the evil powers of the world—the tyrant under which human beings are in bondage and suffering and in him God reconciles the world to himself.

Interestingly, this theory sees the cross as the work of God going forth to battle as our champion. Yung Hwa observes that through the cross the hostile forces however conceived—whether as sin and death, Satan and his hosts, the demonic in society and its structures, the powers of God's wrath

---

132. Macquarie, *Principles of Christian Theology*, 318.
133. Aulen, *Christus Victor*, 75.
134. Aulen, *Christus Victor*, 155.
135. Macquarie, *Principles of Christian Theology*, 318.

and curse, or anything else—are overcome and nullified, so that Christians are not in bondage to them, but share Christ's triumph over them.[136]

The classical theory has its own advantages. The theme of the classical theory, "Christ's victory," is a very important strand in the New Testament understanding of Christ's death. John 12:23 and Colossians 2:15 give the basis for this theory. Macquarie argues that the self-giving of Christ is continuous with the self-giving of God, and the whole work of the atonement is God's.[137] Thus the continuity of the divine work is acknowledged. Further, this theory powerfully acknowledges the nature of human enslavement to sin and the power and rights of evil. James Cone says, "Fellowship with God is now possible because Christ through his death and resurrection has liberated us from the principalities and powers and the rulers of this present world."[138] Wolf admires Aulen saying that he has done a service by recovering a patristic insight into the nature of salvation and atonement.[139]

Nonetheless, Aulen's understanding of the atonement has received criticisms. Though Wolf admired Aulen, he points out a serious defect as well. He says that Aulen admits to the inadequacy of the military metaphor as the sole image when, in describing God's reluctance to use brute force, he writes with the image of sacrifice in his mind. Wolf goes on to say, "He overcomes evil not by an almighty fiat, but by putting in something of His own, through a divine self-oblation."[140] Macquarie observes that one defect in Aulen's rehabilitation of the classical view of the atonement was his failure to come to grips with the mythological background of the principalities and powers. During the temptations of Jesus, he rejects making worldly power his ultimate concern, which is equated with worshiping Satan.[141] Yung Hwa puts forward the following arguments. 1) If the atonement consists essentially of a victory of God in Christ winning a victory over the forces of evil what logical necessity is there for an incarnation?, 2) This theory sets up an unnecessary tension between love and wrath and between grace and justice in God, and 3) The classical theory fails to provide a solution for the moral guilt of man.[142] For Chakkarai, much of the evil considered to be caused by an evil force is actually found to be caused by microbes and bacilli in the

---

136. Hwa, "Theories of Atonement," 545.
137. Macquarie, *Principles of Christian Theology*, 320.
138. Cone, *God of the Oppressed*, 212.
139. Wolf, *No Cross*, 100.
140. Wolf, *No Cross*, 100.
141. Macquarie, *Principles of Christian Theology*, 318–19.
142. Hwa, "Theories of Atonement," 547.

modern world.¹⁴³ Marius Felderhof rightly is of the opinion that it is unclear as to how evil represents a power which God must overcome when it is ultimately under his control and how this theory of victory can be understood when evil is still a virulent reality.¹⁴⁴

The classical theory too remains inadequate in an Indian context. Precisely, Indians cannot think that Christ at the cross overcame evil at one point of time. For example, Rabindranath Tagore, an Indian poet and a Nobel Laureate, whilst speaking on God's generosity in his distribution of Love, stresses that it is false to think it had been restricted to a blind lane abruptly stopping at one narrow point of history.¹⁴⁵ The classical theory views the cross as a singular event as most other theories also look at the cross. The Indian context pushes all theologians to seek the meaning of the cross as a continuing event. Samartha, an Indian theologian, also claims that the interpretation of the cross as a rescue operation should be avoided.¹⁴⁶

Here, to sum up, the classical theory claims that Christ through his atoning work overcame evil powers whilst the saving concept of Brahman underlines that Brahman creates the knowledge that we should be in union with the divine and others in his life and work. Hence, it is clear that the concerns of the classical theory and the saving concept of Brahman are very different.

Having seen that none of the traditional theories of the atonement are adequate enough to address the concerns of the saving necessity of Brahman and thus are perceived to be irrelevant to the Indian context we turn to analyze the theories as they are evolving in modern theology. However, as we had pointed out, we acknowledge that some theories will provide specific insights in the construction of our model of the atonement.

Models of the Atonement in Modern Theology

Although there are several works on the theology of the atonement, we will limit ourselves to the mentioned selected models of the atonement in modern theology.

---

143. Thomas, *Vengal Chakkarai*, 318.
144. Felderhof, *Revisiting Christianity*, 140–44.
145. At the Parliament of Religions in Calcutta, quoted by Gandhi in *Harijan*, 39
146. Sumithra, *Christian Theology*, 183.

The Modified Satisfaction Theory of Karl Barth

The first contribution of Karl Barth on the topic of the atonement is seen in his celebrated work, *Church Dogmatics*.[147] To construe Barth's view of the atonement we need to point out his understanding of divine love. This is because, according to Barth, what is satisfied on the cross is neither the wrath of God nor the honor of God, rather it is the love of God that is satisfied on the cross. Hence, Barth's model can be called as modified satisfaction theory.

For Barth, the holiness and righteousness of God denote the perfections of his love. God's love is unique because of his holiness and righteousness. Also, the holiness and righteousness of God makes his love divine. God loves his creation and God will not let anything to stand in the way of his love. Precisely, God's will to love his creation cannot be blocked by the will of his creation to oppose that love. In fact, God's love is seen as wrath when it is resisted. However, what is more important is that God's love never ceases to be love, even for the moment when it is experienced as wrath. Barth's understanding of the atonement should be analyzed against this background.

Now, what is the meaning of the atoning work of Christ? Barth says that the cross is the expression of wrath and condemnation. It was necessary because of sin. Sin is the obstacle to God's love toward his creation. Once the obstacle is removed God's love is again experienced as love by the creation. Barth writes, "The meaning of the death of Jesus Christ is that there God's condemning and punishing righteousness broke out, really smiting and piercing human sin . . . It did so in such a way that in what happened there . . . the righteousness of God which we have offended was really revealed and satisfied."[148]

Barth is also careful to say that it was not the suffering of an innocent man in the Calvary which is the motive, but it was the suffering of God's own heart. In his words,

> There is no moving of God by the creature on the basis of which God can then decide on a universal amnesty. It is rather God's own heart which moves in creation on the basis of His own good pleasure. It suffers what the creature ought to suffer and could not without being destroyed. It suffers it with omnipotent vicariousness in virtue of the fact that it is the heart of the almighty Lord and Creator, who, since it is His good-pleasure,

---

147. Barth, *Church Dogmatics*, vol. II, 351–406.
148. Barth, *Church Dogmatics*, vol. II, 396.

cannot be prevented from Himself sustaining His creature . . . as He has Himself created it[149]

Barth's claim is that God's wrath is not satisfied on the cross because the offering made is from the human side. But, the love of God is that which is expressed, even when that love expresses itself as wrath, judgment and punishment.

The crux of Barth's understanding of the atonement is found in Volume IV. For Barth, offering satisfaction to the wrath of God is alien to the New Testament.[150] It is the holy love of God that is satisfied in the atonement. The holy love of God is satisfied by the attack on sin and its destruction. Barth says,

> not out of any desire for vengeance and retribution on the part of God, but because of the radical nature of the divine love, which could "satisfy" itself only in the outworking of its wrath against the man of sin, only by killing him, extinguishing him, removing him. Here is the place for the doubtful concept that in the passion of Jesus Christ, in the giving up of His Son to death, God has done that which is "satisfactory" or sufficient in the victorious fighting of sin to make this victory radical and total.[151]

Our salvation is achieved by the satisfaction of God's love. That God's love is holy means that God must do what is worthy of himself in achieving the goals of love. It is true that God's love could not accomplish its purposes with humankind unless God condemned sin and removed it, unless he poured out his wrath upon it. Wrath here is only the means to accomplish the goals of love. The point is to know that the atonement is an act of God's love.

Barth's interpretation of the atonement has its own merits. The atoning work of Christ, no doubt, is heaping coals of fire—on us—it is experiencing love as wrath. Barth powerfully shows that the love of God is deeper than the sufferings of the cross. The New Testament concepts of grace and mercy form the setting of this theory. Also, the evil of sin is adequately acknowledged and is seen as resisting God's love toward us.

Nevertheless, modified satisfaction theory too operates with a juridical framework. Christ takes upon himself our sin by making himself liable for our guilt and consequences. Though, unlike the reformed view, Barth

---

149. Barth, *Church Dogmatics*, vol. II, 402.

150. Barth, *Church Dogmatics*, vol. IV, 253. Barth says, "The concept of punishment has come into the answer given by Christian theology to this question from Is. 53. In the New Testament it does not occur in this connexion."

151. Barth, *Church Dogmatics*, vol. IV, 254.

takes the entire life of Christ as a judgment, it could not escape the human logic of jurisdiction.

Apparently, Barth's does not deal with the intuitive as well as practical knowledge of the four-fold union. Hence, this theory will also not suit the Indian context. However, the profound thinking of Barth should be acknowledged and the atonement can be seen quite differently through his writing. The love of God expressed in the atonement is highlighted in this model. Our model will also see God's love manifest in the atonement but in a different way.

The Moral Authenticity Theory

Vernon White formulates the Moral Authenticity theory in his work, *Atonement and Incarnation*. White takes a comprehensive approach to the atonement drawing from renowned theologians like Maurice Wiles and many others. His main concern is on what way the particular atoning work of Christ can be understood as having a universal appeal. White begins by identifying the trustworthiness of traditional theories and points out the flaws inherent in them. According to him, "the explanation of how a particular event could constitute a universal, or at least widespread, change is precarious."[152] He comes to this conclusion after analyzing the themes of the classical, the moral influence, the sacrificial, and the substitutionary theories of the atonement. This, in fact, encourages us in the direction which we have taken in this work in the formulation of a fresh model for an Indian context.

Nevertheless, as we have seen, White's interest lies in affirming that the particular atonement is significant for all. The question he raises is: how can the particular little local Christ-event be relevant for salvation of the entire world? For him, to make salvation available to all, Christ had come into one part of the world, in one particular time. Thus for the moral authenticity theory the incarnation of Christ is of crucial importance. Also, White is careful to interpret the atonement as constitutive and not as an epistemological one. He says,

> I will examine and defend the claim that the particular event of Jesus Christ is constitutive of universal saving significance, rather than being merely demonstrative. It is the conceptual (and

---

152. White, *Atonement and Incarnation*, 29.

moral) possibilities of such a claim with which I am chiefly concerned, rather than the provision of empirical evidence for it.[153]

Having made clear that it is ontology which should be emphasized rather than demonstration alone, White proposes his model. For him, Christ had to submit himself to suffering, death and resurrection to gain moral authenticity to take us through the same path. It is because Christ underwent the path of suffering he is qualified to be with us in our suffering. An element of Christ's identification with the suffering humanity predominant in liberation theologies is evident here as well. However, White's stress is on the moral authenticity of God. He says that the heart of his model of the atonement rests on the criterion of moral authenticity.[154] In his words,

> unless and until God himself has experienced suffering, death, and the temptation to sin, and overcome them, as a human individual, he has no moral authority to overcome them in and with the rest of humanity. If this is accepted, then the Christ event becomes constitutive action (for God) in his reconciling activity through history, in the sense that it helps form an essential ingredient in God's moral character.[155]

Thus White understands that healing through and from suffering is salvation and Christ has the moral authority to be with us in our suffering to take us across. White points out that a similar perspective is found in the work of Brian Hebblethwaite. For Hebblethwaite,

> Only if we say that God has himself, on the cross, 'borne our sorrows' can we find him universally present 'in' the sufferings of others. It is not a question of 'awareness' and 'sympathy.' It is, as Whitehead put it, a matter of the fellow-sufferer who understands.' This whole dimension of the Christian doctrine of the incarnation, its recognition of the costly nature of God's forgiving love, and its perception that only a suffering God is morally credible, is lost if God's involvement is reduced to a matter of 'awareness' and 'sympathy.'[156]

Nevertheless, White substantiates his theory by saying that it is not only by identifying with the suffering humanity that Christ gets the moral authority but by himself experiencing the suffering. This experience in turn enables Christ to rightly use that moral authenticity in a powerful

---

153. White, *Atonement and Incarnation*, 4.
154. White, *Atonement and Incarnation*, 39.
155. White, *Atonement and Incarnation*, 39.
156. Goulder, *Incarnation and Myth*, 94.

way.[157] The particular Christ event in history, according to White, should be seen not only as revelatory but it should also be deemed constitutive of saving efficacy.[158]

Similar to the saving concept of Brahman White holds that the objective and subjective sides of the atonement should be held together. He says, "we require a model which also illuminates the paradox of salvation by divine grace yet involving our co-operation."[159] Christ is affected by a changed attitude as the agent of salvation and hence the atonement is objective. However, the atonement is also subjective because it affects a changed attitude in the objects of the action as well. By saying this, White argues that the particularity of Christ is universally significant.[160] The claim of White is that, "God in Christ takes into his own divine experience that which qualifies him to reconcile, redeem, and sanctify his relationship with all people everywhere."[161]

Here, we move on to highlight the strengths and weaknesses of this theory. White's argument is consistent and he is careful to hold the objective and subjective sides of the atonement together. This model effectively portrays the need for incarnation, suffering and death of Christ and resurrection in terms of the demand for moral authenticity. Moreover, White's attempt to view the particularity of Christ as universally significant succeeds to a great extent.

However, though the "why" question of Christ's suffering is addressed the "why" question of entire human suffering could not be addressed in this model. Who are we to know the authenticity of God in Christ, unless God informs our understanding, still remains a question. Further, whether undergoing suffering and death is worthy enough just for having moral authenticity is a question.

To sum up, the moral authenticity theory is close to the saving concept of Brahman in the sense that both strive to hold the objective and subjective sides of the atonement together and both try to portray the particular event of the atonement as universally significant. However, whilst the saving concept of Brahman relies on the intuitive and practical knowledge created within us by the divine, the moral authenticity model rests on the experience of Christ in the atonement to restore us to a right relationship with God. Hence, this theory will also prove inadequate for an Indian context.

---

157. White, *Atonement and Incarnation*, 39.
158. White, *Atonement and Incarnation*, 41.
159. White, *Atonement and Incarnation*, 51.
160. White, *Atonement and Incarnation*, 52.
161. White, *Atonement and Incarnation*, 53.

The Narrative Christus Victor Model

J. Denny Weaver formulates a model of the atonement using the principle of non-violence. He calls the model as the Narrative Christus Victor because it is an effort to see the victory of Christ through narration of biblical history, early Christianity and contemporary Christianity. Whilst Aulen's Christus Victor model sketches that the victory of the cross is seen in Christ overcoming evil powers by nailing them on the cross and by the subsequent resurrection of Christ, Weaver's attempt does not portray Christ's victory over evil powers in the form of some mythological wisdom, but in and through real human history. Weaver writes, "Narrative Christus Victor is not the classic image of cosmic beings in conflict. It is rather the event of Jesus and the church around Jesus unfolding in the realm of history as depicted in the biblical story."[162]

Weaver begins to articulate his model by briefly highlighting the weaknesses of Christus Victor motif, Satisfaction motif and Moral influence motif. In fact, we have already seen criticisms of these theories and hence I will not repeat them here.[163] However, the significant contribution of Weaver in relation to criticizing traditional theories is that he uses Black Theology, Feminist Theology and Womanist theology to make his point. According to Weaver, traditional theories are either manipulative trickery as in classical theory, or of minimalist reading of the bible as in satisfaction theory or subjective alone as in moral influence theory. Further, Weaver portrays the nature of violence involved in these theories. Commenting on traditional theories Weaver says, "Atonement theology starts with violence, namely the killing of Jesus."[164] Criticizing the satisfaction theory he says,

> the prevailing assumption behind the criminal justice system is that to 'do justice' means to punish criminal perpetrators appropriately.... Called retributive justice, this system assumes that doing justice consists of administering quid pro quo violence–an evil deed involving some level of violence on one side, balanced by an equivalent violence of punishment on the other.[165]

---

162. Weaver, *Nonviolent Atonement*, 69.

163. For details on Weaver's criticisms of the traditional theories, see Weaver, *Nonviolent Atonement*, 14–19.

164. Weaver, *Nonviolent Atonement*, 2.

165. Weaver, *Nonviolent Atonement*, 2. Weaver is of the opinion that violence can only create a greater violence. In his book, *God's Just Vengeance,* Timothy Gorringe is also of the same view.

Weaver's argument, in fact, is not convincing here because we could say that is precisely what justice and the moral life requires. If I have done wrong, says Socrates in the *Gorgias*, it is better to be punished than not to be punished.

In fact, the narrative Christus victor model begins with the use of the book of Revelation in understanding the atonement. Weaver says that Christ's victory is through non-violence. He writes, "The lion and lamb symbols of Revelation 5, which both refer to Jesus, portray one instance of a conqueror motif—with lion as a symbol of victory while slaughtered lamb signifies the (non-violent) manner of the victory."[166] Here, we could say that this may be the case but the lamb was slaughtered, the lion was the symbol of violence. The transformation has something to do with the slaughtering of the lamb. Weaver interprets different parts of the book of Revelation showing that Christ triumphs through non-violence. Using it to understand the atonement, Weaver is of the opinion that the resurrection of Jesus followed by the cross is worthy of celebration. He goes on to say, "The victory of the reign of God over the rule of evil culminates with the vision of the new Jerusalem, emphasising the restoration of what was destroyed."[167]

Weaver similarly interprets the gospels, particularly of Luke, Old Testament imageries of sacrifice and the book of Hebrews to say that God's victory is through non-violence. Perhaps Weaver would say that Christians were right in tolerating the violence of Rom in early centuries. However, Weaver is careful to argue that Christ's non-violent attitude was not a passive one but an active one. In his words,

> Rejection of violence, however, ought not to be interpreted as passivity. Walter Wink has demonstrated that far from counselling passivity, Jesus' statements about turning the other cheek, giving the cloak, and going the second mile (Matt. 5:39–41; Luke 6:29) actually demonstrated an assertive and confrontational non-violence that provides an opponent with an opportunity for transformation.[168]

Weaver applies his biblical interpretation to the doctrine of atonement and claims that satisfaction theory or other traditional theories cannot in any way be justifiable. His understanding is that the atonement is the victory of Christ through non-violence and should be viewed through the lens of non-violence.

---

166. Weaver, *Nonviolent Atonement*, 20.
167. Weaver, *Nonviolent Atonement*, 31.
168. Weaver, *Nonviolent Atonement*, 36.

It is interesting that Weaver, like many Indian theologians, tries to find the meaning of salvation in the life of Jesus rather than in his death. Commenting on the suffering of Christ he says that God himself suffered in Christ and did not leave Christ to suffer alone. This suffering, according to Weaver, is not the specific mission of Christ. The motif of his atonement model is not to ponder on what happened in Christ's suffering but rather to promote a reading of the Bible in a non-violent perspective.

The heart of Weaver's atonement model is as follows. He says,

> In narrative Christus Victor, individuals as well as the world are saved, although we still await the culmination of that salvation in the eschaton. In the intermediate time, Christians participate in that salvation when they accept God's call and are transformed from creatures aligned with evil to those who become co-laborers with Jesus in making God's rule present and visible on earth. . . . [N]arrative Christus Victor is a viable expression of God's saving work in Christ that makes visible and real in our history the victory of the reign of God and invites our participation in it.[169]

Thus Weaver's attempt is to re-read the Biblical story of the atonement in a way that would not legitimise oppression and violence. His model narrates that the non-violent attitude of Christ brings him victory. Participating in that victory of Christ we ought to make God's reign visible in this world. In this model we find that Christ expects us to be non-violent to participate in the salvation brought by him.

Weaver's attempt is coherent and to the point. He wants to view the non-violent character of Jesus in his life and death. It is a well-known fact that Gandhi was an advocate of non-violent living and would have appreciated this interpretation of Weaver. This model rightly provides continuity in the life of Jesus and his work and more significantly strives to seek for continuity in God's action in history starting from the Old Testament times. Thus the chronological problem of salvation through the atonement is also addressed in this model.

However, Weaver fails to give a logical explanation to the place of suffering in the life of Christ. Moreover, Christ as an energetic person driving away those who bought and sold at the temple after the triumphal entry to Jerusalem cannot be interpreted as non-violent.

Unlike the saving concept of Brahman, the Narrative Christus victor model emphasizes non-violence. In an Indian context after Gandhi, Weaver's model would gain much attention. However, in the philosophical

---

169. Weaver, *Nonviolent Atonement*, 227–28.

context of India the divine is what provides union. Non-violence could be accepted as a good way to live, though not explicitly found in Visistadvaitic Hinduism, but never the means or goal of salvation. Salvation through Brahman is to be one with Brahman, with others, with nature and with oneself. In short, the concern of the saving concept of Brahman is not addressed in the narrative Christus Victor.

The Sacramental Model

Michael Winter prefers to use the word liberation instead of salvation.[170] He understands that the crucifixion of Christ is a sacrament of his intercession. Christ intercedes for forgiveness on behalf of us. The atonement is for a relationship between God and People. He compares it with the sacrament of a wedding. The relationship continues between the bride and the bridegroom even after the act of sacrament is over. Crucifixion remains the quasi-sacramental manifestation of the whole process.[171]

Winter also interprets the atonement in terms of personal relationship. For him, the interaction effected by the atonement can apply to the interaction between human beings, and to their intimacy with, or estrangement from, God.[172]

Winter clarifies that it is not the will of Heavenly Father that caused the death of Jesus but surely it was the hostility of his earthly opponents.[173] He writes, "the uncompromising purity of Jesus' teaching and the integrity of his way of life presented a serious threat to the formalism of the religious observance of both the wealthy and privileged Sadducees and the passionately earnest Pharisees."[174] This made Jesus' death inevitable.

Now, where lies the uniqueness of the atoning work of Christ? For Winter, the atonement is the intercession of Jesus, literally asking for our forgiveness. It is a sacrament. Winter relies on Rahner to say that a sacrament is a visible means of grace. In this sense, the atonement is an act of grace. Analyzing Rahner, Winter says,

> The cross is the signum efficax, the efficacious sign, of the redeeming love that communicates God himself, because the cross establishes God's love in the world in a definitive and

---

170. Winter, *Atonement*, 6.
171. Winter, *Atonement*, 132–33.
172. Winter, *Atonement*, 87.
173. Winter, *Atonement*, 124.
174. Winter, *Atonement*, 125.

historically irreversible way . . . Given these presuppositions the cross of Christ can really be seen as the efficacious sign of God's salvific will in the world.[175]

With this Winter concludes that the atonement is the sign or sacrament of Christ's intercession. Christ neither satisfied an angry God nor did he play a drama. The cross is so real and as an intercession it becomes the means of our salvation. This is the central point of Winter's theory.

However, a sacrament can take place in the absence of suffering and death. Hence, a more comprehensive meaning is to be found in the self-giving act of Christ's atonement. Further, Winter's theory does not deal with the concept of four-fold union as found in the saving concept of Brahman. Hence, this theory too will remain inappropriate for the Indian context. The final theory, which we will look at, in this chapter, is the theory proposed by Vincent Brümmer.

The Divine Forgiveness Theory.

This theory is expounded by the philosopher Vincent Brümmer.[176] For him, we are estranged from God and from one another and estrangement is mainly caused by our ignorance of God as well as ourselves. According to Brümmer, what brings unhappiness is estrangement from God. He is also careful to say that human beings are estranged from each other as well.[177] In contrast, the goal of life, which is eternal happiness, can be achieved by recognizing our state of estrangement from God and the need for reconciliation with Him. There is no other means for achieving eternal happiness other than through fellowship with God. In fact, fellowship with God is realized through divine forgiveness and enlightenment, empowerment and inspiration. In fact, what we really need to know is the will of God by seeking his grace. Further, human repentance is essential toward this achievement. It is in this context Brümmer formulates his theory of the atonement.

Brümmer says that God is a God of love, who seeks restoration and not retributive justice. In his words, "God always remains willing to forgive and to pay the price of forgiveness."[178] For Brümmer, God pays price of forgiveness and the price paid is the sacrifice made by God. God suffers at our

---

175. Winter, *Atonement*, 132.
176. Brümmer, *Atonement, Christology and Trinity*, 1–12.
177. Brümmer, *Atonement, Christology and Trinity*, 36.
178. Brümmer, *Atonement, Christology and Trinity*, 78.

hands to forgive us.[179] This is why we had titled Brümmer's theory as the divine forgiveness theory.

Brümmer contradicts the ancient doctrine of divine impassibility that says God lacks nothing and hence does not suffer.[180] The sacrifice of God portrays divine forgiveness, which is essential for reconciliation. Moreover, Brümmer says that our part in achieving fellowship with God is equally important. In his words,

> Such reconciliation also requires penitence and a change of heart on our part. In order to be reconciled with God we need to change from rebels against God who seek ultimate happiness in finite goods, to children of God who seek our ultimate happiness in the kind of fellowship in which we identify with God by seeking his will as our own.[181]

He goes on to say that there is no merit for our strength for salvation, "because love and forgiveness can never be earned or merited, but by definition remains a free gift of grace."[182] The crux of this theory is that the cross shows divine forgiveness. God suffers to forgive us. This is the objective side. As it is clear, Brümmer emphasizes the subjective side to the atonement as well. God expects change in us to make the fellowship offered on the cross our own.

Thus Brümmer deserves commendation for having done justice in interpreting the atonement taking into consideration both the objective and subjective sides. Brümmer also avoids dualism when he says that the sacrifice is the inevitable suffering of God in forgiving us and he does not say that the sacrifice is made by the Son of God on behalf of us. The atonement is an act of God's love.

Nevertheless, Brümmer does not say why divine forgiveness and eternal happiness cannot be granted by God without Christ's suffering and death on the cross. In other words, the logic of the cross is obscure. In the Indian context too, Brümmer's theory will remain inadequate because this theory never touches on the intuitive and practical knowledge created in us by the divine. Moreover, Brümmer's theory deals only with God-human and human-human union and in effect takes human beings out of their environment as if this environment was not in some way constitutive of our existence. As we

---

179. Brümmer, *Atonement, Christology and Trinity*, 78.

180. In today's theological circles, the rejection of the ancient doctrine of divine impassibility is very common. For example, see Goetz, "The Suffering of God," 385.

181. Brümmer, *Atonement, Christology and Trinity*, 78.

182. Brümmer, *Atonement, Christology and Trinity*, 79.

have noted the Indian context pushes us to see the relevance of the atonement for human-nature and one-oneself unions as well.

Concluding Remarks

In the previous chapter, we have seen that in the Indian context, where Hinduism predominates, salvation is understood as a life with the intuitive and practical knowledge of a four-fold union created within us by the divine. In this chapter, we have analyzed the penal substitutionary and the representative theories in detail and the other existing major theories of the atonement in Christian tradition very briefly and noted that none of the theories exploit the four-fold union in detail. This leaves the existing atonement theories inadequate and inappropriate in the Indian context. We now proceed to outline an atonement model, in an inter-religious perspective, in an Indian context. Our model of the atonement will not only be readily applicable to the Indian-Visistadvaitic Hindu context, but also will help Christians construe the atonement in a fresh dimension.

4

Constructing an Atonement Model in a Hindu-Christian Indian Context

The Atonement Creating Unions

HAVING ESTABLISHED THAT NONE of the existing theories of the atonement do full justice to an Indian context, we venture to outline a model of the atonement that will be relevant, meaningful and motivate the Visistadvaitic-Hindu people of the Indian sub-continent and elsewhere. In chapter 2, we highlighted the Visistadvaitic Hindu concept of Brahman within its religious context with particular reference to Ramanuja, the most notable theologian of that strand of Hinduism. We briefly analyzed the concept of sin (bondage) in Visistadvaitic Hindu theology that emphasizes the problem of "ignorance" (*avidya*) and the consequent alienations. We also noted that salvation is understood as liberation from the bondage of "ignorance" and the three phenomena that constitute the bondage (sin) are *anavam* (egocentricity), *karma* (action-result) and *maya* (illusion). Significantly, we pointed out that Brahman "saves" the soul from the bondage of "sin" by providing the intuitive and practical knowledge necessary for salvation/liberation. Interestingly, we saw that the "knowledge" provided by Brahman is that we ought to be in union with Brahman, with each other, with nature and with ourselves. Following this, we carefully analyzed the three dimensions of Brahman's essence in relation to salvation, i.e.

1) as ongoing, 2) as transcending religious barriers and 3) as providing ground for theological interpretations of the various Visistadvaitic Hindu doctrines.

The saving concept of Brahman, as we have delineated in chapter 2, has in-depth possibilities for interpreting Christ's atoning work for salvation. This interpretation of the work of Christ, which we shall call the atonement creating[1] unions, as we noted, will enrich and enhance the theological understanding of Christ's atonement not only for Visistadvaitic Hindus but also for Christians. It is also our hope that this model of the atonement, though it arises from a (Hindu-Christian) Indian context, will be equally insightful to people of other countries as well, since it deals with more or less the universally germane concepts of alienation and union.

We need to be clear that this theory is not all-encompassing, incorporating the manifold dimensions of the atonement elucidated in the Bible. However, we also do not believe that the immensely sophisticated concept of the atonement, with which theologians have struggled for centuries now, can be fully comprehended in one theory. We believe that our efforts are worthwhile in pointing to a direction in which a fruitful theory of the atonement can be constructed.

Apparently, as we construct our model of the atonement, in a comparative doctrinal perspective, using a Visistadvaitic Hindu concept, it will not only have potentialities but also problems. In fact, whilst maintaining the central motif of the saving concept of Brahman, which is to create the knowledge of the four-fold union, we will go beyond this to say that Christ creates the four-fold union anew and thereby creates the practical knowledge of the four-fold union as well. However, we will not go into details of the potentialities and limitations of our inter-religious doctrinal model of the atonement, in this chapter, since we will devote the next chapter exclusively for that task.

Precisely, our objective here is to interpret the atonement as a doctrine which creates the four-fold union and at the same time inspires us to overcome alienation with the four dimensions. We will first, along the lines of Ramanuja, see that alienation, except from evil, is sin, and salvation is a life in union with God, others, nature and ourselves even in Christian terms. We will then elucidate six principles that underlie the construction of our atonement model. Following this, we will analyze the way in which the atonement creates the four-fold union and thereby the intuitive and practical knowledge of the unions as well. We will also briefly see that the atonement has implications for a union between the past, the present and the future. Finally, we will also point out the implication of the atonement on a union between religious traditions and the implication of the atonement on a union between different theological doctrines in Christianity.

---

1. Here we use the word, "creating" not in the sense of *creatio—ex-nihilio*, but in the sense that there is an inherent union between everything that often is unrecognized, and Christ creates the intuitive and practical knowledge of the union anew.

An Indian Interpretation of the Christian Understanding of Sin: Alienation as Sin

There are varied definitions of sin within Christianity. For example, on the one hand, Karl Barth says that sin is nothingness or an impossible possibility. By nothingness he means that "contradiction of God's positive will and that breach of his covenant which can exist only under the contradiction which is his judgment."[2] On the other hand, for Rahner, the Catholic theologian, sin is clearly a refusal by human beings to share in God's divine nature.[3] Thus, the perception of "sin" is diverse even within the Christian tradition.

Nonetheless, our interest here is to point out that alienation, in its different dimensions: i.e. God-human, human-human, human-nature and one-oneself, can also be understood as sin, in Christian terms. However, before proceeding to do that, we will very briefly re-assert that *avidya* and the consequent four-fold alienation are considered as sin in Visistadvaitic Hinduism.

We would begin by clarifying a common misunderstanding that sin is not taken seriously in Hinduism. For example, Sigfrid Estborn says that, in Indian thought, the idea of *avidya* overlooks the fact that our intellect by no means represents the deepest and strongest forces of our nature.[4] He argues in a manner similar to the traditional Augustinian position that it is with our will that we decide to sin or not.[5] Here there is no doubt that our will "knows" good and evil. St. Paul acknowledges that though he wants to do good the sin in him makes him do evil. However, in Ramanuja's thought, *avidya* is not a lack of knowledge in general terms, and not even a lack of knowledge to distinguish between right and wrong, but it is the lack of the intuitive/tacit knowledge to lead a practical life in union with the divine, others, nature and ourselves. Essentially, this knowledge is never just an abstract and informative knowledge of right and wrong but is ultimately an intuitive and practical knowledge, which is, in this case that of realizing the good union and eschewing evil alienation. Thus *avidya* is not a failure in abstract knowledge or that of a lack in information but a failure of knowing how to realize the good union and eschew evil alienation that inter alia presumes a mastery of the will. This clarifies the position and shows that Ramanuja's Visistadvaitic Hinduism takes sin seriously.

---

2. Barth, *Church Dogmatics*, 358.
3. Rahner, "Sin," 1589.
4. Estborn, *Christian Doctrine of Salvation*, 43.
5. Estborn, *Christian Doctrine of Salvation*, 43.

In short, *avidya* is sin for Visistadvaitic Hindus. Although the literal translation of the term *avidya* is ignorance, as we noted, it is not a mere lack of any kind of knowledge, nor is it an inability to distinguish between good and evil. It is exactly the lack of intuitive and practical knowledge, offered by Brahman that we ought not to live in alienation from the divine, others, nature and ourselves. In other words, it is not knowing intuitively and practically and therefore being unable to live in union with the divine, others, nature and ourselves. For Ramanuja, just as the body is united to the self so we ought to be united with Brahman. Nevertheless, it should be clear that, in Visistadvaitic Hindu thought, *avidya* and alienation harmonize because *avidya* is being ignorant of the four-fold union and consequently embracing alienation. It is precisely this alienation that makes *avidya* sinful.

Analyzing the thought of Sara Grant, K. P. Aleaz says, "avidya is the ascription of a false autonomy to created being."[6] This is simply to say that our egocentricity alienates us from the divine and should be overcome by knowing that we are not our own but we are of the divine. Interpreting Hinduism, Bede Griffiths says that sin is a "divided self."[7] "Divided self" is to understand and will to act in a way that we are alienated from the divine. Obviously, these two definitions stress the need for realizing alienation as sin. Along with divine-human alienation, human-human alienation, human-nature alienation and one-oneself alienation are also sin. We have made this plain in chapter 2. Further, a careful thought will disclose that these four different kinds of alienations are interconnected and interdependent.[8]

Can the Four-Fold Alienation Be Understood as Sin in Christian Terms?

We will answer this question with biblical and theological support. Firstly, biblically, some scholars believe that the idea of sin in the Old Testament starts with the "original sin" caused by the disobedience of Adam and Eve. In this biblical account, the disobedience portrays the will of humanity being alienated from the will of God. However, there are also people who believe that sin is part of human nature.[9] Whatever may be the case, Christians

---

6. Aleaz, *Christian Thought*, 55.

7. Griffiths, *New Vision of Reality*, 98.

8. Persaud rightly suggests that sin is basically a separation from God from which all other societal forms of alienation are derived. See Persaud, *Theology of the Cross*, 252.

9. For example, Arthur Peacocke says that evil is introduced into creation by free human beings. In his words, "For humanity is free to . . . bring into existence disharmonies uniquely of its own—and has perennially done so." Polkinghorne, *The Work of*

generally understand that humans were granted free will to choose between right and wrong. The original sin of alienation and disobedience committed by Adam and Eve was because they chose to do what was wrong instead of right through the exercise of their free will.

The Hebrew root word used to refer to sin is *hata*. This Hebrew word can mean miss, fail and sin. This word has also led to other words like error, fault, sinful and sinner.[10] Though this is the common word used to denote sin, there are also many more Hebrew words that refer to sin in the Old Testament such as *chata, qal, peil* and *hithpael*. This very multiplicity of terms denotes fine distinctions and the importance given to the concept of sin even in Old Testament times. More importantly, it is crucial to note that whether it is missing or failing or error or faultiness, our will estranged from the divine will is at the root of any flaw.

In the New Testament, words such as *hamartia, parabasis* and *asebeia* refer to sin. These Greek words occasionally refer to wrong done to fellow human beings but most of the time they refer to wrong done against God.[11] The New Testament also has sin as one of the dominant themes. This dominance is reflected by the assurance that the purpose of the atonement is to conquer it. It is important for us to note that in the New Testament thought too, alienation is that which underlies all sinful thoughts and deeds.

Paul Tillich explicitly says that alienation is sin. He straightaway uses the word, estrangement in explaining the concept of sin. However, Tillich is reluctant to replace the word sin with estrangement.[12] Certainly, our claim too is not to replace the term sin with alienation or estrangement but to construe the concept of sin using the term, alienation. To move further, Tillich helpfully writes, "Sin expresses most sharply the personal character of estrangement . . . Man's predicament is estrangement, but his estrangement is sin."[13] Thus Tillich, obviously, is not far from our argument.

It is true that in Christianity a breach in divine-human union is often highlighted as sin. But it is no less true that a breach in human-human union, a breach in human-nature union and a breach in one's union with oneself, which is to live selfishly, are also considered sin. Although Tillich combines human-human estrangement and human-nature estrangement with the phrase, "estrangement from one's world," he favors us in unfolding

---

Love, 39.

10. Buttrick, *Interpreter's Dictionary*, 361.
11. Buttrick, *Interpreter's Dictionary*, 371.
12. Tillich, *Systematic Theology*, 52.
13. Tillich, *Systematic Theology*, 53.

the four proportions of alienations. For him, sin is the "state of estrangement from that, to which one belongs—God, one's self, one's world."[14]

Moreover, as Vince claims, it is the problem of alienation or estrangement that is overcome in the cross of Christ.[15] If the problem of alienation is overcome on the cross, then alienation is definitely sin because the cross traditionally and theologically, no doubt, is for liberation from sin.

To sum up, in Christianity, it is usually understood that we are free to choose an alienated life in its four dimensions due to the free-will given by God to his creation. Visistadvaitic Hinduism understands that the craving for alienation in us is due to *maya* (illusion). *Maya* does not mean that we have no understanding of the real, but it means that we become ignorant of the purposes of our creation, which is to be with Brahman. In Christianity, whilst in our free-will we sometimes choose to go astray from being in tune with God's will, in Visistadvaitic Hinduism, it is *maya* which makes us choose ungodly things instead of godly things. This perceptibly is in close relation with Augustine's distinction between freedom of choice and *libertas*. According to Augustine, we act the way we do, neither because our passions drive us nor because our reason apprehends what is best, but ultimately because of what we choose. We have freedom of choice and our freedom to choose is not determined by anything outside our control.[16] On the other hand, *libertas* is a freedom given to us by a superior that is different from us. For Augustine, there is no true *libertas* other than the *libertas* of the happy who cleave to the law of the eternal.[17] In the concept of *maya*, the stress is on *libertas* rather than on the freedom of choice. However, in both Visistadvaitic Hinduism and Christianity, to alienate ourselves and to act contrary to the will of the divine is sin.

Further, the commonalities between the Visistadvaitic Hindu and Christian understanding of sin include that sin is 1) something which is against the divine, 2) something which the divine helps us to overcome, 3) something which is negative, 4) something which destroys harmony and peace and corrupts humanity, 6) something which should be consciously worked against, and 7) something from which salvation is essential. The dissimilarity is that whilst in Visistadvaitic Hinduism *maya* is the cause of

---

14. Tillich, *Systematic Theology*, 52. In relation to one-oneself union, it should be noted that we are not saying that one is ignorant of the self, but our argument is that one is ignorant of the necessity of being in union with oneself, in relation to salvation. Also See Snook, *Anonymous Christ*, 62–63. Snook says that estrangement is a state of being lost.

15. Vince, "Alienation," 15.

16. Augustine, *On Free Choice of Will*, 22.

17. Baillie, *God was in Christ*; Augustine, *On Free Choice of Will*, 132.

avidya and the consequent alienation, in Christianity, free-will gives us the freedom to choose to sin or not to sin.

Nonetheless, what is important for us to bear in mind is that alienation is undesirable. Precisely, both biblically and theologically there is enough room for claiming that four-fold alienation is sin. When alienation is seen as sin then indubitably union is salvation. We will now turn to deal with the concept of salvation.

An Indian Interpretation of the Christian Understanding of Salvation: Four-Fold Union as Salvation

Admittedly, again in Christianity, there is no one understanding of salvation. The different theories of the atonement portray that salvation is achieved for us by Christ, however, in various ways. Further, whilst some theologians support universalism others favor the view that only believers will be saved.[18] This illustrates that salvation is a complex notion.

Our objective in this section is to point out that salvation in Christian tradition, similar to Ramanuja's thought, can be construed in terms of the four-fold union. In Ramanuja's thought, salvation is to attain the intuitive and practical knowledge of our union with Brahman, others, nature and ourselves. How could salvation be understood in terms of the four-fold union in Christian vocabulary?

There are recognized scholars who have expressed the view that salvation implies very different positions in different religions. For example, Mark Heim claims that we cannot talk of a salvation but can only talk of salvations in a pluralistic world. His point is that, in Hinduism, salvation is not liberation from "sin" as Christians understand it but it is the liberation from the "human" condition itself.[19] Nevertheless, we have made it plain that alienation in its four dimensions is considered as sin both in Visistadvaitic Hinduism and Christianity. Moreover, human condition as sin is stressed by Sankara and not by Ramanuja. Whilst for Sankara, the atman (soul) merges and disappears in Brahman during salvation, for Ramanuja, the atman continues to be distinctly different even in the state of union with Brahman. Thus the generalized attack with the distinction between the understandings of salvation in the two different traditions does not prevent us from seeing that salvation is a life with the four-fold union in both the traditions.

---

18. For details, see McGrath, *Christian Theology*, 364–68.
19. Heim, *Salvations*, 129–30.

Klostermaier, who has done extensive study on Hinduism and Christianity, portrays the "union trend" in the understanding of salvation in both traditions. His treatment of the topic is more constructive and practical than Heim's abstract distinction between the idea of liberation from sin and liberation from human condition. Klostermaier writes,

> Kristvidya (Union with Christ) is the revelation of the hidden mystery of Brahmavidya (Union with Brahman) . . . Kristvidya will not exhaust the mystery of Christ . . . it could help the church to become aware of some aspects of Christ which did not come out clearly as yet . . . it will not culminate in a summa of doctrines and definitions but will be largely marga—a systematic liberation of man from all wrong attitudes and concepts to make him 'free' for the ONE, the ultimate experience.[20]

Nevertheless, does the Bible support the view that salvation consists of the four-fold union? Biblically, the divine activity for our salvation is pre-eminent even in the times of the Old Testament. Salvation in the Old Testament is to deliver, to bring to safety, to redeem, to restore and to set free. The beginning chapters of the book of Genesis clearly state that there was a union between God, humanity and nature at the time of creation. God walked with Adam and Eve at the Garden of Eden. This union was soon lost by Adam and Eve alienating themselves from God, expressed in their disobedience. Hence, the term deliver probably could be understood in terms of deliverance from alienation and restoration toward the state of union. Though we do not intend to go into detail, other Old Testament terms also can be construed in a similar way.

In relation with Visistadvaitic Hinduism, a word of caution is necessary. In Visistadvaitic Hinduism, the four-fold union is already present. But the problem is that we are not aware of it and hence are not able to live in accordance with that union. However, in Christianity, "union" is a lost phenomenon and it is only by creating the four-fold union the intuitive and practical knowledge of it can be created. We will later return to this in this work.

Coming to the New Testament, the word salvation can mean to keep from harm, to rescue, to heal and to liberate. The New Testament also puts great emphasis on deliverance from sin (Matt 1:21; Mark 1:5; Acts 2:38, 3:19, 26, 10:43; Rom 6:1–23).[21] It is perceptible that the kingdom of God imagery is related to salvation (Mark 10:23–26; Luke 13:23–30). The New Testament also uses terms like new life, new being, new creation and

---

20. Klostermaier, *Indian Theology*, 111.
21. Klostermaier, *Indian Theology*, 111.

heavenly Jerusalem for salvation. For John, sharing in the life of Christ is salvation. St. Paul, in 2 Corinthians 6:2, writes of a day of salvation and in Ephesians 1:13 records a gospel of salvation. He considers that salvation is freedom from sin (Rom 6:1–23) and freedom from death (Rom 6:21). All these he sums up in the paradigm of "life in Christ" (Rom 8:1, 16:7; 1 Cor 15:21). However, all New Testament understandings of salvation directly imply that a union with God is essential for salvation. J. Atkinson says that the essential truth of the good life to the biblical writers was that good life means communion with God.[22] The New Testament also has passages that talk about human-human union, human-nature union and one's union with oneself that will be pointed out later in this chapter.

St. Paul experiences that it is Christ who lives in him. Bede Griffiths and Sara Grant have understood salvation in a similar fashion. Griffiths says that redemption is a return to unity; it is the awakening to our true being in the "Word."[23] Grant expresses our union with Christ in terms of self-denial. She says, "Christ has brought us redemption in the sense that he became the very anti-thesis of self-assertion."[24]

Moreover, theologically, we could say that salvation is God himself. One could also argue that here is an inner unity between objective and subjective redemption. In fact, Tillich is overt in his understanding that union is salvation he is careful in comprehending salvation as union in all its dimensions as well. For him, salvation is healing from estrangement. In his words, "healing means *reuniting* that which is estranged, giving a center to what is split, overcoming the split between God and man, man and his world, man and himself."[25] Thus, interestingly, theologians have unhesitatingly construed salvation in a union perspective.

In short, in Visistadvaitic Hinduism after Ramanuja, Brahman-atman union is salvation. This involves our union with others, nature and ourselves. Salvation as the four-fold union is thus not contrary to the Christian idea of salvation. We have seen that biblically and theologically it is not wrong to construe salvation in the union perspective. It is significant that even etymologically, the term, salvation means "making whole." In this context, we may point out that the word "Jesus" itself means salvation. Jesus is the union of both divine and human. Two passages will be worth mentioning. In Romans 5:17–21, it is said that Christ's obedience (union with God's will)

---

22. Atkinson, "Salvation," 301.

23. Aleaz analyzes the thought of Griffiths in detail. See Aleaz, *Christian Thought*, 55.

24. Aleaz, *Christian Thought*, 179.

25. Tillich, *Systematic Theology*, 192. Emphasis added.

brought the free gift of righteousness and life for all. In Romans 4:25 and 1 Peter 1:18–19 we read that in Christ's *union* with humanity he was put to death for our sin and raised. Salvation thus involves human union with divine volition, demanding that we abandon our selfishness.

Along with divine-human union and human-human union, human-nature union and one-oneself union also constitute salvation. This will become clear when we consider in detail the atoning work of Christ. Now, we shall move on to the principles of our atonement model.

Principles of Our Atonement Model

Prior to examining how the atonement creates the intuitive and practical knowledge of the four-fold union it is important for us to view at least six principles that underlie the construction of our atonement model.

1) Any atonement model should elucidate a concept of God that underlies the construction of that model. In Christianity, God is understood to be a trinity, yet it is believed that God is one. The dictum, "Three in One and One in Three" well testifies to this fact. Traditionally, the triune God is construed in terms of the metaphors Father, Son and Holy Spirit. However, there is no specific distinction between the three aspects. For example, the spirit of Christ is same as the Holy Spirit. Again, whilst generally, God the Father is thought of creating, God the Son is thought of redeeming and God the Holy Spirit is thought of sustaining—there is also no definite distinction between the "persons" to which these attributes belong. As Ogden says, "What it means to have God as Father is existentially the same as having Jesus Christ as our Lord."[26] Interestingly, the God who unites is Himself a united being and the Doctrine of Trinity reveals this fact.

We have noted that whilst some theories work on the basis that God was in Christ during his atoning work, other theories look at the atonement as Christ's work directed toward God the Father as substitution and representation. Our atonement model is based on the belief that the Father and the Holy Spirit were in Christ throughout his atoning work on the cross and the event of the cross is the experience of the triune God. Precisely, as we will soon see, we understand that Christ substituted and represented us to create the four-fold union and thereby the unique knowledge of the "unions" as well. Our model is also constructed with the traditional understanding that Christ is fully divine and fully human.

26. Ogden, *Reality of God*, 201.

2) The problem of alienation is intense. As we saw in the introductory chapter, Hegel and Marx carefully point out this problem. For Hegel, religion is the source of manifold alienation. G. Baum writes, "Hegel held that the inherited religion was the source of a threefold alienation, man's alienation from nature, from himself, and his fellow man."[27] However, over against Hegel's view, our model of the atonement will assert that it is a four-fold union.

The persuading idea of our atonement model is the Visistadvaitic Hindu thought of four-fold union as salvation. Why is this four-fold union a necessity? Firstly, the four-fold union is to bring peace and harmony overcoming conflicts. Clearly, the four-fold union is necessary for us to be at peace with God, others, nature and ourselves. Secondly, the four-fold union only can help us grow together under the divine, caring for others, nature and ourselves. Thirdly, the four-fold union can help us resist evil together.

3) In Visistadvaitic Hindu thought, Brahman alone can provide the knowledge of four-fold union, no matter what the means is, and thus it is objective. But it is also necessary that we realize the four-fold union and lead a practical life in accordance with it, which means there is a subjective side as well. In relation to Visistadvaitic Hindu logic, one might argue that if one doesn't know about the union there is no union at all. In this sense, it is not wrong to construe that the four-fold union is also created when the knowledge about it is created. However, our model of the atonement will argue that the atoning work of Christ creates the four-fold union and thereby it also creates the intuitive and practical knowledge in us.[28] Moreover, we understand that the atonement expects a change in us. Thus, as we will soon see, our model of the atonement will have both objective and subjective sides.

4) One might ask, how extensive does this knowledge persist? We noted in chapter 2, that the knowledge of Brahman is not an abstract and theoretical knowledge but a knowledge which is intuitive and practical. It is on this understanding of the concept of knowledge we proceed from here. Our model also understands that the removal of sin, guilt, and punishment is through the suffering of Christ and in leading a practical life with the knowledge of the four-fold union created by the atonement.

---

27. Baum, *Religion and Alienation*, 9.

28. Obviously, here there is a difference in the logic between the Hindu and Christian systems of thought. We will return back to this in the next chapter.

5) Although we use the saving concept of Brahman in formulating our model of the atonement, Brahman does not undergo any suffering in creating the intuitive and practical knowledge for salvation.[29] But the suffering and death of Christ on the cross is very central to the understanding of means to salvation in Christianity. As Schillebeeckx says, "In this complex of tradition the suffering and death of Jesus are interpreted, on a basis of Scripture, as a 'salvific economy,' God's plan of salvation."[30] Further, he writes, "At no stage of the tradition are Jesus' suffering and death reported merely as an atrocious and absurd, more or less unholy and baffling event."[31] Our model of the atonement will take the centrality of the suffering and death of Christ seriously, although Brahman does not undergo suffering, just as Patripassionism in Christianity was traditionally regarded as a heresy. We will return to this difference in logic in the next chapter. However, along the lines of Brahman concept, we will maintain that Christ creates the intuitive and practical knowledge of four-fold union.

We will soon see how Christ creates the four-fold union and thereby its knowledge through his atoning work on the cross. We will also soon see how the cross has both objective and subjective sides. Here, we will just point out the utmost use in creating the knowledge, in and through suffering, with the insights of Weil and Popper. We assert that Christ creates the salvific knowledge through his suffering unto death on the cross because reality is revealed in the highest and in the most acute extent in suffering. Simone Weil talks of affliction which unveils the reality to the utmost extent. Though she hailed from a well-to-do Jewish family and was a teacher she took an assumed name and worked as an unskilled worker in an electrical factory. Unused to such physical hard work, she found it an agony, since from childhood on she endured severe head-aches almost constantly. Reflecting on these very painful experiences she writes that in suffering there is no reply for the question "why." In her words,

> When one finds a comforting reply, first of all one has constructed it oneself . . . If the word "why" expressed the search for a cause, the reply would appear easily. But it expresses the search for an end. This whole universe is empty of finality. The

---

29. This is because Hinduism, again, works on a different logic. For Hindus, God cannot suffer at all even in the form of avatars, and if something suffers, that is not God at all. In chapter 2, we noted that Brahman creates the knowledge of union through scriptures, consciousness, and gurus. Again, we will come back to this difference in this logic of both of the traditions in the next chapter.

30. Schillebeeckx, *Jesus*, 282.

31. Schillebeeckx, *Jesus*, 284.

soul which, because it is torn by affliction, cries out continually for this finality, touches the void.[32]

Suffering discloses reality. Christ takes this suffering in union with the Father and the Holy Ghost also to display what is really needed. The deepest and the most passionate way of teaching is through suffering unto death. God suffers for our sake. Only through the God of the cross can we find real meaning for us.

Weil goes on to say that void is the absence of God, as a horror that submerges the entire soul. She writes, "During this absence there is nothing to love . . . It was not only the body of Christ, hanging on the wood, which was accursed, it was his whole soul also."[33] Jesus takes this pain of "nothing to love—including God" in body and soul because God himself was suffering in him. Then Christ's pain is both objective and subjective[34] in the sense that he had to give himself to us, on the cross, to teach us that "practical life of four-fold union is salvation" in the uttermost reality that is manifested only in suffering.

Another insight is Karl Popper's notion that the growth of knowledge comes through the falsification of theories. For him, reality is known when theories are falsified. He says, "What we should do, I suggest, is to give up the ideal of ultimate sources of knowledge, and admit that all knowledge is human: that it is mixed with our errors, our prejudices, our dreams, our hopes; that all we can do is to grope for truth even if it be beyond our reach."[35] Even though metaphysical assertions are not necessarily worthless or even false, Popper rightly stresses a principle of delineation in the criterion of falsification. For him, reality is known when all theories are falsified.

It is a fact that all theories are falsified when one suffers unto death. Reality becomes completely visible in suffering. It is through suffering, which falsifies all theories that Christ brings us salvation. Christ's suffering draws our attention toward him in the most passionate way.

6) Finally, the principles of our atonement model also include viewing the atonement in relation to the complete historical life of Christ. Schillebeeckx says, "It is precisely when the message and conduct of Jesus which led to his death are ignored that the saving significance of this death is obscured . . . the life and death of Jesus must be seen as a single whole."[36]

---

32. Weil, *Intimations of Christianity*, 198–99.

33. Weil, *Waiting on God*, 80–81.

34. We will proceed to see the objective side along with the subjective side in detail, whilst analyzing the four-fold union, soon in this chapter.

35. Popper, *Conjectures and Refutations*, 30.

36. Schillebeeckx, *Interim Report*, 133.

True that theologically speaking, the atonement is not an isolated event in the life of Christ. It is to be construed in conjunction with the incarnation, teachings, suffering, death and resurrection of Christ.[37] Our atonement model will draw support from the incarnation, teachings of Christ, person of Christ and teachings of the church in its construction. We now move on to analyze the intuitive and practical knowledge of divine-human union created in the atonement.

The Atonement and Four-Fold union

a) Arguments in Support of Viewing the Creation of Intuitive and Practical Knowledge of Divine-Human Union in the Atonement

Divine-Human alienation is a problem that has affected us throughout history. In Ephesians 4:18, St. Paul says that people are alienated from the life of God due to their ignorance and their hardness of heart. Gunton portrays this trouble in a different way. He says, "In response to Christendom's often alienated conception of God, we have created a conception of humanity in the very same image and made the alienation even deeper."[38]

Biblically and theologically, it is avowed that the atonement is the resolution of the problem of estrangement between God and humanity. Most theories, analyzed in the previous chapter, seek to address this dilemma of estrangement at some length. However, they do not attempt to offer an intuitive and practical solution to the problem of our alienation from God.[39] If only the atonement is theologized as creating an intuitive and practical knowledge of our essential union with God it serves its purpose by addressing the problem of sin as alienation. We will now point out the arguments in support of construing the atonement as creating this intuitive and practical knowledge of divine-human union.

Firstly, unlike the classical theory and most other objective theories, there can only be a logical necessity for incarnation if the atonement is

---

37. True that it is difficult, if not impossible, to reconstruct a biography of Jesus that will satisfy the demands of our historical and critical minds. For details, see Käsemann, *New Testament Questions*, and Robinson and Koester, *Trajectories Through Early Christianity*. However, we will largely depend on the fragmentary information available in the New Testament for the outlining of our atonement model.

38. Gunton, *Enlightenment and Alienation*, 153.

39. Though Abelard talks of the love of God unveiled in the atonement, which should stimulate us in taking any suffering for God in Christ's sake, it does not confer our union with God.

viewed as necessarily creating a divine-human union. For example, if the atonement was merely a defeat of the evil then God could possibly have overcome the evil with a word or phrase and certainly without the incarnation. It must also create a subjective response in human beings. If there is no subjective dimension to the atonement why should the incarnation and the atoning work of Christ happen in this world at all. Indeed, to portray a practical knowledge of the divine-human union, the incarnation is essential.[40] Gunton says, "The transcendent is not that from which we have to escape if we are to be human. It is rather that through which the immanent is enabled to bloom and flourish."[41] In fact, it should be stated that the problem of divine-human alienation is already confronted in the incarnation itself. The New Testament repeatedly states that the incarnated Jesus is both God and Human. More precisely, as we have noted, the Christian tradition has interpreted that Christ is fully God and fully human. Christians believe that in an unusual way, by the Holy Spirit, the Virgin Mary conceived and gave birth to Christ. Thus, reading the incarnation from a perspective of union is more logical than any other perspective. Our model construes the possibility that the incarnation enables us to realize our union with the divine, through Christ, just as Christ was himself completely a human like us and yet was also completely divine. In the words of J. Mattam, "The union between man and God achieved in Christ is the pledge of our union with God."[42] If incarnation portrays divine-human union it is logical that we need to learn to look for the manifestation of this union even in the atoning work of Christ.

Since we are exploiting a union theory of the atonement using the saving concept of Brahman, a word of caution in relation to the concept of incarnation is needed here. As we noted in chapter 2, the knowledge of divine-human union created by Brahman is not through incarnation. Actually, the different *avatars*, in Visistadvaitic Hindu tradition, were completely divine and did not share human nature. In Visistadvaitic Hinduism, it is believed that Brahman creates this knowledge through scriptures, *gurus* (saints/teachers) and/or through reason.

Secondly, most traditional atonement theories do not deal with the teachings of Jesus. On the contrary, we argue that the atonement should be viewed in continuity with the teachings of Jesus. We now attempt to describe how the teachings of Jesus encompassed an account of the need of divine-human union. We begin by saying that, according to Swami Vivekananda,

---

40. The incarnation is necessary to affect reconciliation between humanity and God. See, Meadowcroft, "between AuthorialIntent and Indeterminacy," 199–200.

41. Gunton, *Enlightenment and Alienation*, 155.

42. Mattam, *Modern Approaches to Hinduism*, 132.

the highest teaching of Christ is the essential unity of the soul with God.[43] It is also worthwhile to point out J. Mattam's comment of the divine-human union aspect in comparison with Gita and the New Testament. He finds that the teaching on divine-human union is common to both the teaching of Gita and that of Jesus. In his words,

> The Gita recognizes God as someone distinct from man and creation, who can be approached as a friend, with whom union is at least possible . . . in Christ the great desire of the Gita is fulfillled for here we have a God with whom a relation of friendship is possible: I have called you friends (John 15:15). Not only will the believer be a friend, but he can become one with Him (John 17:21).[44]

It is a fact that Jesus summarized the vision of divine-human union for salvation in his teachings on the kingdom of God. St. Mark commences Jesus' ministry with the words, "Jesus came to Galilee, proclaiming the good news of God, and saying, the time is fulfilled, and the kingdom of God has come near; repent and believe in the good news."[45] The kingdom of God is the state of affairs in which the divine and human are living in union. There are theologians who have identified the divine-human union aspect in relation to the reign of God teaching of Jesus. For instance, Thomas Thangaraj, an Indian Christian theologian says, "The guru's [Christ's] proclamation of the reign of God liberates the disciples to be themselves "under" God and to be "with" others.[46]

Jesus taught about the divine-human union through parables. For example, Christ affirmed that he came to save the lost through the parable of the lost sheep. He says that when one sheep that is lost gets "united" with the shepherd there is great joy. He compares it with people and says that when one sinner repents (realizes that he needs to be in union with the divine) there will be joy in heaven.[47] The parable of the prodigal son illustrates the joy of the Father and the prodigal son when the lost son is "united" with the father.[48] Thus Jesus' parables contain a strong emphasis on the need for a divine-human union.

---

43. Samartha analyzes the thought of Swami Vivekananda. Samartha, *Hindu Response*, 55

44. Mattam, *Modern Christian Approaches* 131–32.

45. Mark 1:14–15, NRSV.

46. Thangaraj, *Crucified*, 98.

47. Luke 15:6.

48. Luke 15:15–24.

Jesus also taught that the kingdom of God is within us.[49] The divine-human union, as in Ramanuja's thought, is to be realized within us. This is in agreement with our argument that the knowledge of unions should not be viewed as merely an external piece of information but is an intuitive knowledge of the unions that is to be lived.

One might wonder about the need for a divine-human union when one materially has everything that they need to live. However, Jesus' teaching was always about bearing fruit by means of the constructive union. He makes this clear through the imagery of vine and branches. He says, "Abide in me as I abide in you. Just as the branch (of vine) cannot bear fruit by itself unless it abides in the vine, neither can you unless you abide in me."[50] Here Jesus' emphasis is on bearing spiritual fruit and not merely on being materially sustained.

A powerful bond that can sustain our union with the divine is love. Defending religion against Marx, Girardi says, "The affirmation of God [may], in fact, be alienating if our relationship with him were exhausted in the master-slave dialectic . . . but it ceases to be so if the relationship is understood in terms of a dialectic of love, as an encounter between two liberties."[51] Jesus expresses God's love to us. At the same time, he says, "The Lord our God is one; you shall love the Lord your God with all your heart and . . . You shall love your neighbor as yourself."[52] To love God is to will God's interest and this is in effect to be in unity with his will.

The divine-human union aspect, taught by Jesus has also a dynamic and progressive nature. For instance, Jesus points out, "With what can we compare the kingdom of God, or what parable will we use for it? It is like a mustard seed, which, when sown upon the ground, is the smallest of all the seeds on earth; yet when it is sown it grows up and becomes the greatest of all shrubs, and puts forth large branches, so that the birds of the air can make nests in its shade."[53] Just as the kingdom of God is about growth, the knowledge of our union with the divine involves growth.

Interestingly, an element of grace and judgment goes hand in hand both in Visistadvaitic Hinduism and Christianity. Brahman as a God of grace creates the knowledge that we ought to be in union with the divine. But still whoever acts selfishly is subject to the bondage of *samsara* (rebirth). Though

---

49. Luke 17:21.
50. John 15:4, NRSV.
51. Girardi, *Marxism and Christianity*, 78–79.
52. Mark 12:29–31, NRSV.
53. Mark 4:30–32, NRSV.

the rebirth concept, as understood in Visistadvaitic Hinduism,[54] is not part of Jesus' teachings, God in Christ accepts the son (daughter) who goes astray (Luke 15:30). He accepts sinners whilst judging and condemning sin. The identification of Jesus with the ostracized, such as tax collectors and harlots illuminates the gracious aspect of God. However, the kingdom of God calls us for obedience to the will of God as well. Jesus' proclamation of the jubilee year epitomizes the judgmental aspect of God's kingdom (Luke 4:16). The parables in Matt 13:24, 47, and 25:3 also show the judgmental character of God. Hence, the divine-human union is a product of grace and judgment both in Visistadvaitic Hinduism and Christianity.[55] It is now clear that the teachings of Jesus certainly emphasize the divine-human union. This implies that we need to look to the atonement to learn how it creates the intuitive and practical knowledge of "divine-human union."

Thirdly, we will draw support for understanding that the atonement is for divine-human union using traditional teachings in Christology. In the Christian tradition, Christ portrays all that needs to be said about God. In Jesus' own words, "The Father and I are one."[56] St. Paul goes on to say that in Christ the fullness of God was pleased to dwell.[57] At the same time, Christ was fully human. The symbol of Christ shows fully all that needs to be said about humanity as well. In the words of S. Clarke, an Indian Christian theologian, "Christ . . . is the lens through which all aspects of the symbol of God and humanity are viewed."[58] The Christian tradition, through various councils, affirms Christ as fully divine and fully human. For instance, the Chalcedonian statement (451 AD) says,

> We all with one accord teach men to acknowledge one and the same Son, our Lord Jesus Christ, . . . of *One substance with the Father*, . . . of *one substance with us*, . . . recognized in two natures, without confusion, without change, without division, without separation, . . . not as parted or separated into two persons, but

---

54. However, the concept of reappearing is part of Christ's teaching. Jesus' words in John 3:7 is an example for this.

55. In relation to Hinduism, it should be noted that the teachings of Jesus took place at a particular period in human history, and his teachings had a public character. The gospel writers stress that Jesus taught with authority. However, in Hinduism, Brahman is beyond human history and the creation of the enlightening knowledge is spontaneous through the scriptures, *gurus,* and consciousness. In Hinduism, *gurus* teach their disciples on a one-to-one basis and their teachings do not have a public character.

56. John 10:30, NRSV.

57. Col 1:15a and 19.

58. Clarke, *Dalits*, 182.

one and the same son, the only begotten God the word, Lord Jesus Christ.[59]

Thus, the symbol of Christ itself is understood as creating the knowledge of divine-human unity. St. Paul says that Christ was before all things, and in him all things are held together.[60] We will soon view the atonement as necessary for creating divine-human union.

Fourthly, we venture to gain support from the concept of the church. The church is interpreted as the body of Christ and it represents the presence of Christ with us. In the words of Hans Frei,

> when Christians speak of the Spirit as the indirect presence now of Jesus Christ and of God who is one with him, they refer to the church. The church is both the witness to that presence and the public and communal form the indirect presence of Christ now takes, in contrast to his direct presence in his earthly days.[61]

Persaud says, "the church dares to proclaim Jesus Christ and him crucified, that God was in Christ reconciling the alienated world to God."[62] The divine-human union is symbolized in the two sacraments, namely Baptism and Eucharist, established by Christ and carried out by the church. Here, we need to point out the difference in the Hindu way of expressing divine-human union. In Visistadvaitic Hinduism, union with Brahman is not expressed through sacraments like Baptism and Eucharist. Nevertheless, Hindus realize humanity's union with Brahman by the proper and often sustained pronunciation of the divine-sound OM/AUM, which from a Christian perspective may be perceived as a kind of sacramental act.

It is in this context that the atoning work of Christ should be construed in the present time. It is clear that Christ proclaimed our union with the divine in the vision of the kingdom of God. The vision of divine-human union explicated in the paradigm of the kingdom of God resulted in conflict with the existing leaderships and powers of both religious and political groups at the time of Christ in history. Eventually, Christ was put to suffering and death on the cross.

---

59. Bettenson, *Documents of Christian*, 73. Emphasis added.
60. Col 1:17.
61. Frei, *Identity of Jesus Christ*, 157.
62. Persaud, *Theology of the Cross*, 266.

The Atonement as Creating the Intuitive and Practical Knowledge of Divine-Human Union

In Visistadvaitic Hinduism, Brahman alone can provide the knowledge of divine-human union. This function is done by grace alone. Thus the objective side of the saving concept of Brahman is manifest. Nevertheless, we need to go further to analyze the significance of suffering whilst dealing with the atonement.[63] One strength of an atonement model lies in holding the objective and subjective sides of the cross together. We will begin by analyzing the objective side of our model of the atonement.

The crucial point is this. Obviously, if two incompatible substances need to be united one substance needs to undergo change. And it is absolutely better if the weaker substance is empowered to be united with the stronger one. Humanity, alienating itself from God, has committed sin against the almighty and the most holy. This alienation cannot be overcome by human effort because of our frailty. God's help is needed for us to be united with God again. Now, how does the cross recreate divine-human union? On the cross, Christ, in his humanity—substituting and representing entire humanity, takes the pain unto death to himself so that human beings will become worthy enough to be united with God. God too suffers in Christ, on the cross, out of his love for humanity so that they will be united with him. Apparently, Jesus alone can fulfill the work on the cross because he alone is fully divine and fully human. Unlike the substitutionary model that is God-ward, which portrays God as an angry monster, our model is *alienation-ward* in the following way.[64]

We will portray the atonement using an analogy. We know that if impure gold is to be "united" with pure gold, it should be melted in fire. Unless the impure gold suffers in fire the impurities will not be removed and it cannot be "united" with pure gold. If God, the most high, is considered as the purest gold obviously we are the most impure gold and unless we suffer to remove our impurity we cannot become united with God.

Again, the pure gold also needs to suffer in fire if any other purified gold needs to be "united" with it. Thus, it is clear that the impure gold alone cannot work for its becoming "united" with pure gold.

---

63. As we noted, there is a difference between Hinduism and Christianity in relation to creation of knowledge. In Hinduism, it is understood that Brahman creates the knowledge of union, which is already present. The problem is that we are ignorant of that union. However, we will understand that Christ brings the knowledge by creating the union anew. We will come back to this issue in the next chapter.

64. Apparently, since we construct a model of the atonement using the saving concept of Brahman, it should overcome the problem of divine-human alienation.

Like the impure gold that cannot become pure unless it bears suffering, we cannot become united with God unless we take suffering unto melting to death. We will only perish if we make this effort due to our frailty. Christ takes our suffering unto himself, to get us united with God, substituting and representing us on the cross. Further, just like pure gold also needs to suffer to "unite" the purified gold unto itself, God in Christ also suffers for uniting us with him.

The more the impure gold suffers the more it becomes pure. In the days of Jesus, the most terrible and the most humiliated form of suffering and death was crucifixion on the cross. Christ takes this utmost suffering and death on the cross on behalf of entire humanity for the sin of alienation. He could very well substitute us because he is fully human. On the other hand, Christ is also fully divine. God in Christ too, out of his love for humanity, suffers so that we may be united with him in and through Christ. Thus, the cross unites God and humanity and it has an objective side.

The atonement also has an objective side because it is through this suffering that God creates the intuitive and practical knowledge of divine-human union in us. As we have noted, reality is best known in suffering,[65] and all theories are falsified in suffering unto death, except the theory of the cross.

Now, what is the subjective side? No serious theologian argues that the cross is an expression of God-human alienation, but most argue, either directly or indirectly, how the divine-human union aspect is made evident on the cross. Before we go into more precise detail of how the atonement creates the intuitive and practical knowledge in us, we will briefly highlight the insights of three theologians, in the Indian context, who have viewed that the atonement expects us to live in union with the divine. Firstly, Klostermaier writes,

> According to Christian theology Christ died a real, human death—as bitter and painful as any other death. But because it was a death undergone in obedience (union) to God's will it became the beginning of Christ's glory . . . Man, in union with Christ, is able to give to his own death the redeeming quality of Christ's death. The analysis of the human situation in Christian theology essentially includes the element of faith in Christ and the acceptance of Christ as the 'archetype' of man. The basic experiences of birth, life and death are in themselves

---

65. Some accounts of people who self-harm, flagellate themselves, or who endure great hardships in pursuit of some goal, will report that they never felt more alive than at that point. This is not to recommend it, but to observe why people might be attracted to such activities.

ambivalent—their definite meaning is revealed in their relationship to Christ.[66]

Secondly, J. Peringalloor says that the atonement expects us to live in union with the divine. Interpreting the atonement, he claims, "there was perfect unity of will between Jesus and his heavenly Father."[67] Thirdly, J. Mattam too says that the cross is a path of our union with the divine. To quote him,

> Through His Crucifixion Christ shows the type of mystical path the soul must tread if it is to rise to union with God. The Crucifixion of Christ is in Indian terminology not merely the total giving up of the ego, but even an abandon of the eternal essence, and the refusal to accept beatitude apart from God.[68]

Along these lines, our model of the atonement also construes that the cross creates the knowledge of the divine union with humanity to the greatest extent possible that human beings can comprehend. It creates the knowledge that the divine is with humanity and humanity ought to be with the divine even unto and beyond death. The vision of the cross of Christ in relation to the subjective side is that at the time when Christ was thoroughly on the cross—accepting divine sovereignty, giving himself to do the will of God and at the same time accepting human solidarity in pain and suffering unto death—created the intuitive and practical knowledge of the need of divine-human union—in the most intense way—unto death and beyond.

Precisely, how does the cross create the intuitive and practical knowledge of divine-human union? Here, a similar logic like that of Abelard will help us.[69] We need to understand that, though the atonement has an objective side, Christ also takes the suffering unto himself to change us. The atonement reveals God's sacrificial love in Christ, in creating the divine-human union. It should be noted that God was fully in Christ during the atonement. We will elucidate the divine-human union that was prevalent on the cross, by interpreting one of Jesus' sayings on the cross. He says, "My God, My God, why have you forsaken me?"[70] It is a cry of utter helplessness and intolerable pain. An outward reading of the verse may mean that the divine-human union is completely lost here. However, a potentially deeper

---

66. Klostermaier, *Indian Theology*, 206.
67. Peringalloor, *Salvation Through Gita*, 84.
68. Mattam, *Land of Trinity*, 132.
69. However, the serious criticism against Abelard is overcome in our model of the atonement since it has a strong objective side to it, along with the subjective side.
70. Matt 27:46; Mark 15:34, NRSV.

reading of this verse can mean that it is here that Jesus totally abandons his will to carry out God's will. This abandoning of himself to be with God evidently results in giving his spirit into the hands of God.[71]

It is also here that the pain of God becomes manifest. God was so much in Jesus, that Jesus feels forsaken. In fact, God takes the suffering unto himself so that Jesus has lost himself unto the hands of God. It is similar to the familiar story of Jesus and his friend walking on the seashore. Jesus says that the one footprint is mine, since I carried you. God did not allow Jesus to suffer alone but took the suffering unto himself to the extent that Jesus feels that he is lost on the cross. This manifestation of God suffering with Jesus is the portrayal of God suffering with entire humanity as well. In contrast to a "theology of glory," Moltmann speaks of a "theology of the cross," in which healing and wholeness are paradoxically present. He says, "It alienates alienated man."[72]

This self-giving love of God obviously will want our response to it. Any ideal person would respond, from the bottom of their heart, to such a self-giving love of Christ. We understand that through his love for us, expressed in the suffering on the cross, Christ teaches us to lead a practical life with the constant conscience that we need to be in union with God.

In Visistadvaitic Hindu thought, we need to bear in mind that, although an event like the cross in a particular point in history is not provided by Brahman to create the knowledge of the need of divine-human union, Brahman creates the knowledge of the union through one or more different ways to individuals. Whilst Christianity insists on a historical event in creating the divine-human union, Visistadvaitic Hinduism insists that the function of Brahman cannot be limited to history. Here, Christianity and Visistadvaitic Hinduism mutually enrich each other by highlighting the significance of a historical revelation in Christ and the significance of keeping the divine beyond history in Brahman respectively. Besides this, Christ continued to symbolise the divine-human union in his resurrection and ascension. Schillebeeckx acknowledges the prolongation of Jesus' living communion with God in resurrection.[73] However, we shall not go into the details of that here.

It is important to understand that over against human-divine alienation in history, in biblical terms, which began at the Garden of Eden, the cross creates a practical knowledge, in the utmost way that we ought to live

---

71. Luke 23:46.
72. Moltmann, *Crucified*, 71.
73. Schillebeeckx, *Interim Report*, 135.

in union with God in all situations of our life. There is also the hope that in times of suffering the divine is with us to share in our pains.

Another relevant issue we need to analyze is the nature of divine-human union created on the cross. As we saw in chapter 2, Ramanuja understands the nature of divine-human union with the help of a self-body union analogy. This is a powerful insight for understanding the nature of divine-human union. We will come back to analyze the nature of union in the next chapter. However, here we need to say that divine-human union is a dualistic union. We end by reiterating that the knowledge created in the atonement is about mastering our will and not a mere informative one.

b) Arguments in Support of Viewing the Creation of Intuitive and Practical Knowledge of Human-Human Union in the Atonement

Divine-human union and human-human union go hand in hand. Precisely, Human-Human union is an essential component of the human dialogical symbolic interaction both within a community and between communities. But, evidently, alienation between human individuals and alienation between human communities are prevalent almost everywhere. Biblical evidence for the undesirable alienation between humans is abundant, beginning from the story of Cain and Abel. Karl Marx has written much on human-human alienation caused by labor and economic power.[74] This alienation has been obvious in our world, even up to the present time.

Regarding Hinduism, in general, Klostermaier writes, "Individuality itself is seen by some schools as intrinsically sorrowful and unhappy ... This individuality is even called a state of sinfulness."[75] Ramanuja clearly finds the need for human-human union which we made clear in chapter 2. We need to acknowledge that it is the Visistadvaitic Hindu thought which provokes us to ponder the arguments for viewing human-human union aspect in the atonement as well.

Firstly, the incarnation is not only about a divine-human union but also has an inference for the creation of the intuitive and practical knowledge of a human-human union. In fact, the incarnation of Christ is an act which shows that Christ gave up his heavenly glory in order to be in union with humanity as a human. The New Testament witnesses that he lived in human flesh. He, therefore, knows our thoughts and feelings. He knows what it is to be in union with our fellow beings. The incarnation creates the

---

74. For instance, see Israel, *Alienation*; and Schacht, *Alienation*, 94.
75. Klostermaier, *Indian Theology*, 197.

knowledge of human-human union not in a utopian dream but in the very practical coming of Christ to this world as a human being and dwelling amongst humanity. In the words of Gunton, "We belong with each other, because he made us for each other, and brings about our reconciliation: 'the Holy One in our midst' who does 'not come to destroy' (Hos 11:9) but to restore our true humanity."[76] It is along these lines we need to understand the atonement. With regard to Visistadvaitic Hinduism, although Brahman is not incarnate its essence creates the knowledge that all humanity ought to be in union with one another in and through Brahman.

Secondly, as we noted, the atonement also needs to be construed in tune with the teaching of Jesus. Jesus never teaches that human-human alienation is virtuous. On the contrary, he upholds the need for human-human union. The words of Jesus stress that human-human union is a fundamental need. He says, "So when you are offering your gift at the altar, if you remember that your brother or sister has something against you, leave your gift there before the altar and go; first be reconciled to your brother or sister, and then come and offer your gift."[77]

Moreover, the kingdom of God imagery, taught by Jesus, is certainly not a condition in which human beings live in union with the divine alone but also with each other. Jesus began his ministry by inviting his first disciples Simon and Andrew to follow him.[78] Thus, the kingdom of God is not a life in isolation but a life in union with others.

Interestingly, a glance at Jesus' parables discloses the teaching that we ought to be in union with each other. For instance, in the parable of the lost son, in Luke 15:25–31, the story doesn't end with the union of the father and the prodigal son. But the father expects the elder one and the younger one also to be in union with each other. Furthermore, the parables of the mustard seed and of the yeast portray the fact that the kingdom of God is for many.[79]

How could the "human-human union" teaching of Jesus be expressed in our lives? According to Jesus, it should be expressed by love, forgiveness and sharing. For example, Jesus says that we have to love our neighbor as we love ourselves.[80] It is challenging that Jesus teaches to love even one's enemies.[81] Again, Jesus incorporates the theme of loving enemies in his

---

76. Gunton, *Enlightenment and Alienation*, 155.
77. Matt 5:23–24, NRSV.
78. Mark 1:17.
79. Luke 13:18–21.
80. Mark 12:31.
81. Matt 5:43–47.

teaching in a functional and realistic sense. This is evident when he asks us to forgive those who sin against us.[82] This he practice by forgiving even those who crucified him.

In Visistadvaitic Hinduism, even though the presence of Brahman in everyone is acknowledged, it also teaches that the righteous should flourish and the evil ones should be destroyed and put to rebirth. Thus, "loving enemies" is alien to Visistadvaitic Hindu teaching. But, it could be noted that there are pious Hindus who did overcome evil with good works. For example, Sri Ramakrishna gave away his utensils to the burglar who had taken them from him, not withstanding the fact that Sri Ramakrishna himself caught hold of the thief. It is said that the burglar later repented and became a disciple of Sri Ramakrishna.

The need of human-human union is found in Jesus' teaching on sharing as well. He taught that everyone should be the salt and light of the world.[83] Sharing with fellow beings is very much related to salvation. In Luke 19 we read about Zachaeus. As soon as Zachaeus says that he will share his possessions with others, Jesus replies, "Today salvation has come to this house, because he too is a son of Abraham for the Son of Man came to seek out and to save the lost."[84] Sharing obviously is the product of our concern for others and thus directly portrays the human-human union aspect involved in it.

Does Jesus pray for a human-human union? Jesus' prayers are unique and specific. Certainly, he prayed for a human-human union. Thus he prays, "that *all of them may be one*, Father, just as you are in me and I am in you . . . I have given the glory that you gave me, that *they may be one* as we are one."[85] With this, we move on to view the deeds of Jesus.

Thirdly, Jesus' longing for human-human union can be delineated in his actions. He loved and cared for the people who lived during his time. His miracles found in the early chapters of all the four gospels portray the concern and fellowship Jesus had in working toward a union with the people around him.

Jesus' life portrays that human-human union should not be limited to one's own community or race alone. We live in an age where conflicts between communities and races generally are on the increase. During Jesus' time the Samaritans were excluded by the Jews. Christ went through the province of Samaria which no Jew of his time entered wittingly and held a

---

82. Matt 6:14.
83. Matt 5:13–16.
84. Luke 19:9–10, NRSV.
85. John 17:21, NIV. Emphasis added.

conversation with a Samaritan woman.[86] Thus the need for unity between humans, transcending community boundaries, was expressed and shown by Jesus. Further, during his ministry he warned the Pharisees and Sadducees but never hated them. Human-human union, in fact, in Jesus' view had to be established between the entire humanity.

Fourthly, we will draw support for our atonement model from the church's teaching. Although Visistadvaitic Hindu teaching emphasizes human-human union, it is not reflected in popular worship at temples. In contrast to individual worship, worship in union with others is encouraged by the church. The Church is a symbolic-expression not only of divine-human union but also of human-human union. It is a place where human-human union is practice. When people praise God together, they feel a sense of oneness. When they pray together, read the biblical verses together, and sing hymns together, they not only derive a new strength in Christ, but also realize their union with one another.

In fact, the church portrays the nature of human-human union taught in the New Testament.[87] St. Paul tells that every person is like a part of body and all together constitute the whole body of Christ. In his words,

> For just as the body is one and has many members of the body, through many, are one body, so it is with Christ. For by one Spirit we were all baptized into one body—Jews or Greeks, slaves or free—and all were made to drink of one Spirit . . . If one member suffers, all suffer together with it; if one member is honored, all rejoice together. Now you are the body of Christ and individually members of it.[88]

The church is a place where we meet others and seek to understand their existential problems. In all possible ways we help them. When we are in need we are also helped by them. This implies that human-human union involves commitment. Now, we shall analyze how the atonement does create human-human union and thereby the intuitive and practical knowledge of it.

---

86. John 4.

87. Bonhoeffer says, "It is the unity of the whole church which makes each member what he is and the fellowship what it is, just as it is Christ and his Body which makes the Church what it is." See, Bonhoeffer, *The Cost of Discipleship*, 219.

88. 1 Cor 12:12–27, NRSV.

The Atonement as Creating an Intuitive and Practical Knowledge of Human-Human Union

We have noted that Christ undergoes suffering to make us worthy of being united with the divine. Since, Christ suffers for the entire humanity, substituting and representing all—in and through his humanity, we have not only become worthy of having a union with the divine but also have been united with each other in Christ. Further, just as brothers and sisters have an inherent union between themselves for the simple reason that they have a common union with their parents, since Christ has created a union between the entire humanity and the divine—entire humanity also has obtained an inherent union between themselves. Thus, the cross has an objective side in the creation of human-human union as well.

How does the cross create the intuitive and practical knowledge of human-human union? As Moltmann writes, "Whether or not Christianity, in an alienated, divided and oppressive society, itself becomes alienated, divided and an accomplice of oppression, is ultimately decided only by whether the crucified Christ is a stranger to it or the Lord who determines the form of its existence."[89] The pain of alienation can be addressed only by taking pain into oneself. Christ underwent suffering and gave himself to death on the cross. For Simone Weil, as we have noted, reality is known in and through suffering. Notably, even unto death, Christ was completely human—revealing his solidarity with humankind. The knowledge given at the cross by Christ is that he is fully human and is with humanity in its sufferings. Christ expects us to live in union with others even to the extent of taking pain for the welfare of others.

Precisely, Jesus foretells the knowledge of human-human union created on the cross. At the Lord's Supper, on the very day before Christ's death, he expressed his death on the cross as sharing his body and blood. Gospel writers quote Christ's words, "This is my blood of the covenant, which is poured out for many."[90]

Christ symbolized on the cross that we all share in the same body and blood. Hence, the human-human union, established on the cross, is not external but at the very core of being a human.

The atonement is sometimes understood as a sacrament. John Macquarie says that sacrament without the accompanying word cannot be truly Christian and will easily degenerate into a sort of magical rite.[91] The atone-

---

89. Moltmann, *Crucified*, 3. Moltmann says that the theology of the cross should liberate men from political alienation as well.

90. Mark 14:24, NRSV.

91. Macquarie, *Principles of Christian Theology*, 396–430.

ment is not a sacrament without the word. Christ, on the cross, gives himself to be the uniting code of human beings with each other. The human-human union is symbolized in the rites of Baptism and Eucharist by Christians.

Thus, the atonement unites people through baptism and more frequently through the Eucharist. As argued in the course of this section, it is true that the human-human union aspect of the atonement inspires us to live in harmony and peace. This theology is inclusive and representative of the symbolic interaction of humanity. We are not only members of the divine but also members of the common humanity so much so that to cause suffering and hurt to others is to do it to the divine. Our realization of this encourages us to resist racial conflict, caste conflict, bitter poverty and conspicuous waste. Such theology fosters essential values of health, beauty, friendship and empathy amongst humanity.

Moreover, it is when all of us live not only for ourselves but also for others that the ideal situation of the kingdom can come in this world. Finally, since human-human union is created in and through the divine, it is a trinitarian union. We shall briefly analyze the nature of this union in the next chapter.

c) Arguments in Support of Viewing the Creation of Intuitive and Practical Knowledge of Human-Nature Union in the Atonement

Having gained an understanding of divine-human union and human-human union created in the atonement, our task now is to analyze the extent to which the knowledge of human-nature union is in the atonement. In chapter 2, we noted that in the Visistadvaitic Hindu concept of Brahman, there is an inevitable union between humanity and nature because both are held together in and through Brahman. Precisely, human-nature union is the unity of the being, Brahman. However, the concept of atonement is not as explicit as the concept of Brahman in creating the intuitive and practical knowledge of human-nature union, though it has sufficient room for such an interpretation.

It is true that we become more and more alienated from nature. G. Baum says, "Since Hegel's day social thinkers have greatly extended the critique of people's alienation from nature."[92] Our model of the atonement tackles this issue as well.

---

92. Baum, *Religion and Alienation*, 12. Schacht talks of three types of alienation from nature: 1) through making nature a slave, 2) through disengagement from immediate immersion in nature, and 3) through the inability to relate fully to nature. For details, see Schacht, *Alienation*, 120–21.

Firstly, how does the incarnation help in viewing the atonement as creating an intuitive and practical knowledge of human-nature union? The incarnation is an act through which Christ gave up his heavenly glory not only to be with humanity but also with the entire creation. He lived using the products of nature, preserving nature and caring for it. Thus Christ set an example for us to be in union with nature and the incarnation made this possible.

Secondly, Sugirtharajah claims that Christian tradition has sometimes seen God as the totally other, as one who exists over against the created order.[93] However, as Sugirtharajah himself goes on to say that a more in-depth reading will unveil the scope of biblical relevance in upholding the desirable human-nature union.[94] Evidently, Jesus taught about human-nature union. He said that God cares even for lilies and sparrows.[95] In Matt 10:29 it is said that not even one sparrow will fall to the ground apart from the will of God. God's concern for nature makes it explicit that we ought to be in union with it. In fact, an interdependency between humanity and nature sustains both nature and our lives.

Again, with regard to Jesus' teachings, it should be pointed out that in almost all parables, the kingdom of God message is taught with the help of imageries drawn from nature. To mention a few: the parable of the shepherd and the sheep (John 10:1–39), the parable of mustard seed (Matt 13:13–38), and the parable of the sower (Matt 13:18–30). The teachings of Jesus only indirectly tell of a human-nature union. We should bear in mind that at the time of Jesus in history, ecological destruction was less evident. His teaching would probably have had more direct implications for human-nature union if the present environmental crisis had been a reality at that time.

Thirdly, Jesus did not live an alienated life from nature but lived in union with nature. Nature spoke of divine presence to him. For example, at the baptism of Jesus at the river of Jordan the divine spirit is depicted as descending on him in the form of a dove. Moreover, Jesus loved the seas, the mountains, the trees and the beasts and they won a vital place in his ministry.

St. Paul believes that precisely in Christ the entire universe is held together. In his words, "He [Christ] himself is before all things, and in him all things hold together."[96] It is also St. Paul who finds a direct bearing of the cross on human-nature union, which we will view soon.

---

93. Kirk, *Contemporary Issues in Mission*, 52–54.
94. For details, see Kirk, *Contemporary Issues in Mission*, 56–59.
95. Matt 6:26–30; Luke 12:24–28.
96. Col 1:17, NRSV.

Since we exploit our model of the atonement using the saving concept of Brahman it needs to be pointed out here that in Visistadvaitic Hinduism, all things are held together in Brahman and nothing is present apart from him. Significantly, natural sciences share this Hindu view of life and portray our close relatedness with nature. For instance, Sallie McFague claims that the natural world and humanity are intrinsically interrelated and interdependent. She writes, "For if everything that we are came from our roots in nature and if we cannot live a day without the plants and the micro organisms in the sea, then 'we are like it' and 'it is like us.'"[97] It is also in this context that the atonement should be understood.

The Atonement as Creating an Intuitive and Practical Knowledge of Human-Nature Union

Biblically and traditionally it is construed that the cross is imperative for our salvation. Going beyond that, St. Paul stresses that the cross is for the entire creation.[98] If the cross is understood as the means to salvation for the entire creation then we are also united with nature in Christ. Notably, interpreting the cross, St. Paul writes, "God was reconciling the world to himself in Christ."[99] St. Paul's claim is that as the cross is decisive for our salvation it is crucial for the salvation of the entire creation. Thus, St. Paul's understanding of the cross definitely claims that there is an inherent unity between us and nature.

Precisely, if we understand that the entire creation fell along with humanity, then the suffering and death of Christ has not only created the divine-human union and human-human union, but also a human-nature union. Thus there is an objective side in the creation of human-nature union as well.

Arthur Peacocke suggests that God suffers to bring into being a kingdom of living organic creatures. Interestingly, he too puts this dream of his

---

97. McFague, *Super, Natural Christians*, 48. Furthermore, although it is generally understood that the concept of *imago dei* appears to set human beings apart, in recent decades there are scholars who consider that *imago dei* is part of other creations as well. For example, Gilkey says, "I believe that nature also represents an *imago dei*, an image and likeness of its creator. This point is important because if nature be in truth an image or mirror of the divine, then—as is the case with humans—nature has integrity in itself, a value for itself." See, Gilkey, "Nature as Image of God," 489. This way of arguing, although is alien to traditional theology, will have a direct impact on ecology and, in our case, gives an emphasis for the need of human-nature union.

98. Rom 8:19–23.

99. 2 Cor 5:19, NRSV.

beside the possibility of God-human and human-human union. According to him,

> God, we find ourselves having to conjecture, 'suffers' the natural evils of the world along with ourselves because—we can but tentatively suggest at this stage—God purposes inter alia to bring about a greater good thereby, namely, the kingdom of living organic creatures . . . and even free-willing, loving persons who have the possibility of communion with God and with each other.[100]

Moreover, it may be incidentally pointed out that even during the destruction in Noah's time, it was not only humanity which was saved by God's orders. Noah protected every species. This Old Testament episode too tells us that salvation is equally significant for both humanity and other creations.

However, the death of Christ on the cross is remembered through the Eucharist. Poet W. C. Williams, in the light of present ecological crisis writes that nature should be viewed as the body of Christ. In his words,

> There is nothing to eat—seek it where you will,
> but the body of the Lord. The blessed plants
> and the sea yield it—to the imagination intact.[101]

This powerful poem not only claims that any meal is a Eucharist since nature is the body of the Lord but also has implications for us to be in union with nature with the same spirit of leading a life in union with the divine. G. Baum says, "If people listen to the divine call and act in keeping with the divine impulse, they will discern the harmony between themselves and nature and thus create a garden in this world."[102]

Nevertheless, human-nature union is a complex phenomenon because although the atonement is for our union with nature, we see nature red in tooth and claw. Here, we need to assert that God has created us not only to preserve nature but also has lovingly gifted nature to us to use it responsibly. Using nature for food is obviously permitted in the Bible. Our point is that unnecessary killings and cruelty toward animals and birds should be avoided. Further, Jesus held humanity as superior to nature as

---

100. Polkinghorne, *The Work of Love*, 38. Peacocke also explains this with the help of a figure. For details, see Peacocke, *God and Science*, 25.

101. The poem can be found in Clark, *Our Sustainable Table*, 131.

102. Baum, *Religion and Alienation*, 16.

might be illustrated in his sending of an evil spirit from a man to pigs.[103] In relation to Visistadvaitic Hinduism, we have seen that Brahman is closer to humanity than to nature—paving the way for this kind of interpretation. This again does not mean that we can misuse nature. We need to live in union with nature, loving it and preserving it, though we may also depend on it for our livelihood.

To conclude this section, we have seen that the intuitive and practical knowledge of our union with nature, with particular reference to the cross, is portrayed by St. Paul. However, we have also seen that there are references in the gospel to uphold the necessary human-nature union. We end with the insight of Charles Hartshorne, a process theologian. For him, God's body or sphere of interaction is the whole universe.[104] In other words, God includes everything. He says, "we must agree with modern absolutism and orthodox Hinduism that the Supreme Being must be all-inclusive."[105] This theology of nature, like the concept of Brahman, highlights the realization of the need of human-nature union since humanity and nature together constitute God's body. Brahman's union with nature also helps us to criticize theism for its stress on absoluteness of the divine to the neglect of his union to nature. It is a fact that the cross has relevance for entire creation. Any abuse of nature should be avoided and we need to use nature responsibly.[106] With this we move on to deal with the final dimension of the four-fold union, which is one-oneself union.

d) Arguments in Support of Viewing the Creation of Intuitive and Practical Knowledge of One-Oneself Union in the Atonement

Kierkegaard says,

> The self is a relation which relates itself to its own self, or it is that in the relation which accounts for it that the relation relates itself to its own self; the self is not the relation but consists in the fact that the relation relates itself to its own self. Man is a

---

103. This act may justify the use of animals in analyzing the function and use of medicines and surgery, although we need to argue to keep the cruelty against animals to the minimum as much as possible.

104. Hartshorne, *Divine Relativity*, 165.

105. Hartshorne, *Divine Relativity*, 76.

106. Human-nature union is also trinitarian in its nature and we will return to discuss this in the next chapter.

synthesis of the infinite and the finite, of the temporal and the eternal, of freedom and necessity, in short it is a synthesis.[107]

This definition makes it clear that the self consists of a synthesis of the "infinite-divine" and the "finite-me" in us. Now what is one-oneself alienation? One-oneself alienation refers to a disparity between a person's actual condition and their essential or ideal nature. It means being split and estranged from something that is essential or intrinsic to one's nature. In the light of Kierkegaard's definition of the self, any breach between the "infinite" and the "finite" in us can be said as one-oneself alienation. Hence, we are again dealing with divine-human union in different words. However, we do this in a different section because the alienation which we address here is not caused by sin but the after-effect of sin such as guilt, guilt feeling and fear.

It is true that many don't live freely or they live in conflict with themselves. Along with guilt, guilt feelings and fear—one-oneself alienation can be caused by sufferings of various kinds, failures, depression and inferiority and superiority complexes. Marx identifies that self-alienation can be caused by labor. For him, alienated labor alienates a person from his spiritual life and his human life.[108] Self-alienation can lead one to self-deception and vice-versa. In fact, the problem of self-alienation is largely related to psychology. Psychologists want their clients to become their "real selves."[109]

Before analyzing the arguments in support of construing the atonement as creating the intuitive and practical knowledge of one-oneself union and as helping in overcoming one-oneself alienation, we need to guard against another cause of this alienation put forward by Feuerbach. Feuerbach takes the view that human beings credit all their good qualities to God. When all of a person's good qualities are ascribed to God, he becomes alienated from himself because all his best qualities are moved from him and are attributed to God.[110]

However, anyone would admit that human beings have good as well as bad qualities within themselves. It is also true that there is a struggle between the inherent good and evil within us. The basic question that can be directed against Feuerbach is; why human beings ascribe good qualities to God and not evil ones. Gunton writes, "But to transfer the predicates to humanity is even more alienating, encouraging us to act a part that befits

---

107. Bretall, *A Kierkegaard Anthology*, 340.
108. Schacht, *Alienation*, 101.
109. Hall and Lindzey, *Theories of Personality*, 529.
110. Feuerbach, *Essence of Christianity*, 1. Also see, Israel, *Alienation*, 31.

God, if it can be put that way."[111] Nevertheless, the fundamental thesis of Feuerbach is attacking the very existence of God. Though we do not intend to go in that direction we need to be careful to note that it is not this kind of alienation we are dealing with here. On the other hand, we will focus on Kierkegaard's definition of self and the alienation caused by the many effects of sin as well as self-deception.

Now what do we mean by one-oneself union? Theologically, it is the realization that it is no longer we who live, but it is the divine who lives in us. In Visistadvaitic Hinduism, living in union with oneself is abandoning selfish will and realizing that one is of the divine Brahman. In the New Testament, St. Paul says that it is no longer he who lives, but it is Christ who lives in him. Similarly, Bonhoeffer says, "In Christ we no longer live our lives, but he lives his life in us."[112] It is this experience that we are engaged with here.

Firstly, the doctrine of incarnation motivates us to understand that the atonement creates a one-oneself union as well. In fact, the incarnation portrays that Christ was fully divine and fully human whilst he lived in human history. It is because he became human we know that we as humans can partake in his divinity and live selflessly. The union in terms of one-oneself thus is seen in the incarnation. Jesus sets an example to us of how a human can live in union with themselves. He was always free in his consciousness because he chose to be himself.

Secondly, we need to construe the atonement in the context of Jesus' teaching. Jesus taught that one should live in union with oneself. This is simply to say "be honest to yourself." The kingdom of God is a state of mind where one lives in union with oneself. Jesus teaches us to love our neighbors as we love ourselves.[113] To love oneself is a prerequisite to loving others. This means that to live in union with oneself it is necessary to love oneself. Though human beings have free- will the divine guides and expects each one to be true to one's real self, which is of the divine.

Thirdly, the life of Jesus illustrates that he was always in union with himself. He never lived with a feeling of guilt. Even though he was tempted just like others and even though he underwent pain and suffering, he never led a selfish life. In other words, he never lived with a divided self. He was always aware that he belonged to God, the Father. In this sense, it is only when one lives in union with oneself, one lives in union with the divine. The atonement should be understood in this context as well.

---

111. Gunton, *Enlightenment and Alienation*, 154.
112. Bonhoeffer, *The Cost of Discipleship*, 219.
113. Luke 10:27.

The Atonement as Creating an Intuitive and Practical Knowledge of One's Union With Oneself

How does the cross create one's union with one-self and thereby create the knowledge of one-oneself union? Obviously, one-oneself union is related to the divine-human union because, as we have noted, we understand that it is the divine who lives in us. As we have noted, for Paul, "It is no longer me, but it is Christ who lives in him." The suffering of Jesus has direct relevance here too because it is through his substituting and representing us he makes us worthy of living in union with our real self, which is of the divine in us. Thus the cross is objective is bringing one's union with oneself.

Further, the cross also portrays that we need to hate the sinful nature within ourselves and love ourselves because it is the divine who lives in us. This needs an explanation because many who take an exclusive scientific approach to life need not believe that it is the divine who lives in us. Our claim is that theologically it is the divine who lives in us because we do not know where "our essential self" comes from and where it goes. It is also a fact that we can realize a struggle going on between the evil and the good within us. We believe that the good spark in us is of the divine and the other is of our selfishness. The cross teaches that selfishness should vanish and we need to grow Christ-like in being united with the essential and divine self in us.

Moreover, the cross manifests that no believer need be ashamed or be guilty in one's self. This is because, in union with Christ, we die to our sin and selfishness and rise to a selfless life.[114] The cross symbolizes that our sins are forgiven by our union with Christ and we therefore belong to the divine.

In Christ we have a model of how we should live in union with ourselves in order to live for others. Like Christ we may have to suffer when we seek to live in union with our real self, which is of the divine. In that sense, whether happy or miserable—the message of the cross is to live in union with oneself because the real self in us is of the divine. The nature of one-oneself union is dualistic and we will briefly analyze this too in the next chapter.

---

114. Rom 6:3.

Three implications of the Atonement for Theology

The Implication of the Atonement On Union between the Past, the Present, and the Future

In Visistadvaitic Hindu thought, Brahman is the one that effects salvation for all. Brahman creates the saving knowledge in humanity at all times. This "saving function of Brahman" has neither beginning nor end. Unlike the saving concept of Brahman, the atonement is considered as an act in history at one particular point in time. This historical particularity of the atonement, no doubt, has been a problem with which theologians struggle. For example, on Christian theology, O. V. Jathanna, an Indian Christian theologian writes, "Christian theology worth its name should hold . . . that the Christ-event is decisive for the whole of mankind, and in fact for the entire cosmos, and not only for a fraction of it, either geographically or temporally."[115] Similarly, Cupitt says, "No one should claim that the historical method alone can validate a Christological statement."[116] However, the question raised in relation to the atonement is: how does it save people who lived before the atoning act and how does it save in the present times?

Theologians have ventured to solve this predicament. Firstly, the idea of rebirth is considered as a possibility to solve the problem of the salvation of all who lived in the *ante christum natum*. In this understanding, God will cause all who lived and died before the time of the atonement in human history to be born again in the *post christum natum*. This idea of rebirth has been widespread in the ancient world.[117] Even in present times, in countries like India, the concept of rebirth (*punarjanma*) plays a vital role. Jathanna proposes that the concept of rebirth can enhance the possibility of universal salvific will of God. He writes,

> The decisiveness of the Christ-event and the universality of Christianity on the one hand, and the universal salvific will of God on the other, when held together, call a rigidly conceived only-one-life-on-earth hypothesis in question. They demand both as a hermeneutical bridge and as a Christian expectation springing from Christian hope—a hope which is inspired by Christian love and informed by the Christian faith—some kind of belief in "Rebirth" i.e., re-incarnation of human beings on earth.[118]

---

115. Jathanna, *Decisiveness of Christ-Event*, 436.
116. Cupitt, *Christ*, 123.
117. Richardson, "Reincarnation," 288–89.
118. Jathanna, *Decisiveness of Christ-Event*, 471.

The concept of rebirth offers a possible solution to the problem of relevance of the atoning work of Christ to all transcending chronological barriers. Nevertheless, this view of Jathanna cannot be stressed for the reason that the New Testament does not propose a concept of rebirth in this sense. It may be added that though Jesus would probably have been aware of the "rebirth concept," he did not use it in his teaching and preaching. In fact, the concept of rebirth could minimize the value of our present life. It is also not logical because we do not remember anything of a previous life. The Christian story of salvation is both temporal and eternal, the one for all comes from the reality of an atonement in eternity, the temporal is always either anticipated or recollected no matter where you are in the spatio-temporal realm. Eternity is not perpetual time or everlasting time; it is more the absence of time, and that is why rebirth is no guarantee of eternity.

Secondly, some Christians claim that the time of last judgment is the time when salvation through the cross will be granted to the unevangelized. This understanding is based on the hope that is derived from the all-encompassing love of the Christian faith. In this view, all who lived before the time of historical Christ and all who were not privileged to know the atoning work of Christ will have an opportunity to know about the salvation created in the atonement during the time of last judgment. However, this view that postpones salvation for the vast majority and locates it outside of history also needs to be rejected since it diminishes the significance of a historical life lived under the divine grace in this world.

Thirdly, the texts in 1 Peter 3:19, 20, and 4:6 are useful in explaining the relevance of the atonement for all times. In 1 Peter 3:19–20, we read that Christ went and preached to the spirits in prison who disobeyed God during the time of Noah. In 1 Peter 4:6, it is also said that the gospel is preached to those who are now dead, so that they might be judged according to men in regard to the body, but live according to God in regard to the spirit. We can suppose that the good news of salvation, as given in the atonement, was preached by Christ to all who lived and died before the historical event of the cross. The New Testament scholar, Charles Bigg is of the opinion that these texts portray that Christ gave a chance of repentance for all the sinners who were in Hades at the time of Christ's descensus.[119] Using these texts, Wolfhart Pannenberg makes a similar comment that Peter affirms the universal significance of Jesus' atonement. In his words, "The symbolic language of Jesus' descent into hell expresses the extent to which those men

---

119. Bigg, *Critical and Exegetical Commentary*, 162.

who lived before Jesus' activity and those who did not know him have a share in the salvation that has appeared in him."[120]

Hence, if the texts of 1 Peter 3:19, 20, and 4:6 are broadly interpreted, the relevance of the atonement for all who lived *ante christum natum* can be discerned. No doubt these texts shed some light on the relevance of the atonement for all times transcending chronological barriers. Thus even those who did not live a life anticipating salvation in Christ are given a chance to participate in the salvific life through Christ. Nevertheless, these texts do not talk of the *post christum natum* situation and hence fail to bring a union between the past, the present and the future.

Fourthly, should the objective side of the atonement be radically interpreted the relevance of the atonement for all times is brought out. In this perception, Christ brings salvation to all through his atoning work either by surmounting the evil powers once and for all or by satisfying God's wrath once and for all. The creation's response to the atonement does not play any role at all. Here though the atonement took place at a particular time in history it is considered as having relevance for all times because there is no subjective dimension to it. The two times prevalent in this understanding are the past and the present. We need only to believe that the creation was once under the power of evil oppressive force or was subject to destruction by the wrath of God due to its sin. Christ through the atoning work overcame the evil powers or satisfied God by his sacrifice. The creation once under bondage is now free.

However, the New Testament holds the objective and subjective sides of the atonement together. The church also vigilantly holds both the objective and subjective sides of the atonement together. Thus it is clear that the subjective side of the atonement should be given equal significance as its objective side. Though, in this view, the objective side of the atonement can be easily construed as relevant for all times, this view has not got adequate acceptance among Christians and theological circles precisely because the subjective side is completely left out.

Fifthly, the church understood as a universal sacrament of salvation deserves our attention here. Often the church is seen as being an instrument in bringing salvation to all through the atonement. In this view, the church is thought to represent the whole of God's creation. This is to say that the church represents all not only who live after the atoning work of Christ but also who lived in the *ante christum natum*. In fact, the church represents not only the ones who come into contact with a particular church as its members but also those who have not had any contact with the institutional

---

120. Pannenberg, *Jesus-God and Man*, 272.

church. Precisely, a part of God's creation, the church, represents the whole of it. However, this understanding too does not give adequate attention to the subjective side of the atonement.

It may also be noted that some churches do intercessory prayers for all—no matter when they lived. They pray that by the grace of God, the atonement may cause salvation to all who lived and died even before the atoning event in human history. On universal salvation and on intercessory prayers, Jerome P. Theissen, a Benedictine theologian says,

> Thus perhaps the weightiest argument in support of the universal effectiveness of the church in the salvation of those outside its boundaries is the matter of prayer to the Father in Christ Jesus. The prayer of the faithful, whether in solemn liturgies or in private aspiration, is addressed to the Lord God on behalf of all men. It is prayer to the Father through Christ. According to traditional Christian teaching the Father urges us to pray and is affected by prayer. It can be argued persuasively, therefore, that the church exercises through its mission of prayer some effectiveness in the process of salvation.[121]

Thus, Theissen is careful in seeing the intercessory prayer of the church as an instrument in effecting salvation beyond historical boundaries. However, though the validity of the concept of church and intercessory prayers are well-taken, here too, the subjective dimension of the atonement is not addressed.

Having rejected the "rebirth notion" and "the last judgment understanding" and having pointed out that the texts in 1 Peter do not address salvation in *post Christum natum* and having claimed that the objective is not to be separated from the subjective side, we shall very briefly outline how our model of the atonement addresses this difficulty. The claim of the atonement creating unions model is that the relevance of the atonement for all times is by the understanding that even before the historical event of the cross, there are those who lived a life in anticipation of salvation in and through Christ. In other words, people like Abraham of Old Testament times, even before the time of historical Jesus, lived a life in union with the divine, with one another, with the wider creation and with themselves making salvation accessible to them.

Karl Rahner calls the people who lived a Christian life, though they have not known Christ, as "anonymous Christians." It is true that always and everywhere human beings are in an objective salvific situation whilst they also always have the possibility of subjectively responding to the divine

---

121. Theissen, *Ultimate Church*, 130.

appropriately. Here, we may construe that God's saving activity is intrinsically related to the atonement, and hence salvation is necessarily Christian even before the historical time of atonement. Jathanna helpfully writes,

> The Christ-event cannot, therefore, be viewed as the moral cause of God's universal salvific will, but as its effect: as its manifestation and the highest point of realization or actualisation in history. For in the incarnation God's absolute offer was received absolutely on the human level, and thereby it has become irrevocable . . . The revelation of Christ, thus, makes explicit what may be implicitly experienced before the event of Christ.[122]

Thus the problem of the possibility of salvation in *ante Christum natum* is solved because the effect of the atonement was always explicit and an anticipatory life toward this should be seen as adequate to share in the salvific life created by Christ. In the *post Christum natum* period, we live with the knowledge of the atonement. Paul S. Fiddes rightly says that as we think and meditate on the past event of atonement we are grasped by it making salvation possible in present times.[123] Precisely, our model will understand that humanity after the time of atonement is being saved by their response to the intuitive and practical knowledge of four-fold union created within us through the atonement.

In sum, just as Brahman provides the necessary knowledge for salvation of all at all times, so also the atonement creating unions model is adequate enough to portray the atonement as relevant for salvation of all times. Nevertheless, Brahman's "salvific function" transcends history and the atonement in an important sense remains historical even if it is also an eternal reality.

No doubt, it is the saving concept of Brahman that prompted us to analyze the relevance of the atonement for all times and bringing a union between the past, present and future through the atonement. However, I end this section by stating that Visistadvaitic Hinduism should strive to find ways to make the concept of Brahman's saving function more historical and concrete whilst Christianity should try to understand the atonement as transcending chronology and bringing union between the past, present, and future.

---

122. Jathanna, *Decisiveness of Christ-Event*, 452.
123. Fiddes, *Past Event and Present Salvation*, 220.

Implication of the Atonement on a Union between Religious Traditions

Religious pluralism has been a fact throughout history even from the Old Testament period and early Christianity. In recent decades, religious pluralism has captured the attention of theologians of every hue. However, theology of the atonement, in general terms, remains unique to Christianity. This uniqueness, in fact, may be viewed as a stumbling block to a union between Christianity and other religious traditions.

Nevertheless, the atonement can be very well viewed in a different light. As we shall soon see, an in-depth look at the theology of the atonement reveals that this very doctrine can remain as a foundation for union between religious traditions.

In chapter 2, we pointed out that the saving concept of Brahman can be construed as a uniting factor between Visistadvaitic Hindu and other religious traditions. Hindu philosophers from ancient times have understood the saving function of Brahman as a universal phenomenon. They have not circumscribed it as if it was for Hindus alone. In this context, our task is to analyze the relevance of the atonement to all in a religiously plural world with a view to bringing a union amongst religions.

How does the atonement work as a uniting factor? Unfortunately, none of the other atonement models deal with this issue. On the contrary, our model includes this concern as well.

Firstly, the Bible portrays that the atonement is for everyone. The New Testament affirms that the atonement is for all, and in fact, for all creations. For instance, Jesus proclaims that his blood is shed for many. This statement of Christ means that salvation effected through the atonement is not limited to a particular religious, racial, class or caste group. Furthermore, Jesus teaches his disciples to go and make disciples for him in all nations, which means that salvation through the atonement is extended to people of all nations.[124]

Secondly, at least three notable theologians have worked on this theme. Wesley Ariarajah, a Sri Lankan theologian says,

> If we say that those who do not believe in Christ and do not belong to the Christian community are outside the saving providence and power of God, we are talking about a God who is not the God of Jesus Christ . . . The belief that people of other faiths are outside the saving activity of God is not only a comment

---

124. This discipleship need not mean the abandoning of the religious positions and insights of another faith. But it definitely means to engage with others in conversation and learn to grow in friendship.

about the people, but also about God. The God of the Bible, the God whom Jesus called Father, rules over all and is in all. All things have their being in God.[125]

Thus Ariarajah makes it plain that salvation through Christ is not limited to any one religious tradition. Referring to the objective side of Christ's work Ariarajah says, "Christ is universal in so far as the salvation offered in him is available to all persons."[126] Similar views are evident in other theologians as well.

Donald G. Dave is another theologian who understands the implication of the atonement as transcending religious barriers. He expounds that salvation through Jesus is possible for all—no matter which religious tradition one belongs to because the "name of Jesus" can be translated in many ways. To quote him,

> the "name of Jesus" is the disclosure of the structure of new being. It is the pattern of salvation. So the universality of Christianity is grounded in the translatability of the "name of Jesus," not in the imposition of particular formularies on others. This power of new being operates throughout the world under the names of many religious traditions.[127]

Thus Dave construes that salvation is possible in all religions but through Christ alone. This is very close to the "anonymous Christians" understanding of Rahner.

Next, for Panikkar everyone is redeemed by Christ. He claims,

> He (Christ) has redeemed mankind and the whole cosmos, and not only Christians, i.e. those who consciously acknowledge him. Christ's sacrifice is universal also for non-believers, and the opinion that non-Christians do not share in Christ's redeeming influence has been explicitly condemned by the Church.[128]

In a stimulating way, Panikkar also interprets the sacrament of Eucharist being effective to all implying that salvation through the atonement is beyond any one religion. He says,

> Christian consciousness today is realizing more and more that Christ "became" Eucharist, not only for the Christians who receive it, but for the entire world, which receives it through the

---

125. Ariarajah, *Bible and People,* 32–33.
126. Ariarajah, *Bible and People,* 37.
127. Dave and Carman, *Christian Faith,* 30.
128. Elwood, *What Asian Christians are Thinking,* 358.

communion of Christians. Communion is not just a private devotion or an exclusively individual act of Christians: it is a cosmic act . . . This process of divine assimilation descends to those people who do not believe explicitly in Christ, through the sacramental action of the Christian who, having "received" Christ, is subsequently "received" by others in the stresses and strains of daily life. The Christian receives Christ and, as it were brings him down to other people, who enter into contact with the Eucharist through contact with their Christian brethren.[129]

Thus for Panikkar too the implication of the atonement should not be limited to Christians alone but should be understood as a universal phenomenon. This understanding of universal salvific will of God is increasingly recognized in the world today.

Along the lines of Ariarajah, Dave, and Panikkar our model of the atonement claims that the atoning work of Christ is for every one and is not limited to one religious community. The New Testament prompts us to perceive the atonement as an inclusive concept, avoiding inter-religious alienation based on this concept.

The Implication of the Atonement On a Union between Different Theological Doctrines in Christianity

We have already pointed out that the saving concept of Brahman is the ground on which other theological doctrines get their intrinsic meaning in Visistadvaitic Hinduism. We have analyzed this using Visistadvaitic Hindu doctrines of creation and revelation. This facilitated us to conclude that the saving concept of Brahman brings a union between the different theological doctrines in Visistadvaitic Hinduism.

Does the concept of atonement provide such a union between various theological doctrines in Christianity? It is a fact that even in Christianity, the concept of atonement shapes all other related doctrines. If one doctrine should be highlighted as the central one, it should be the doctrine of the atonement. Students who begin their studies in Christian theology are taught the doctrines of revelation, God, Christology, Holy Spirit, Trinity, Atonement, Church, Worship, Providence, Problem of Evil, and Eschatology. All these doctrines are interrelated and interdependent yet they are learnt under different titles for the sake of greater erudition and originality. Now, what can be the most central string that brings continuity in the specific meanings of the doctrines? Arguably, the shapes of all other Christian

129. Elwood, *What Asian Christians are Thinking*, 368–69.

doctrines are dependent on the concept of atonement. We do not say this to undermine the profound importance of all Christian theological doctrines but we say this only to portray the shape which the doctrine of the atonement provides to the various Christian doctrines. Several theologians recognize the centrality of the doctrine of atonement in the whole scheme of Christian doctrines. For instance, Steve Holmes rightly says, "the cross . . . is so basic to any properly theological account of the nature of true humanity, true justice, true sacrifice, true relationship, or a host of other realities."[130] Dillistone also comments on the centrality of the atonement. According to him, among the doctrines of Christian faith it is the atonement which has more points of contact with life. In his words,

> If Paul Tillich is in any way right in his assertions that 'the Christian message provides the answers to the questions implied in human existence'; that the Christian answers are, so far as their form is concerned, directly dependent upon the questions which they answer; if, in other words, it is true that the leading questions of any particular era supply the language-forms necessary for expressing the essential Christian affirmations within that era, then everything points to the fact that it is precisely the doctrine of the Atonement (even though the actual word 'atonement' may not be used) which is needed to answer the most pressing enquiries of our own time.[131]

Thus the atonement definitely has a bearing in providing a union between the different theological doctrines within Christianity.

To conclude this chapter, we will make a few remarks. We have not considered the event of the cross alone as the atonement. Instead we have included in the atonement all the matters which are centered on the life, ministry, death and resurrection of Christ. The significance of the atonement for the salvation of all is well affirmed. Both the divine and the human have their part in establishing the four-fold unions thus making our model both objective and subjective. We have also noted the implication of the atonement for a union between the past, present and future, between different religious traditions and between the different doctrines within Christianity.

Obviously, the direction we have shown is using the saving concept of Brahman in Visistadvaitic Hinduism. Nevertheless, we should comment on how the atonement creating unions differ from the saving concept of Brahman. Jesus' life and the event of the cross is an historical act. The saving concept of Brahman is transhistorical and exists at a philosophical plane. Jesus

---

130. Holmes, "Can Punishment Bring Peace?," 105.
131. Dillistone, *Christian Understanding*, 2. Also see Moltmann, *Crucified*, 72.

himself said that he has come for the salvation of many. This, he made clear by teaching about the kingdom of God. On the other hand, Brahman speaks through scriptures, reason, and gurus. It is also remarkable that whilst in Christianity the atonement, which creates the unions, is remembered through the sacrament of the Eucharist, in Visistadvaitic Hinduism, Brahman who provides the liberating knowledge is realized through the sound Om. Whilst, in Christianity, the salvation created through the atonement is often realized in a community or church, in Visistadvaitic Hinduism, the liberating essence of Brahman is realized individually during worship or through a guru. Furthermore, the possibility of the divine becoming a human, as in Christ, is a concept alien to Visistadvaitic Hinduism.

How far can these differences be accommodated within the means to salvation/liberation? This question is addressed in the next chapter.

5

The Atonement Creating Unions

Potentialities and Problems

BEFORE WE CONCLUDE THIS project, it is significant for us to highlight the potentialities and problems of our outlined atonement model. No theology can be accepted without a very careful, critical analysis and scrutiny. And our atonement model cannot be an exception to it. Obviously, our model of the atonement has to do with both the Indian Visistadvaitic-Hindu context as well as the Biblical tradition. Hence, anyone could expect both potentialities and problems to emerge from our outlined theology. In this chapter, we will briefly portray the anticipated pre-dominant possibilities and problems of our atonement model.

Even in a general sense potentialities and problems become apparent when one deals with both the Visistadvaitic Hindu and the Christian traditions. Kim says,

> The Christian and the Hindu traditions, each have a unique theological understanding of faith and practice and a distinctive historical development. But though the differences are great, similarities are also perceived, not only at the level of human commonality, but also at the theological level of the two religions.[1]

Further theologians have already written on the inevitable confessional and apologetic nature of theology whilst dealing with comparative doctrinal concepts. For instance, Francis Clooney says,

> The deeper, more difficult, and more acute differences become, the more slender the distinction between a "confessional" theology, where one pronounces and explains the truth of one's

---

1. Kim, *In Search of Identity*, 196.

positions, and an "apologetic" theology, where one also asserts the error of the other's positions. For this reason I speak of an inter-religious theology's "confessional and even apologetic" dimension. Strong arguments in favor of one's own tradition often go along with critiques of other's theological positions, and theologies are often confessional and apologetic at the same time, testifying and criticizing, explaining and arguing, persuading and disproving. But even criticisms need not be a problem if it is offered respectfully and professionally. That is, the theologian must actually know something about the theological tradition being criticized, become engaged in a receptive dialog with theologians of that other tradition, admit that areas of disagreement are probably far fewer than area of consensus, and concede that one's own theology is not beyond criticism. Such is the high price for a mutual apologetics today.[2]

We admit that an apologetical approach from both sides could be justified in a comparative doctrinal theology. However, though we agree with Clooney on all other points we need not agree with him that disagreements are likely to be fewer than agreements. It may be or may not be the case. It is not our primary concern here, but in this chapter, as well as in the next chapter, we will precisely conclude that though there are significant similarities as well as dissimilarities, our fresh model of the atonement can be fruitful in taking Christian thinking in a new direction as well as useful and meaningful in an Indian context where Christianity and Visistadvaitic Hinduism exist together.

In fact, in a work like this we need to be open to the different religious traditions involved. Openness to other religions means, we should stop evaluating other religions based on a priori theological presuppositions. The situation, in which we recognize the unique nature of the two major theological traditions[3] and take into account that the people who belong to Visistadvaitic Hinduism and Christianity are equally intelligent and capable, compels us to be impartial, as far as possible and to respect the integrity of both traditions. A genuine conversation between the two theological traditions will be of mutual help and will promote an enhanced life together under the divine.[4]

---

2. Clooney, *Hindu God, Christian God*, 11.

3. Obviously, Christianity has existed for many centuries now and it lives in almost every part of the world. Regarding Hinduism, Kim rightly says, "It challenges . . . any theology or philosophy contradicting Hindu dharma." See, Kim, *In Search of Identity*, 192.

4. In recent decades, scholars like Arun Shourie and the propagators of Hindutva

One objective of this chapter can be clarified in the following way. The saving concept of Brahman in Visistadvaitic Hinduism, presented with great vigor and thought by Visistadvaitic Hindu theologians, particularly by Ramanuja, is used to formulate a model of the atonement. Then, we attempt to evaluate critically the constructed model of the atonement. For instance, only a God who allows himself to be a human amongst humanity, and to suffer with humanity, as portrayed in the atonement creating unions, can serve as a corrective to the abstraction of the Visistadvaitic Hindu understanding of the saving concept of Brahman. In other words, the portrayal of God in Christ suffering, dying, and raising provides a critique of, and suggestion to, the ideological and metaphysical picturing of the saving concept of Brahman.

In the construction of this chapter, still another important consideration is that even though the concept of Brahman's saving grace is present in both reflective and popular literature of the Visistadvaitic Hindu tradition, the former will be given priority because theology chiefly arises in the reflective mode. Giving attention to a reflective construction of theology, our concern in this chapter is also to contribute to the ongoing discussion between theologians of the two distinct theological traditions. We also need to be clear that in this chapter we will only briefly highlight the major potentialities and problems, so that we understand the fruitfulness of our atonement model with a note of caution.

In portraying the potentialities and problems of the atonement creating unions model, we will in a broad sense give attention to (1) contextual and interpretative concerns, and (2) theological concerns—although these concerns often overlap between one other. Whilst dealing with contextual and interpretative concerns we will give particular attention to (a) metaphysical concerns, (b) inter-contextual concerns, (c) economic and political concerns, (d) ecological concerns, (e) psychological concerns, and (f) belief and understanding. Whilst dealing with theological concerns we will take into account (a) nature of union, (b) particularity and universality, (c) pluralism and unity, (d) tradition and reformation, and (e) compatibility with the central biblical concepts of the Torah and the new covenant. The questions which this chapter will address are: Does the atonement creating unions model maintain the decisive nature of salvation in and through

---

movements have criticized Christian theologians who do Hindu-Christian studies saying that they are aimed at a fine and delicate form of conversion. We, in fact, in this study, aim to look at our own traditions differently and do not intend to engage in any subtle form of conversion. We have already said that each tradition has its own merits and weaknesses. However, in my view, conversion can happen anytime and it should be a voluntary decision.

Christ? Is this model only applicable to the Indian context where Hinduism predominates? Does this model help to enhance life? Does this model provide adequate space for a world-wide conversation on the concerns of a theology of the atonement?

1) Contextual and Interpretative Concerns

a) Metaphysical Concerns

Theology is an intellectual and practical matter which involves making an intangible model of our apprehension in faith; a model which in the case of the theory of the atonement must be 1. critically coherent, 2. externally coherent with other major doctrines, 3. rooted in scripture and in the history of the church(tradition), and 4. applicable and useful in the contemporary church and the wider world.

We have ventured to understand the salvific work of Christ in the language of Brahman's saving knowledge, which belongs to another cultural and religious tradition. Now, whether the atonement creating unions model is useful for the church is a question before us. The Bible clearly says that it is the work of God's spirit to translate and contextualize the word of God to render it understandable in people's cultural and vernacular background. The event at the time of Pentecost is an inspiring example of this claim. On Acts 2, as Stackhouse writes,

> The first thing that needs to be said is that 'contextualizing the faith' has been a part of the mission of the church from the beginning. If we take Pentecost, as reported in Acts 2 as the birthday of the church, we will have to note that the disciples were filled with the Holy Spirit and began to preach in such a way that 'each one heard them speaking in his own language.' The faith was being contextualized. . . . These concerns are not only ones of language, but are social, economic, political, familial, and ideological in character.[5]

Thus the crux of this project falls within the boundaries of Christian tradition. Furthermore, it is a fact that the exposition of the importance of the atonement has been developed and interpreted several times throughout the centuries within the Jewish, Greek, Roman, Latin, and Western systems of thought. The understanding of the atonement in these contexts manifests the peculiarities of these contexts.

5. Costa, *One Faith, Many Cultures*, 4.

The peculiarities of the said contexts are mostly alien to the saving concept of Brahman developed and taught in the history of Visistadvaitic Hindu theological tradition in India. On the other hand, our model of the atonement is relevant and immediately applicable to an Indian context because it bears the peculiarities of that context.

Now we will move to comment on the potential of understanding the atonement in terms of knowledge. It is often claimed that at times knowledge can bring grief and ignorance is bliss. Here again, as we noted, we are not dealing with the concept of ignorance on the whole but precisely with the ignorance of the intuitive and practical knowledge of the four-fold union and the resultant alienation. The knowledge of Brahman is about mastering the will. In theological terms, it is not knowing about God but knowing God.

Another fruitful aspect of the atonement creating unions model is that it clearly shifts the soteriological concern to a unique and decisive level. In chapter 2, we mentioned that salvation by the grace of Brahman eventually means to be with Brahman. In this same sense, the salvific work of Christ is to enable us to be with him. However, we do need to mention that the saving concept of Brahman works at a metaphysical level because it deals with the ultimate condition of human existence, though a foretaste of salvation is possible here and now Brahman is seen as essential for a salvation that implies union. Understanding the life and work of Christ using the lens of the saving concept of Brahman tells us that we are dealing not only with practical concerns but also with a metaphysical reality. Although we do not strive for liberation at a metaphysical level, dealing with metaphysics is part of theology because it has implications for practical life.

Nonetheless, when one applies the saving concept of Brahman to the atonement, it is carried out at a philosophical, or rather at a metaphysical, level not only in the eschatological sense but also in the sense that the saving concept of Brahman has a contemplative dimension and not just a popular one. Arbis B. Collins says, "the need to know what accounts for the reality or being of what we know became associated with the need to know the 'metaphysical' i.e., what is 'beyond the physical' and separate from it."[6] In short, metaphysics can be construed as a system to explain the ultimate principles of human existence through imaginative or contemplative concepts, images, and symbols. It is true that human beings use the language of metaphysics to discern, as well as, to illustrate theological concepts. Nevertheless, what is significant here is not to know whether something really exists or not, but to know whether some imaginative concepts or symbols help to convey what

---

6. Collins, "Metaphysics," 655.

one really wants to convey. Human beings, in general, are emotional beings and there are those who want to understand others as well as interact with them. Clifford Geertz, an anthropologist says,

> Their [Human Beings'] world view is their picture of the way things in sheer actuality are, their concept of nature, of self, of society. It contains their most comprehensive ideas of order ... the ethos is made intellectually reasonable by being shown to represent a way of life implied by the actual state of affairs which the world view describes, and the world view is made emotionally acceptable by being presented as an image of an actual state of affairs of which such a way of life is an authentic expression ... Whatever else religion may be, it is an attempt ... to conserve the fund of general meanings in terms of which each individual interprets his experience and organizes his conduct.[7]

In the light of Geertz's argument, one knows that there is a particular worldview underlying the construction of any theological or religious concept. Here, it is significant for us to note that there is a specific worldview with a soteriological dimension for human beings which leads to, and influences, the idea of the saving concept of Brahman within Visistadvaitic Hinduism. Three interrelated categories, which are evident in the construction of the saving concept of Brahman, are the concepts of *maya*, *avidya*, and the Brahman-atman union. Furthermore, the concept of Brahman cannot be extricated from the concept of *karma-samsara*, which says that human actions lead them to their future and rebirth. Thus it is apparent that the Visistadvaitic Hindu visions of soteriology and eschatology are notably different from the metaphysical contexts with which the doctrine of the atonement was conversant and formulated throughout many centuries.

Nevertheless, Christian theologians are well aware of the absence of a unified vision of human condition and salvation that has shaped the doctrine of the atonement. We will illustrate our point with an example. The metaphysical vision that underlies the formulation of the classical theory—acknowledging the problem of evil in a realistic way is completely different from the metaphysics that informed and shaped the subjective theory. Precisely, the classical theory presupposes that an evil force exists apart from us which causes us to sin and brings us suffering. Deliverance from the evil, which binds us, is brought through the atoning work of Christ. On the other hand, the subjective theory is based on the understanding that we sin because our sense of the good and moral will is not strong enough. Christ, through his atoning work on the cross sets an example for us to grow more

7. Geertz, *Interpretation of Cultures*, 127.

Christ-like. Hence it is clear that theology of the atonement is not limited to or contained within the boundaries of any specific knowledge of Christianity. It should be reasserted that the church, up to the present, does not have an accepted formula of the atonement.[8]

The fact, however, remains that a model of the atonement cannot be constructed on a metaphysical conception alone for that cannot sustain and uphold the unique factors of the import of the life, death, and resurrection of Christ. The question that arises here is whether the Visistadvaitic Hindu vision of human existence in this world and the Visistadvaitic Hindu notion of salvation are able to support and sustain the atonement creating unions model with a Christian substance—as outlined in chapter 4. Certainly, there are problems here. We will point out seven of the main ones.

First, the notion of God suffering as human is not found in the Visistadvaitic Hindu tradition. Hence, we cannot assume that the saving concept of Brahman will be useful in adequately portraying all the dimensions relating to the life and work of Christ though it accommodates many distinctive features of the atonement because of its immediate and apparent intelligibility. However, although the idea of God suffering as a human being is alien to the Visistadvaitic Hindu tradition, salvation/liberation is basically understandable as the four-fold union and hence this model of the atonement is not completely incomprehensible to people of the Visistadvaitic Hindu tradition.

But God suffering in Christ is crucial to the interpretation of the atoning work of Christ in Christian tradition. In Christianity, Christ is portrayed as the God of compassion and love and as the God who identifies himself with the sufferings and trials of humanity through his sufferings on the cross.[9] Admittedly, suffering is part of our experience as well, which makes

---

8. Burnaby points out that though the early church fathers were concerned about the nature of Christ and the doctrine of Trinity, there wasn't any need realized to formulate an "orthodox" doctrine of the atonement. In his words, "There have been many theories of the meaning and method of this Atonement, but none of them has been found so defective or so misleading as to evoke from the Church a formal statement of 'orthodox' doctrine." Burnaby, *The Belief of Christendom*, 115. Also, see Kelly, *Early Christian Doctrines*, 375. Kelly writes, "The student who seeks to understand the soteriology of the fourth and early fifth centuries will be sharply disappointed if he expects to find anything corresponding to the elaborately worked out syntheses which the contemporary theology of the Trinity and the Incarnation presents. In both these latter departments controversy forced fairly exact definition on the Church, whereas the redemption did not become a battle-ground for rival schools until the twelfth century, when Anselm's *Cur deus homo* (c. 1097) focused attention on it." We may add that until today, the Church has not formulated or agreed on an "orthodox" theory of the atonement.

9. God's identification with us in our suffering is particularly emphasized by

the atonement relevant to our day to day life. Suffering transforms our will. No doubt, the cross has provided not only consolation but also hope to many throughout the centuries. For instance, as it is well known Luther's confidence and faith were founded on a revealed God in Christ, which implied a God who participates in human suffering and history. Moltmann writes, "[For Luther,] as the cross of the outcast and forsaken Christ it is the visible revelation of God's being for man in the reality of his world."[10] Here, we might persuade Visistadvaitic Hindu theologians to see the vitality of the notion of God suffering in bringing us salvation and incorporate this idea in the Visistadvaitic Hindu system so that the saving concept will be liberated from being part of metaphysics alone through its relation to suffering.

Second, there is the problem related to the Visistadvaitic Hindu notion of atman (soul). In Visistadvaitic Hinduism, when one refers to a human being, particularly in relation to salvation, it is only the soul or atman to which one refers. The physical body is ignored because it is considered to be mortal and of no use after death. On the other hand, in Christianity, the whole human being including the physical body is considered important. In short, the word human and soul/atman are too easily interchangeable in Visistadvaitic Hinduism.

Visistadvaitic Hindu understanding of salvation, then, revolves around the fact that atman, which is divine and everlasting in its very nature, is present in physical bodies and hence is in a state of bondage, akin to the Stoic doctrine of *soma sema*. Salvation then is the freedom or release of atman from physical bodies and rebirth, toward union with Brahman. In fact, the profound sense of Brahman-atman union reveals the idea that atman is closer to Brahman than to physical body in which we live. In the words of James Stutley, "the concept of Atman . . . cannot be isolated and separated from the cosmic Brahman-principle."[11] However, this does not mean that bodily existence is totally devoid of significance because it is seen as a time when one may receive the grace of Brahman for salvation. Nonetheless, on a conceptual level, the priority is for Brahman-atman union over against life in a physical body. This makes Visistadvaitic Hindu understanding of

---

Moltmann. He says that even death cannot separate us from God because Christ himself underwent this experience. In his words, "In the cross of his Son, God took upon himself not only death, so that man might be able to die comforted with the certainty that even death could not separate him from God, but still more, in order to make the crucified Christ the ground of his new creation, in which death itself is swallowed up in the victory of life and there will be 'no sorrow, no crying, and not more tears.'" Though this is a challenge to faith, it has provided comfort to many throughout centuries. Moltmann, *Crucified*, 217.

10. Moltmann, *Crucified*, 208.
11. Margaret and Stutley, *A Dictionary of Hinduism*, 31.

the saving concept of Brahman exclusively a supernatural and spiritual concern; its this-worldly sense is underplayed.

In Christian understanding of human salvation, on the other hand, there is manifestly an interdependence of the physical and the spiritual. Thus after death there is an emphasis on human salvation as being in a transfigured body, if not a physical body. There are theologians who say that we are saved to be in our physical body. For example, the church father, Irenaeus writes,

> Those who deny that the flesh can be saved and are scornful about its regeneration, alleging that it is not capable of becoming incorruptible, are utterly mistaken. They treat the whole providence of God as though it were of no account. If the flesh is not saved then, obviously, neither did the Lord redeem us with his blood, nor is the cup of the Eucharist the communion of his blood, nor the bread which we break the communion of his body . . . Apostle Paul also says . . . For we are members of his body, of his flesh, and of his bones.[12]

Further, the kingdom of God imagery, as expounded by Jesus, envisages human beings to be with the divine, with others and with nature, not absolutely in a spiritual sense and not without a physical body but in a physical body. The ultimate aim is not a supernatural and spiritual one, but union with Christ in human history. Specifically, "the Nazareth manifesto of Jesus," recorded in Luke 4:16, deals with historical liberation of the oppressed, marginalized and suffering people of this world. Our union with the divine, with others, with nature and with ourselves should be reflected in helping others participate in this union and it is meant to be in bodily existence as much as in a spiritual existence. Thus there is a problem when one ascribes the saving concept of Brahman to the atoning work of Christ. One could misunderstand that even in Christianity—our union with the divine, with others, with nature and with ourselves is in the sphere of the soul alone and not in the existence of our physical bodies.

Third, Christians like Griffiths and Staffner were delighted by the insights of Hinduism and they sought for commonalities and differences between the two traditions. However, this particular Hindu-Christian synthesis is largely criticized by Dalit theologians saying that the liberative motifs of Christian theology are not used to criticize the caste system of Hinduism[13] as they ought to do. Thus it is now obvious that whilst constru-

---

12. Galloway, *Basic Readings in Theology*, 21.

13. For example, in his work on Dalits and Christianity, Clarke vehemently argues that Indian Christian theologians largely ignore the concerns of Dalits in their

ing the atonement using a Visistadvaitic Hindu concept there is a problem which revolves around the inherent implication of legitimizing the existing structures of caste hierarchy and domination in the society. Referring to outcast people, Clarke says, "they are an economically oppressed and religiously and culturally marginalized community, mainly because their distinctive heritage is not in conformity with the traditions of the Hindu caste communities."[14] There are theologians who have vehemently fought against the caste system. For instance, Bishop V. S. Azariah contrasting Hindu society's caste centeredness writes,

> But what is Christianity? It is often said that Christianity is Christ. That is true; but it is also a way of life. 'The way' was the name given to it in the days of the apostles. Christianity is not a doctrine about God; it is not hero-worship of Jesus, it is a scheme of life in a society; it is an organism, a family, a fellowship, a brotherhood—whose center, radius and circumference is Christ. In fellowship with all others who are attached to the Lord, bound together by outward rules and rites and throbbing with one inward pulse and purpose, men and women of all ages, races, tongues, colors and nationalities who have accepted this scheme of life, and separated from all others are more and more experiencing in this fellowship the impetus and power issuing from the Spirit who is its in dweller and life-giver.[15]

Nevertheless, it is true that in spite of the ostensible objection against the caste system by Christian theologians, Buddhist leaders[16] and a few within the Hindu tradition itself, the Hindu system, including Visistadvaitic strand, largely tolerates and continues to exist with the caste system. It even sanctifies the caste system. It divides people according to different stages in the process of liberation/salvation. However, the caste taxonomy begins in a creation story itself. It is understood that people who came out of the head of Brahman are *Brahmins*, people who came out of Brahman's chest are *Kshatriyars*, those who came from the thighs are *Vashiyas* and those who came from Brahman's feet are *Sudhras*. In relation to liberation/salvation one's place in the caste system is usually confirmed on the basis of what one did in one's previous birth. For example, the Brahmins are

---

theologizing. In his view, only the theology that includes the liberative concerns of Dalit theology can be an inclusive theology in India. Clarke, *Dalits*, 10.

14. Clarke, *Dalits*, 3.

15. Azariah, quoted in Harper, *In the Shadow of the Mahatma*, 248.

16. Following Dr. Ambedkar, many low-caste people converted themselves from Hinduism to Buddhism. This trend continues even up to the present day.

closer to Brahman than the *Sudhras*. This is made wholly explicit because it is only the Brahmins who, having been taught scriptures in the original language, are entitled to become priests. The reason is also because, in Visistadvaitic Hinduism, liberation/salvation is based on knowledge. On the other hand, in the teachings of Christ we see an equal access to the divine for all human beings. When one formulates a model of the atonement through the eyes of the saving concept of Brahman there is a danger of understanding humanity in a hierarchical way which could begin to affect Christian life adversely. For instance, the "Evangelical" Christians may be thought to be superior to "Liberal" ones or vice versa. Nevertheless, the fact remains that for Christ, the so-called sinners (tax collectors and prostitutes), who readily repented, are closer to the kingdom of God. We see a radical reversal of hierarchy here. This is because the stress is on volition and love, not on knowledge. More importantly, the vision of Christ was a community of service, peace, love, grace, justice and righteousness without any sense of hierarchy like that of caste. In the words of St. Paul, "there is no longer Jew or Greek . . . in Christ."[17]

Fourth, another problem lies in the Visistadvaitic Hindu understanding of the world. Though Ramanuja teaches that the world is real, after liberation/salvation one does not live in this world. One lives in union with Brahman in another world. On the other hand, for Christ, salvation is an affair of this world. He teaches us to pray, "Your kingdom come." The danger then is that when one construes salvation by the atoning work of Christ using the saving concept of Brahman, salvation could be misunderstood as a phenomenon of an other-worldly life alone and not of this world.

Fifth, the saving concept of Brahman, as it does not adequately deal with human existence in a physical body, does not provide a proper in-depth analysis of life in this world. For example, Visistadvaitic Hinduism teaches that our suffering is due to our ignorance and *karma*. However, we know that suffering is a reality that is independent of these. Christianity affirms that Christ himself underwent suffering, death and resurrection, without simultaneously attributing ignorance and selfishness to Him. Hence, whilst interpreting the atonement using the saving concept of Brahman one should be cautious and bear in mind the difference in Visistadvaitic Hindu and Christian understanding of the concerns of everyday life.

Sixth, Brahman as a philosophical and theological concept is transhistorical and Brahman has not lived as a person in a world of flesh and blood with its political struggle. On the other hand, the suffering and death of Christ is a historical fact. Thus, when one understands the atonement

---

17. Gal 3:28.

as a factor for union, using the saving concept of Brahman, the historical concerns are left out. In Christianity, it is understood that through his death Jesus becomes relevant to humanity—identifying himself with the pains and struggles of humankind in the march of history.

Seventh, the design of rebirth is part of Visistadvaitic Hindu theology. In Visistadvaitic Hinduism, an atman is given several lives to have the opportunity of being saved by Brahman. On the other hand, Christian theology does not have a notion of re-incarnation. It is replaced instead with the idea of heaven and hell.[18] The former tends to undermine the seriousness of the moment whereas the latter tends to make the character of this life absolutely decisive.

In sum, the most important purpose of metaphysics is to offer direction to human life seeking union with the divine. Our analysis of the use of the saving concept of Brahman for understanding the atoning work of Christ, in this section, has provided a few possibilities. In the meanwhile, we have portrayed at least seven problems. The problems give a direction to the criticism of the metaphysics of Visistadvaitic Hinduism. However, we should make it plain that we have criticized the Visistadvaitic Hindu metaphysical system predominantly by taking into consideration the contribution of liberation theology. Liberation theology emphasizes that the total human being should be liberated and it should be a historical liberation in this historical world. In other words, our evaluation of Visistadvaitic Hindu metaphysics is based on orthopraxis. Nevertheless, we also need to be aware that liberation theology also exists as a claim rather than a practice. What can be practice is of crucial importance to us. Obviously, our model claims to practice the four-fold union created in the atonement which then becomes our way of fully appropriating the meaning of the atonement. This will become clearer as we proceed to deal with the following sections of this chapter.

Finally, the pointed out problems of using the saving concept of Brahman to explicate the atonement, however, does not lead us to reject the atonement creating unions model, but we have mentioned them only to introduce a note of caution in attempting to understand the atonement using an Indian conceptual world. As we have seen in chapter 3, all models of the atonement are colored with the cultural values in which they were

---

18. Since the Christian idea of heaven and hell is replaced with the Hindu concepts of *moksha* and rebirth, the notion of forgiveness is left out in Hindu system of thought. In Christianity, the stress on forgiveness has helped many to forgive others on different instances. It should be acknowledged that this important idea is not accommodated in our atonement model. However, it should be noted that since sin is understood in terms of estrangement, what is required is union—forgiveness is replaced with reconciliation.

formulated. No doubt, the atonement creating unions model will relate most easily to the Visistadvaitic Hindu context.

b) Inter-Contextual Concerns

We now analyze the potentialities and problems revolving around inter-contextual considerations. The term Brahman is part of everyday talk of Visistadvaitic Hindus in India, whom we are attempting to address. It is notable that the saving concept of Brahman is part of the basic education for Visistadvaitic Hindus. Almost all languages in India use the term Brahman in articulating religious and theological messages. Thus it is evident that when we apply the features of the saving concept of Brahman to the atoning work of Christ for our salvation, such theological language is more comprehensible and acceptable to the majority of the Indians. Gunton says that using understandable metaphorical language in dealing with a concept like the atonement is important.[19] The theological vocabulary and language of our fresh model of the atonement is obviously apt for an Indian context.

As Brahman is not only a religious word but also an important concept of Indian philosophy, our formulated atonement model should also be intelligible to philosophers in India. The atonement creating unions model should have enormous potential for interpreting the salvific work of Christ—for the reader. Moreover, the saving concept of Brahman was highlighted in chapter 2, within the context of the concepts of God, humanity and nature. The atonement creating unions model too is communicated in the same context. It is because of this immediate and apparent intelligibility, the atonement creating unions model is potentially useful to the people of India.

The central claim is that the atonement creating unions model is comprehensible to Visistadvaitic Hindus and is of interest to Christians in India. In the previous chapter, we pointed out that Indian theologians have already used the word Brahman to understand the significance and meaning of Christ. Therefore, the interpretation of the atonement using the saving concept of Brahman will be equally intelligible to both Visistadvaitic Hindus and Christians of India. Tiliander helpfully points out,

> *It is therefore no surprise that the question of Brahman as name for the highest and absolute reality has come up in connection with the efforts to create an indigenous theology and to express*

---

19. Gunton, *Actuality of Atonement*, 27–29.

the Biblical message in a language which more directly speaks to the Indian mind.[20]

The atonement understood by using the saving concept of Brahman can certainly promote a more successful and plausible conversation between Christians and Visistadvaitic Hindus in India.

Having established that the atonement creating unions model is understandable to both Visistadvaitic Hindus and Christians of India, we would suggest that the concept of Brahman and its function as providing the four-fold union is not entirely new to the Western society. It is worthwhile here to stress that the term Brahman itself stands for unity. Margaret Stutley says, "*brahman* is equated with cosmic unity, a notion rooted in the age-old problem of man's relation to his immediate, and subsequently to his supramundane environment."[21] Furthermore, the term Brahman can be found today in various writings of the West. It is generally used to denote the ultimate or the divine or the unifying factor. For example, in the works of Western scholars like John Carman, Eric Lott and Julius Lipner, to which we have referred in this work, the term Brahman plays a significant role. Also, notably, the Oxford Paperback Dictionary has included the word Brahman and defines it as "the supreme divine Hindu reality."[22] The arrival of Hindus from the East to the West with their philosophies, from 1960s or earlier onwards, has helped people of the West to become familiar with this concept. Thus the concept of Brahman and its function in relation to salvation is more or less a recognizable idea in most parts of the East as well as the West.

The credibility of our argument becomes clearer if viewed in the light of our discussion in chapter 3. For instance, as we noted, when one applies the classical theory of the atonement, in an Indian context, the discussion instantly becomes unacceptable because people of the Visistadvaitic Hindu tradition never think of an evil power to which the divine is obligated. Or, as we pointed out, the satisfaction theory is not readily applicable to an Indian context because the idea of satisfaction is not found within the framework of Visistadvaitic Hindu theological system. We do not presume that people cannot take on board new ideas and conceptions. But our argument is that the Indian context doesn't immediately relate to the classical or the satisfaction theory because it is so utterly alien to current ways of Indian thinking. On the other hand, the saving concept of Brahman links the discourse to the

---

20. Tiliander, *Christian and Hindu Terminology*, 138.
21. Margaret and Stutley, *A Dictionary of Hinduism*, 49.
22. Pollard, *The Oxford Paperback Dictionary*, 94.

theological tradition within Visistadvaitic Hinduism and helps our constructed model of the atonement to be readily applicable. Samartha says,

> The scope of the saving work of Christ is larger than the redemption of individuals. As the Agent of creation and as the Savior of mankind, his work is continuing until all things are summed up in him. Here therefore the advaita emphasis on the unity of all life, where history and nature are seen together in the totality of the life of God, is not irrelevant.[23]

Though Samartha here focuses on the advaitic Hindu thought, it is also readily applicable to Ramanuja's Visistadvaitic Hindu thought if the unity is understood in terms of self-body union. Moreover, it would have been more appropriate if Samartha had used the phrase, Savior of creation instead of Savior of mankind. After all in the Christian tradition there is the conception of the redemption of the whole of creation—the whole of creation fell with humanity and the whole of creation is redeemed with them. There is no sense of a de-contextualized person. We will return to this whilst dealing with ecology in this chapter.

An interesting feature of our created model of the atonement is that it revolves around the concepts of alienation and union. We have discussed them in a four-fold dimension. Arguably, the problem of four-fold alienation is part of most cultures. Even if one argues that any particular culture does not have the problem of a four-fold alienation, our model can still be fruitful by re-emphasizing the need of this four-fold union. Amaladoss notes that this kind of useful comparative study can help in reduction of tension and to look for common social concerns.[24]

However, there are two problems in relation to inter-contextual concerns. Obviously, our model of the atonement will not be directly meaningful to people of other religions like Islam, Buddhism, Confucianism and so on. Thus this model of the atonement need not necessarily be equally meaningful in the near-eastern context or in China, but most traditions may have sufficient capacities to view the concept of the atonement in diverse ways. However, it is beyond the limited scope of this work to establish this in detail and we will leave the task to other scholars.

Another problem is related to vernacular language. More than 70 percent of Indians do not read or write in English but are acquainted with different, local, vernacular languages. Obviously, this work, being in English, will not be fruitful to them. The importance of translation is evident here. However, these problems do not completely deny the credibility of

---

23. Samartha, *Hindu Response*, 193.
24. Amaladoss, "Dialogue as Conflict Resolution," 21–36.

the atonement creating unions model. With this we move on to analyze the potentialities and problems related to economics and politics.

c) Economics and Politics

Despite the enormous quantity of products, especially of food that the Indian sub-continent produces (second place in the production of wheat and rice) hunger and starvation are part of the life of the poor in the country. No Indian economist can fail to highlight the glaring gap between the rich and the poor in the country. Moreover, it is often said that the poor should be mobilized to fight against the dominant and ruling classes to ensure a fair distribution of resources. C. T. Kurien, a leading economist of the country writes,

> A plan to fight poverty does not rely mainly on technical competence. Neither can it be the product of mere formal exercises. It begins with the awareness that a fight against poverty is in the first instance a fight against the power of the beneficiaries of the plans to accelerate 'growth.' . . . The challenge in the fight against poverty is to mobilize the masses against such a mighty combination of powers and principalities.[25]

Nevertheless, the rich and affluent continuing to prosper and the poor and vulnerable continuing to suffer is a problem of other countries as well, including the West. For example, the homeless and the refugees in big cities like London and Birmingham need to be mobilized to achieve their fullness of life in the country.

The socio-economic problem of India and other countries is such that any theology or soteriology to be meaningful and relevant should consider the economic reality seriously. The human-human union established in salvation in the Visistadvaitic Hindu system of thought or established in the atonement creating unions model has its direct relevance here. Brahman/Christ is the basis on which this union is made possible and the intuitive and practical knowledge provided by Brahman/Christ is the crucial factor for this union. If there is to be real union there should be a commonality and equality amongst humanity, particularly in economic terms, to realize this union. Thus there is a direct possibility that the intuitive and practical knowledge created by Brahman/Christ includes economic concern and promotes reformation of society toward a fairer distribution of resources. However, economics obviously is a very wide

---

25. Kurien, *Poverty and Development*, 90.

field and we have only provided a direction which the atonement creating unions model can give to this area of life in society.

However, an apparent problem that again arises here is with the Visistadvaitic Hindu idea of salvation of atman alone. In Visistadvaitic Hinduism, as we saw, when one refers to a human being, particularly in relation to salvation, it is only the soul or atman which is referred to. On the other hand, in Christianity, the whole being of a human, including their physical body, is considered important. The Christian view of total human salvation should be taken as a corrective here of the Visistadvaitic Hindu system. Only a salvation that deals with the entire human being is obviously plausible as well as pragmatic.

Christ's life and message evidently puts forward the human-human union on the basis of equality. In Solle's words, "What is binding on his [Christ's] followers is his cause, his kingdom."[26] An equality included in the process of salvation is expressed by the prophet Isa and later it is attributed to John the Baptist. John the Baptist is recorded as saying,

> As is written in the book of the words of Isa the prophet: A voice of one calling in the desert, Prepare the way for the Lord, make straight paths for him. Every valley shall be filled in, every mountain and hill made low. The crooked roads shall become straight, the rough ways smooth. And all mankind will see God's salvation.[27]

Perhaps John the Baptist equates "the valley" with the poor and "the mountain" and "hill" are those who accumulate more wealth than needed. These words of John are a passionate cry for the required equality amongst humanity in our present times as well.

Another similar insight for economic and political equality comes from Gabrielle Dietrich. She, in fact, argues that such an equality could come from a joint effort of Christians and Hindus in the society. In her words,

> To renounce the fruits of one's action, to renounce the personal gains of a privileged position in the society and to work shoulder to shoulder with the poor and deprived, is exactly what is needed, not only from an idealistic point of view, but also an economic one . . . Sacrifice can be advocated from a Christian,

---

26. Solle, *Christ the Representative*, 117.
27. Luke 3:4–6, NIV.

Hindu or Communist background but needs the effort of cooperation to make the various attempts more fruitful.[28]

Interestingly, as both the saving concept of Brahman and the atonement creating unions model maintain a need of human-human union for salvation it is possible that people of both the traditions work together for economic equality and development. This struggle revolving around economics should be an ongoing struggle and is not confined to a particular period in history. The identification of Christ with the poor and suffering in history should be viewed as a corrective for the more ontological concept of Brahman's saving function and lead to more development works aimed at salvation of the whole person through the four-fold union.

In terms of potentialities and problems with regard to politics, both the traditions strive for a just society of equality and harmony. The human-human union which is emphasized by both the traditions stress that laws should be responsible and helpful for the society.

However, whilst Christ's death on the cross is as a result of political and religious cause, Brahman does not directly relate to the political arena of the society. This does not mean that Hinduism keeps it away from politics, but one of the major political sects of India, namely the *Bharatiya Janata* Party, is based on Hindu religious beliefs. Thus our model of the atonement, claiming to have implications for politics is justified by the active participation of Hindus in politics.

d) Ecology

India is a country which also faces a serious ecological crisis. Deforestation and unnecessary killing of different species are rampant and go unchecked. Nonetheless, ecology is a concern of other Asian countries and most countries around the globe as well. Russell Chandran, an Indian theologian writes,

> During the last two or three decades there has been a growing concern, expressed globally, about the threats to life on our planet . . . Warnings about the seriousness of the pollution caused to the environment, air, land and water have been given by scientists, economists and politicians . . . Humans have interfered with eco-systems through indiscriminate use of land, deforestation, pollution of water, air etc . . . The concern for ecology today is not a luxury concern but a matter of survival . . .[29]

28. Dietrich, "Educational Situation in India," 19.
29. Nehring, *Ecology*, 3–4.

Helpfully, there is an increasing awareness found among the writings of Chandran and other theologians on ecological concerns. Sallie McFague points out that humanity in the past have considered nature as valuable and as part of human life. In her words,

> Strange as it may seem, it is only during the last few hundred years that human beings have considered nature more like an object than like another subject. For most of human history we have believed that nature is more like us than we are like it . . . Nature was not merely a natural resource for human gain.[30]

Interestingly, the saving concept of Brahman has pushed us to find a meaning through the atonement not only in relation to the divine and fellow human beings but also with nature. Visistadvatic Hinduism undoubtedly has a strong emphasis on the divinity of nature. In fact, nature is always thought of as matter that is to be in union with Brahman. Sankara goes further, to say that nature is part of Brahman itself. However, Ramanuja's philosophy, which we follow here, acknowledges only the divinity of nature and he sees Brahman and nature in union with the self-body analogy. This directly implies that we ought to be in union with nature as we understand it comes within the purview of the trinitarian union. In this context, the potentiality of including the importance of nature in the analysis of the atonement emerges powerfully from Visistadvaitic Hindu thought.

Nonetheless, Christianity is not far from understanding nature as essential for human existence. McFague points out the intrinsic union between us and nature by claiming that if we are like a fish in the ocean, nature is like the ocean.[31] Attractively, McFague goes on to put forward that nature should be included in soteriological discussions. She writes,

> While the picture was anthropocentric and hierarchical, with its focus on the salvation of human individuals, it can still provide us with an interesting case study in God-human-nature integration as we attempt to undo the much more devastating effects of the Newtonian worldview, the one that dominates contemporary thinking.[32]

Thus there are theologians who have already seen nature as significant in soteriological-talk. The atonement creating unions model has the potential to include a human-nature union in a world grappling with the ecological crisis. Our union with nature can be of mutual nourishment

30. McFague, *Super, Natural Christians*, 46
31. McFague, *Super, Natural Christians*, 16.
32. McFague, *Super, Natural Christians*, 23.

when we love nature. McFague again says that nature should be loved in incarnational terms. She writes,

> Christians should love nature—a way in keeping with the earthly, bodily theology suggested by the tradition's incarnationalism, a way that allows us to love the natural world for its intrinsic worth, to love it, in all its differences and detail, in itself, for itself ... How Christians should love nature is by obeying a simple but very difficult axiom: pay attention to it.[33]

The atonement creating unions model insists that humanity needs to be in union with nature by loving it, something that includes promoting its wellbeing. Though McFague's insight of loving nature is illuminating, her claim of mere paying attention to it is too simplistic. Being in union bound by love is not just a matter of attention alone, but it is manifest by loving nature—expressed in our action toward assisting it to flourish. We ought to love nature as we love ourselves because nature is part of us and we are part of it. The saving concept of Brahman portrays that the divine is in union with nature in the same way as the divine is in union with humanity. Here we see a corrective to Christianity known for its predominant emphasis on divine-human union from Visistadvaitic Hinduism that lays great emphasis on divine-nature union. None of the traditional Christian theories have sufficient potential to include the human-nature union in the atonement. Potentially there are further possibilities. We have already seen how Jesus loved nature. The atonement creating model is justified in insisting human-nature union not only in terms of contextual insight but by the gravity of today's ecological crisis too.

e) Psychology

Next we deal with the potentialities and problems in relation to psychology. Psychology makes it plain that one can live in a self-alienated state. In other words, one can sometimes experience a split within the self. This is often referred to as the split between the "bad self" and the "good self." For example, Hinshel Wood writes, "These developments have come about as a result of recognizing that the ego can come to organize a 'bad self' which is endowed with especially large quantities of death-instinct impulses, which can then dominate the 'good self' by intimidation or seduction."[34] Thus it is clear that

---

33. McFague, *Super, Natural Christians*, 27.
34. Wood, *Dictionary of Kleinian Thought*, 421.

in psychological terms a split can occur within one's self. This deformation of the self is caused largely by depression, fear, guilt and guilt feelings.

The saving concept of Brahman persuades one to be in union with one's self. Nevertheless, in Visistadvaitic Hinduism, it is not getting away from guilt and sin but it is transcending *maya* and *avidya*. On the other hand, in Christianity, one-oneself union is caused by the assurance of forgiveness through the atonement. However, both traditions view one's union with oneself as a state of mind within a liberated/saved human existence. The overcoming of double-mindedness or alienation of one with oneself is an important contribution of the atonement model formulated using the saving concept of Brahman. John Hick says, "If one believes that one is in one's deepest being, identical with the infinite and eternal Brahman, one will seek to negate the present false ego and its distorting vision in order to attain that which both transcends and underlies it."[35] We see a similar thought in Christianity when St. Paul says that it is not he but it is Christ who lives in him. Moreover, as Moltmann says, "The knowledge of the cross . . . alienates alienated man. And in this way, it restores the humanity of dehumanized man."[36] Thus, we have made it clear that one-oneself union is dualistic in its nature.

f) Belief and Understanding

The saving concept of Brahman revolves around the four-fold union. Using this concept, we had outlined a model of the atonement. An element of belief is essential to experience and understand the divine initiative of grace for salvation in both the traditions. Anselm says, "I believe so that I understand." Daniel Migiliore adopts *Faith Seeking Understanding* as the title of one of his books to show that both should go together.[37] In Visistadvaitic Hinduism as well as in Christianity, belief in the divine is essential to understand the purposes of our lives in this world. Hence, in relation to the aspects of belief and understanding, there is no obvious reason why both of the theological traditions should not be compatible at a fundamental level. There are other parallels.

Both the traditions base their belief on scripture. Clooney points out that for advaitins, Brahman is knowledge and scripture is the path to this knowledge.[38] This is true to Visistadvaitins too. Thus there is no problem

---

35. Hick, *Problems of Religious Pluralism*, 70.
36. Moltmann, *Crucified*, 71.
37. Migiliore, *Faith Seeking Understanding*, 1.
38. Clooney, *Theology After Vedanta*, 20.

with the importance given to scriptures both in Visistadvaitic Hinduism and Christianity. Both Christians and Visistadvaitic Hindus believe in revelation of God's word as the scripture. Further, God is personal both in the Christian tradition and for Ramanuja.

Ramanuja believes that there is an objective as well as a subjective side in salvation becoming possible. This we analyzed with the help of the *Tengalai* and *Vadagalai* Hindus. As we used the saving concept of Brahman in explicating the atonement creating unions model, our model re-asserted that there is an objective as well as a subjective dimension to the atoning work of Christ. Thus the potentiality of the objective and subjective sides of the atonement is brought out in our model of the atonement.

In Christianity, faith is affirmed by repeating the Apostles and the Nicene Creed. Now, one could ask us if the Apostles creed, which is used more often in churches, can include the dimension of union in relation to salvation in Christ. Any change should be acceptable to believers and our model is not final but is open to change and is to be judged by others. However, repeating the need of union, using the creed could help us in applying it in practical life as well.

Certainly, the atonement understood by using the saving concept of Brahman receives the insight of basing belief in historical facts like testimonies and reiteration of truths by religious teachers throughout centuries. But there is a problem because Brahman itself is not a historical character. Thus whilst the atoning work of Christ is mainly evident in a historical sense using the historical life of Christ the concept of the saving knowledge in Visistadvaitic Hinduism is understood in manifold ways. For Visistadvaitic Hinduism, faith is established through intuitive or transcendent experience of an individual, study of scriptures and hearing the testimony of the many wise rishis speaking out the same truths over thousands of years. The inner conviction is based in the divine sight of the third eye center, ajna chakra. Rightly founded, faith transcends reason, but does not conflict with reason.

Thus, Visistadvaitic Hinduism teaches Christianity to re-emphasize the human experiences of intuition and learning from *gurus* (priests/teachers). However, Visistadvaitic Hinduism could learn from Christianity to seek ways in which the concept of Brahman can have a concrete historical basis because it is history that teaches us of practical realities. Significantly, it is also *historical particularity* that brings about the importance of each human being living in a particular period of time.

Another problem which needs to be pointed out is in relation to understanding. Whilst the atonement aims for universal, trans-contextual understanding derived from a particular contextualized fact, the saving concept of Brahman is intended for universal, trans-contextual understanding and is not derived from a particular contextual fact as such. Thus when one seeks to understand the atonement, using the saving concept of Brahman one needs to be aware of the difference in understanding evolved in both the traditions. Whilst, the atoning work of Christ has a contextual particularity of Golgotha, the saving concept of Brahman transcends any geographical context.

2) Theological Concerns

a) Nature of Four-Fold Union

In Christianity, divine-human union is largely understood with both the analogies of father-child union and bridegroom-bride union. In John 14 Jesus says, "I am going to prepare room for you so that you can be with me . . . there is enough place in my father's house." This is like a life of a happy bridegroom and bride living in union. Thus, the divine-human union is based on love. Ramanuja understands that a human, in a saved state, will be in union with Brahman as a self is in union with the body. Samartha says,

> To Ramanuja, God is all-inclusive in the sense that all things are in him and within the Godhead there is both cit (conscious spirit) and acit (unconscious matter) . . . To Ramanuja, because of his doctrine of inseparability, both matter and consciousness are within the Godhead itself.[39]

This poses a problem for Christian understanding of divine-human union. Both the analogies of father-child union and bridegroom-bride union, imply that one does not include the other and they can be in union whilst still they are distinctively different from each other. Madhava, another philosopher of (dvaitic) Hinduism says that a human can be in "union" with Brahman in terms of relationship alone. A Brahman-atman merging of any sort is not possible at all. Generally, it is understood that Madhava is closer to the Christian understanding of salvation. Nevertheless, we have followed Ramanuja's thought on the means to salvation because of his unique self-body union philosophy that gives a basis for reflection and practice of the four-fold union. Julius Lipner rightly says that a Hindu Christian can have firm faith in Christ, but at the same time can be enriched and transformed by the Hindu meaning of life.[40] Further, Ramanuja's thought is not completely different from a Christian view. It is at times argued that in the framework

---

39. Samartha, *Hindu Response*, 163.
40. Forward, *Ultimate Visions*, 167–75.

of an Indian's religious reflection the theistic-advaita of Ramanuja, with its emphasis on self-body union is more suitable for working out a Christology than any other system of thought. The significant experience, which both the analogies hold, is of a wholistic life worth living in union with the divine. Both Visistadvaitic Hinduism and Christianity further expand the need for a human-human union, human-nature union and one-oneself union. Thus mutual enrichment is possible with the self-body analogy of Ramanuja and bridegroom-bride analogy of the New Testament.

Further, in relation to the notion of the church, St. Paul says that it is the body of Christ. Though St. Paul understands that Christ is the head and the church is his body it has a direct bearing on the self-body analogy of Ramanuja.[41] Also, the idea of absorption into the divine as a drop of water into the ocean so that one can no longer identify it is generally inimical to Western Christian thought. However, the self-body image does have the potential and will relate directly to the notion of being filled with the mind of Christ, letting one's life be directed by the spirit of God. Finally, as both divine and human are being united in both the traditions this union is of "dualistic" nature.

Regarding human-human union it is not wrong to say that both the traditions see it in terms of brotherhood. Ramanuja says that it is the same Brahman who lives in all of us and it is that which provides the ground for human-human union. St. Paul's understanding that it is Christ who lives in him, is not far from the thought of Ramanuja. Further, in both the traditions the nature of human-human union is trinitarian in the sense that the union is established in and through the divine who lives in all. In fact, it is a human-divine-human union.

When it comes to human-nature union, in Visistadvaitic Hinduism, it is again the same Brahman who lives in all beings, not just in human beings. But in Christianity, Christ is generally not thought of as living in other beings. However, Christ loved nature and it is Christ's love toward nature that motivates us to live in union with nature around us. Thus it may not

---

41. Brockington comments, "Were it not that Ramanuja sees this relationship in at least quasi-physical terms, there would also be some analogy with St. Paul's use of the image of the Church as the Body of Christ, when he talks of Christians as being incorporated in Christ and envisages the Christian community as a harmoniously coordinated organism, even regarding Christ as the living body of which Christians are the limbs." Brockington goes on to say that Ramanuja is a panentheist. However, this would be too simple a description of Ramanuja because, though Ramanuja uses the self-body analogy, as we have noted in chapter 2, he is careful to insist that the world as the body of Brahman is dependent on Brahman. He is also careful to say that Brahman is not dependent on the world. Brockington, *Hinduism and Christianity*, 10

be wrong to discern this union as a trinitarian union in the sense that it is a human-divine-nature union.

Finally, one-oneself union is also well emphasized and given appropriate importance in both the traditions. The nature of one-oneself union in both the traditions is a dualistic one since it is again a union of our essential self with the divine who lives in us.

b) Particularity and Universality

Although there is significance in stressing the historical particularity of the atonement, it cannot be denied that the same particularity also poses vital problems for Christian theology. Historical particularity remains a problem for Christianity throughout history as expressed by Lucien Richard. Richard claims,

> The constraints of history are basically the constraints of context; they are essentially those of time and space. Dietrich Bonhoeffer captured quite well the constraint of history by affirming that all historical events are 'penultimate' that their ultimate significance lies in a reality that transcends them and transcends all the empirical coordinates of human existence. Few would dispute the observation that our contemporary understanding of history poses a fundamental challenge to traditional orthodox Christianity. That challenge is the challenge of the constraints of history on everything that touches human reality as human.[42]

It is here that we need to re-affirm that the atonement should be construed as relevant for all times and not for a particular period in history, though the life, death and resurrection of Christ occurred in a particular point in history. Galloway says that redemption is cosmic since Christ took the experience of the world unto himself.[43] The atonement creating unions model outlined in the previous chapter, unlike most other theories of the atonement, considers this problem seriously. It may be pointed out that whilst Christians believe in a linear history, Visistadvaitic Hindus believe in a cyclic history.[44] Here, Visistadvaitic Hinduism stresses that the atonement should be seen as that which has universal significance for all times.

42. Costa, *One Faith, Many Cultures*, 54. For a discussion of personal redemption and cosmic redemption see, Galloway, *Cosmic Christ*, 99. Galloway points out that Irenaeus, like most Westerners, restricts "the work of the Devil to that of tempting the heart of man, rather than as being related to the fallen state of the cosmos as a whole."

43. Galloway, *Cosmic Christ*, 250.

44. For a brief understanding of the cosmic cycles see Harre, *One Thousand Years*, 40.

THE ATONEMENT CREATING UNIONS

However, the particularity of the atonement is of crucial importance in Christianity and it has profound validity as well. Theologians like Gunton and White insist on the particularity of the atonement. Gunton writes,

> The distinctiveness of the Christian theology of the atonement, its particularity, derives from the distinctive way in which it construes the human condition and identifies its redemption: its unique combination of historical dynamic and moral realism . . . the universality is historically focussed because only so can the dynamic of history, the nature of man and woman as created in the image of God, the radicality of evil and the redemption of the world be held together.[45]

Similar to Gunton, White also after an extensive analysis of the universal and particular nature of the atonement writes, "In this area of doctrine at least, credibility arises precisely from particularity."[46] The atonement being an event in history has its own merits. On the importance of history, Schillebeeckx says,

> faith utterances must have a basis in the history of Jesus something must have issued which people could, should and in the end were compelled by their faith to express, and rightly express, in those faith-utterances. There must have been something in the historical situation to indicate that anyone who sees Jesus has actually seen the Father.[47]

Here the saving concept of Brahman should realize the validity of having a historical basis for the understanding of the means to salvation. As Samartha says,

> The discussion is in connection with the nature of Jesus Christ, his relation to God and to man understood historically. Both the existential understanding of the self as a 'Being-next-to God' as Heidegger remarks and the mystical description of the atman as being identical with Brahman himself do not seem to give sufficient importance to man as a historical personality . . .[48]

We conclude that the saving concept of Brahman should consider correcting itself recognizing the significance of historical particularity.

---

45. Gill, *Readings in Modern Theology*, 161.

46. White insists that unless God enters into one part of the world in particular, and in one part of the time in history, he cannot touch the whole world effectively. See White, *Atonement and Incarnation*, 116.

47. Schillebeeckx, *Jesus*, 604.

48. Samartha, *Hindu Response*, 187.

Particularity becomes significant because we live in a particular period of history with all human experiences. The incarnation and the cross portray the love of God. Only when the love of God is seen in the particular can it be seen anywhere and always. In fact, the worst possible thing that can happen to us is suffering and death. But Christianity claims that it is here we find God in Christ. It is a paradox and a challenge to faith. Particularity matters because it is what makes the ideal real. This further enables us to find God in the sufferings of poverty, unattractiveness and marginalization without this possibility one could give no sense to the claim of the omnipresence of the Divine reality. Here, there is definitely a Christian contribution to the saving concept of Brahman, for a transformation of its conceptions.

c) Pluralism and Unity

Interestingly, the saving concept of Brahman has helped us to discuss the unity which the atonement brings between the past, the present and the future. The saving function of Brahman as an ongoing process has helped us to analyze the relevance of the atonement to the *ante-christum natum* and the *post-christum natum* situations. It is true that the relevance of the atonement should be found in all periods. In this sense our model of the atonement has helpfully brought a unity between the different times of history.

We have also noted that the "saving function of Brahman" transcends religious identities and brings a unity on the basis of being human. This vision is particularly important in a world blighted by hostility in the name of religion. Thomas Thangaraj, in his work on mission, argues that being human and not belonging to one religion should be the basis of theologizing in a multi-religious world.[49] Thangaraj gives his creative proposal of a *missio humanitas*, arguing that a genuine dialog with those from other traditions best proceeds from an appreciation of a common humanity. The particularities of tradition—theism, Christocentrism, trinitarianism, incarnation and emphasis on revelation in scripture can follow only after participants recognize a common humanity.[50] Our "union" model of the atonement, based on the intuitive and practical knowledge of a four-fold union, envisions the atonement as a doctrine which can fervently call for a unity on the basis of being human and on a wider unity. Thus our model of the atonement moves beyond the narrow understandings of mere intellectual faith in Christ, being the basis of salvation, to a practical life with four-fold union as the foundation of salvation in Christ.

49. Thangaraj, *Common Task*, 20.
50. Thangaraj, *Common Task*, 20.

Moreover, the saving concept of Brahman provides a unity between the different theological doctrines within Visistadvaitic Hinduism. Similarly, with regard to Christianity, Moltmann says, "The death of Jesus on the cross is the *center* of all Christian theology."[51] This insight has provoked us to analyze the unity which the doctrine of the atonement can bring between the various doctrines within Christianity.

Here, we end by recollecting that the church has not formally formulated a standard understanding of the doctrine of the atonement. And if the church formulates a doctrine of the atonement, amongst other ways in which the atonement is fathomed, our model needs to be given adequate consideration because it explores and analyses in detail the crucial issue of manifold alienations, which hinders the development, peace, harmony and indeed salvation itself.

d) Tradition and Reformation

Another significant area which we attempt to identify is the potentialities and problems revolving around the theme of tradition and reformation. Any theologian who ventures to outline a model of the atonement should ask if the model maintains the uniqueness and decisiveness of the life and work of Christ. Precisely, in what ways the atonement creating unions model are authentic in the light of Christian tradition is the question for us to answer. Brahman is the ultimate factor and is decisive in the Visistadvaitic Hindu tradition. Further, the atonement creating unions model takes into account the totality of the life and work of Christ into consideration. Hence, the possibility of viewing the atonement through the lens of the saving concept of Brahman must portray Christ and his work as unique and decisive.

In the previous sections, we have evaluated the atonement creating unions model in terms of its metaphysical, inter-contextual, economic, political, ecological and psychological, particularity and universal, and pluralism and unity dimensions. Nevertheless, we should go beyond these dimensions to analyze and include the spiritual dimension of humanity. Thus the question before us is whether this model of the atonement is sufficiently appropriate for worship and the liturgy of the church.

There are theologians who see the uniqueness of Christ as a problem in a world of pluralism. For instance, Paul Knitter says that the stumbling block to any real conversation with other religious traditions is "the central Christian belief in the uniqueness of Christ."[52] Interestingly, Knitter

---

51. Moltmann, *Crucified*, 204.
52. Knitter, *No Other Name?*, 17.

himself has been keen on observing that the uniqueness of Christ is central to Christianity. We do not think that the center can be changed, for if the center is changed then Christianity will be like bread without yeast. Further, there will not be any matter for conversation. The uniqueness of Christ is what renders the theology of the atonement central to Christian life and thought. Salvation is assured because God himself suffered in Christ. It is the life, suffering, death and resurrection that bring the assurance and confidence of salvation in and through Christ, based on faith.

An outward study of the doctrine of atonement in the history of Christianity itself will show that theology of the atonement is constructed in such a way as to enable a devotional and contemplative worship. Worship is again based on the belief in the uniqueness of Christ. Notably, theologians throughout the centuries have taken care to articulate theology of the atonement in a way that has enormous potentiality to invite humanity for a poignant response and inspire them to bearing witness in church and society. For example, Athanasius writes,

> Even the very creation broke silence at His behest and, marvellous to relate, confessed with one voice before the cross, the monument of victory, that He who suffered thereon in the body was not man only, but Son of God and Savior of all. The sun veiled his face, the earth quaked, the mountains were rent asunder, all men were stricken with awe. These things showed that Christ on the cross was God, and that all creation was His slave and was bearing witness by its fear to the presence of its Master.[53]

Does the atonement creating unions model have this kind of an appeal for worship and witness? There is a problem here which, however, can be set aside. The interpretation of Christ as Brahman itself does not have a place for worship and adoration because Brahman is beyond any personality. However, Brahman, when personified is called *Isvara*. Hindu literature is full of praise and adoration for *Isvara*. For example, a folk song goes like this,

> *I went in search of Isvara*
> *I did not find him anywhere else*
> *But only in abiding love.*[54]

This song is often used for worship in churches. Moreover, as we noted earlier, there are Christian theologians who have attempted to perceive

---

53. Athanasius, *On the Incarnation*, 48.
54. Folk song—often sung in worship services.

Christ as Brahman. Hence, properly interpreted, the atonement creating unions model has enough space to maintain the uniqueness and decisiveness of Christ for the worshiping community of Christians.

It is also important for us to re-assert that the atonement creating unions model, as outlined in chapter 4, is provided as an additional alternative in an Indian context to the existing traditional theories of the atonement. The inadequacy of the traditional models was elucidated in chapter 3 and here we will not repeat the details. Here it is worth noting that this model safeguards the doctrine of the atonement from the dominant criticisms devised in an Indian context. Thus the primary function of atonement creating unions model, evolving in an Indian context, is a reformation in construing theology of the atonement in that context in the first instance.

Another interesting phenomenon is that the atonement, traditionally, is accepted as an expression of the love of God. For example, Felix Podimattam, a Catholic theologian of India says, "the life and death of Jesus are not just convenient ways of letting us know that God loves us. They reveal the innermost nature of God as love, compassion, communication—an infinitely gentle, infinitely suffering being."[55] Further, in 1 John 4:8 we read that whoever does not love his brothers/fellow men does not know God, for God is love.[56] Does the atonement creating unions model include the concern of the love of God? Brahman, as the divine ultimate being is understood as both without qualities (*nirguna*) and with all good qualities (*saguna*). The *nirguna* Brahman is problematic here, but the *saguna* Brahman is with all good qualities including love. Ramanuja emphasizes that Brahman is a reality with attributes (*saguna* Brahman). Brahman provides grace to humanity because of its manifest love toward the creation. This implies that when the atonement is construed using the saving concept of Brahman, the atonement can be understood as the manifestation of God's love in Christ toward his creation. The very nature of the divine allowing the possibility of human union with the divine itself shows God's love toward humanity. Moreover, his love for all creatures is seen when he becomes the ground of the four-fold union. In fact, humanity can have a life in its fullness only when a human-nature union is possible. Thus this model of the atonement obviously is potential enough to safeguard the dimension of the love of God revealed in the atoning work of Christ.

We need to comment on the use of the word, liberation by Hindu theologians and on the use of the word, salvation in Christian thought. The word, liberation used in theological terminology implicitly suggests that humanity

---

55. Podimattam, "Why Would a Good God?," 205
56. 1 John 4:8.

is in a state of bondage. On the other hand, the word, salvation puts emphasis on deliverance from danger. Though the Visistadvaitic Hindu emphasis is on liberation from *avidya* and *maya* and the Christian emphasis is on salvation from sin—liberation and salvation are obviously related concepts. Nonetheless, theologians within the Christian tradition have preferred to use the word liberation in the place of salvation. For example, Michael Winter prefers to use the word liberation instead of salvation.[57] Further, all liberation theologians use the word, liberation instead of salvation. Hence, it is clear that the words liberation and salvation can convey a difference in emphasis, yet ultimately they can be interchangeably used without a major change in their meaning. Thus the difference in the use of the words—liberation in Visistadvaitic Hinduism and salvation in Christianity—does not pose any serious problem in viewing the atoning work of Christ through the lens of the liberating concept of Brahman.

Finally, is the atonement creating unions model acceptable to traditional Christians or people who are Christians for several generations? Remarkably, within the New Testament itself there are several understandings of the atonement. Further, as we noted, the Christian tradition does not offer us with one standard version of the atonement, but rather a set of diverse and distinct understandings of the atonement. It is in this context, a theologian becomes aware of flexibility and the need to interpret the atonement to suit different religious contexts. Thus, the atonement creating unions model of the atonement is justified by the relevance it has to an Indian religious context where Visistadvaitic Hindus and Christians live together as neighbors.

Nonetheless, the atonement creating unions model is not justified by contextual relevance alone. The aspect of four-fold unions, though not brought out in its full extent, has been part of Christian writing. For example, Christ's union with humanity, particularly at his time of death is pointed out by St. Athanasius. He says, "Wherefore, the Word, as I said, being Himself incapable of death, assumed a mortal body, that He might offer it as His own in place of all, and suffering for the sake of all through His *union* with it."[58] Further, Jesus' vision of the kingdom of God is a life of unity. This concept of union is found in the Old Testament itself. The prophet Isa envisages a life together not only as humans but with all creation.[59]

It has become clear that some traditional theories flourished in the Greek and Roman societies of the past. However, the space for understanding

---

57. Winter, *Atonement*, 6.
58. Athanasius, *On the Incarnation*, 49. Emphasis added.
59. Isa 40.

the atonement in terms of union is seen more clearly in some recent theologians. For instance, Maurice says,

> If the Gospel be the revelation or unveiling of a mystery hidden from ages and generations; if this mystery be the true constitution of humanity in Christ, so that a man believes and acts a lie who does not claim for himself union with Christ, we can understand why the deepest writings of the New Testament, instead of being digests of doctrine, are epistles, explaining to those who had been admitted into the church of Christ their own position, bringing out that side of it which had reference to the circumstances in which they were placed, or to their most besetting sins, and showing what life was in consistency, what life at variance with it . . . The fact of a union between Godhead and humanity is thus set forth as the one which the Apostle felt himself appointed to proclaim, ...[60]

As we have said in chapter 3, there are no models of atonement in relation to the four-fold union. However, the principle of union, as we have pointed out, is part of Christian tradition. In this sense, when we ascribe the principle of union to the atonement it is concurrent with an existing tradition, which, indeed has been marginalized and obscured by the various theories of the atonement. The atonement creating unions model highlights a line of thought through which the atonement can be understood. Whilst it is a model that evolves from an Indian context of Visistadvaitic Hinduism, it is also a model that can be immensely useful in the conversation between theologians interested in the doctrine of the atonement around the globe.

Theology should not be a one-way street in which thought-provoking insights concerning the atonement are purely translated or transliterated in today's set phrase. It is a two-way street in which theological concerns and the anxieties of the situation interact and persuade each other. As Ernst Troeltsch says from a Christian point of view, "We cannot live without a religion, yet the only religion that we can endure is Christianity, for Christianity has grown up with us and has become part of our very being."[61] This belonging to Christianity is part of tradition. Obviously, a Visistadvaitic Hindu would see that they totally belong to that Hindu tradition and will not be able to think of anything that ignores that tradition. However, our model of the atonement is a reformed model since we have moved beyond one tradition, in fact, to look at another tradition and, to look at our own tradition differently. The concern for the significance of the atonement brings

60. Galloway, *Basic Readings in Theology*, 297.
61. Hick and Hebblethwaite, *Christianity and Other Religions*, 25.

new connotations and correctives into the saving concept of Brahman, and the saving concept of Brahman, in turn, enriches and makes relevant the theology of the atonement to an Indian context. Indubitably, this effort will help theologians to probe for new directions to explicate the significance of the atonement. It is our hope that the atonement creating unions model will help theology of the atonement to be relevant to an Indian context and elsewhere in terms of plausibility and reformation in understanding as well as in terms of fruitful human existence in the society under the divine. The atonement creating unions model obviously is a model of the atonement that is adequate for teaching oneself a life that is enriching and fulfilling and envisages an individual living in union with oneself, in a world with other fellow human beings, with nature and with the divine.

In sum, the knowledge of two different religions has helped us in the formulation and the evaluation of a fresh model of the atonement. Today's world is enriched by the knowledge of different religions meeting together. The atonement creating unions model is broadly a theological construction where the West and the East meet. It is here we need to comment on how our analysis of the means to salvation in two different traditions is one of mutual transformation.

Kim suggests that an uncritical synthesis of Hindu and Christian traditions is to be unfaithful to both Hinduism and Christianity.[62] We have overcome this problem by analyzing both similarities and differences. Having made clear the similarities and differences between a Hindu and a Christian view of understanding the means of salvation, it is also significant to note that a dialectic approach to a subject should have as its goal mutual enrichment and mutual transformation. Visistadvaitic Hinduism believes in cognition and knowledge for salvation whereas Christianity is based on volition. There are advantages and disadvantages in stressing either knowledge or choice/freewill. Transcending the differences between Visistadvaitic Hindu and Christian understandings of the means to salvation, we are certain that examination of the human mind and the advancement of wisdom to overcome blind impulses would help humanity face all crises.

Nevertheless, the plurality of constructions of atonement theology only tells us that different atonement theologies are relevant to different cultures. When many atonement theologies are possible, the criterion for judging our model of atonement theology is by seeing if it is applicable to the Indian context where Christians and Visistadvaitic Hindus live and grow together. Other atonement theologies need not be judged by this criterion because they are constructed for different contexts, times and from

---

62. Kim, *In Search of Identity*, 196.

different perspectives. Also, our criterion of judgment is a tentative one because the future of religions is not open to us. A total merging of religions could be possible in a multi-religious world as they exist side by side. Here, we conclude that although our model of the atonement has a few problems it is useful in a context where Christians and Visistadvaitic Hindus live together as brothers and sisters. No doubt, our model views the atonement in a fresh and fruitful direction.

e) The Atonement Creating Unions and Central Biblical Notions

Finally, we very briefly outline that our atonement model falls within the central biblical thrusts of *Torah* and *new covenant* and this should be seen as a potentiality of our model. The Bible portrays that humanity alienated itself from God by disobeying his commandments. The Torah too could not deliver humanity from its fallen state. A new covenant was essential. Alan Torrance says,

> the recognition of God and the divine purpose suggests, however, that sure access to God's purpose will involve access to God's expressly disclosed and endorsed purpose, namely, his covenant purposes for humanity as these are defined in the *kaine diutheke*, the New Covenant and which is the fulfillment of all that may properly be described as "law" (Torah), that is, as the divinely declared objective will of God. What this implies is that *synteresis* and *suneidesis*, theologically conceived, must properly refer to our reconciled participation *en Christo* as this includes the subjective epistemic transformation that attends and characterizes it.[63]

In fact, the Bible as well as the Christian tradition insist that God has done everything for our salvation on the cross. Hence, both the objective and subjective sides of the atonement should be understood in the light of the fully accomplished work of Christ. On the atonement, Alan Torrance writes,

> It is to speak of a "new humanity" characterized by a new apperception where the paradigms that mould and condition every dimension of our being (our relating, our interpreting and our understanding) are transformed and reconciled and reconstituted in and through that event of epistemic at-one-ment between God and humanity—an at-one-ment of mind which is

63. Torrance and Banner, *Doctrine of God*, 171.

Christ's and which is only realized in us as we are recreated by the Spirit to participate *en Christo*.[64]

In relation to the concepts of covenant and Torah Alan Torrance goes on to say, "the grammar of the categories of *berit* (covenant) *hesed* (covenant faithfulness) and torah are fundamentally filial (and not legal) in character. They are koinonial and participative and any legislative function requires to be interpreted in this context."[65] The atonement creating unions model strives to point out that the four-fold union created in and through the atonement. The grace and love of God manifested on the cross powerfully teaches us the objective side of the atonement. In the words of Ellen Charry, "Disregarding our sins because of the sacrifice of Christ's life on our behalf is good news. We can let go of our shame before God if, indeed, that is what we suffer from, trusting that God accepts us, warts and all."[66] Again, as Torrance stresses the subjective side of the cross should also be interpreted within the "fully accomplished" understanding of the cross. Precisely, forgiveness comes first and not sin. God in Christ has already granted us himself so that we might be reconciled and united with him, with one-another, with nature and with ourselves. In the light of our atonement model humanity's moral obligation is not to work toward salvation—but to live in the joy, assurance, recognition and confidence that Christ has already done everything needed for our salvation. This is not to say that we need to sin more so that grace will abound more. As Paul cautions us,

> What then are we to say? Should we continue in sin in order that grace may abound? By no means! How can we who died to sin go on living in it? . . . For if we are united with him in a death like his, we will certainly be united with him in a resurrection like his.[67]

In Visistadvaitic thought, this idea is not prevalent. The notion of subjective response to Brahman's initiative is more or less seen outside the realm of Brahman's grace. Here again, in my view, Visistadvaitic Hinduism could seek to work of a way in which humanity could live in the joy, assurance and confidence of salvation/liberation.

---

64. Torrance and Banner, *Doctrine of God*, 171. Interpreting Paul, Torrance says, "to make ethical discernments is, for Paul, simply to recognize our place within the epic story of redemption."

65. Torrance and Banner, *Doctrine of God*, 173.

66. Charry, *Inquiring After God*, 232.

67. Rom 6:1–5.

Thus, although our model of the atonement is fruitful, meaningful, creative and enhancing it should be used with caution. It is also our hope that our work on the atonement will initiate a plausible conversation between Christian and Visistadvaitic traditions. On this note, we will conclude this project, after briefly highlighting the nature and use of our comparative model of the atonement. It is apt that Clooney remarks, "learned leaders must compose their own conclusions."[68] Nonetheless, we will end by highlighting the nature and use of our fresh model of the atonement with a contextual relevance.

---

68. Clooney, *Theology after Vedanta*, 208.

6

Conclusion

The Atonement Creating Unions:
Its Nature and Use

WE BEGAN BY BRIEFLY pointing out the problem of atonement theology in an Hindu-Christian Indian context. Then we outlined a background analysis of atonement theology with reference to selected New Testament themes. We also pointed out that in the Hindu context of Visistadvaitic philosophy, the New Testament theme of "union" should be emphasized if atonement theology should be readily applicable in that context. We anticipated that this understanding of the atonement will be useful not only to the Visistadvaitic Hindus but also to the Christians, because it will illuminate the atonement concept in a fresh direction. We then moved on to elucidate the concept of the means to salvation in Visistadvaitic Hinduism with special reference to Ramanuja. Further, we pointed out the inadequacy of selected models of the atonement in an Indian context or another similar inter-religious context elsewhere. This motivated us to outline a fresh model of the atonement, in a comparative doctrinal perspective, which we called the atonement creating unions. In the previous chapter, we analyzed the potentialities and problems of our model of the atonement.

In this chapter, we attempt to conclude our work by highlighting the nature of the atonement creating unions model and its usefulness in an Indian context as well as in the world context. As we mentioned in the introductory chapter, this work on the atonement with contextual relevance will also help in filling a gap in comparative theology between Christianity and Visistadvaitic Hinduism.

The Nature of the Atonement Creating Unions model.

Can Christian faith be reasonably expressed, in an inter-religious or comparative religious perspective, using the concepts and idioms of non-Christian faiths? One response is to observe that our traditional understandings of Christian doctrines have from the beginning been flavored and colored by the Greek and Roman religious symbols and attitudes in which they were first formulated. Theologians world-wide are aware of the wider cultural impact today. In a world of different religions, it is plausible to seek what each religious tradition with its own distinctiveness and uniqueness has to contribute to the understanding found within the Christian faith. Gordon Kaufman rightly says,

> it is a mistake to suppose that the universality of Christianity resides in the orthodoxy of some bygone age; on the contrary, it is something still coming into being—something still being created!—through the processes of cultural [religious] and linguistic diffusion, as new aspects and dimensions of human life and experience become incorporated into the continuing growth of the Christian vision of the world and the human.[1]

Understanding Christianity using an alien religious system enables theology to be renewed and refreshed in a world of different religions. Comparative doctrinal theology can seek to construe the meaning of divine reality through different symbols and concepts arising from the different religions. The symbol or concept of the atonement, for instance, does not convey the same meaning at the moment as it did in the second or third centuries, mainly because our intellectual and practical contexts have changed. However, it is quite possible that the meaning which the atonement had for the people of the second or third centuries was as evident to their context as the new meaning of the atonement that we hold is to today's context. Similarly, a Western understanding of the atonement need not suit an Eastern context and vice versa because the contexts are different. As Stackhouse points out, "Only theologies able to live by the power of the word, by reasonable communication able to reach across barriers of culture, civilization, and context and to call people to conviction, will be compelling."[2] Our fresh model of the atonement is a compelling theology because it adequately communicates the atoning work of Christ to people of the Visistadvaitic Hindu religious and cultural tradition.

---

1. Thangaraj, *Crucified*, 15.
2. Stackhouse, *God and Globalization*, 18.

There are those who think that the atonement is no longer a relevant concept in the present age. As Dillistone in the introduction to his work on the atonement points out, the word, atonement is hardly used in modern society.[3] Even as I began to work on the doctrine of the atonement there were theologians who said that the atonement is a dreary concept and asked me: why don't you work on something else, which is more modern?[4] But I could not agree that the concept of atonement is not exciting or has no value for us today and my passion for atonement theology has not diminished, so this work began to take shape. However, the goal I want to achieve is to show, in this work, how the atonement can speak to us even today. Although some may think the concept of atonement is irrelevant and outmoded our analysis evidently demonstrates that the atonement can be fruitfully understood in our times as it was by the New Testament writers and by the Christians of early centuries. Our hope is that it will remain as one amongst the crucial doctrines of Christianity till the very end.

The doctrine of the atonement apparently is the attempt to articulate the apprehension of faith that through Christ we are reconciled to God. The Christian faith states that our reconciliation with God is conditional on what Christ does, on his work on the cross. The accounts may and do vary but each is moved and judged by the faith that we are reconciled to God through Christ, so that the weaknesses and inadequacies of the account of Christ's work that we may give should not affect the assurance of faith.

Our work points out a fresh direction in which the atonement can be viewed in the Visistadvaitic Hindu context of India. It is our hope that our work will motivate and inspire theologians all around the globe to re-interpret the doctrine of atonement, in comparative doctrinal perspectives, drawing new meanings from it for the different religious contexts of the globe. As we noted in the introductory chapter, a similar methodology can be applied to other doctrines as well to help us find deeper meanings and purposes for our lives in this world. Thus our "unions" model of the atonement is also intended to be an inspiring one. Theologically, it is when we take pains to re-visit the different doctrines, evolving from the scripture, and clarify their use in our day to day lives that we join the holy will of God which wants us to be united with God, others, nature and ourselves.

Moreover, our attempt to outline a fresh model of the atonement, in this book, using the Visistadvaitic Hindu conception of the means to salvation, provides just a promising direction for the construction of a theology of the

---

3. Dillistone, *Christian Understanding*, 1.

4. In yet more recent years, however, it is interesting to see that the attention of theologians has turned to the concept of atonement again. The works of Brümmer and Spence, to which we have referred in this work, amongst others, testify to this fact.

atonement using other religious traditions, in comparative doctrinal perspective, and we do not claim any finality in the understanding of the atonement.[5] For that matter, no theology is ever final but all theology must always flourish through plausible conversation and the capacity relentlessly to promote life. It is here that the plurality of religions needs to be considered in constructing comparative doctrinal theology in a multi-religious world.

Throughout the Christian tradition, particularly from the sixteenth century to the end of the twentieth century, Christian theology generally maintained that only through the traditional understandings of the theology of the atonement is salvation possible. Absolute claims of this kind do not seem to be reasonable in our penultimate state and is actually socially, and hence spiritually, destructive in today's religiously plural world. Religious pluralism, in the present times, raises several questions for Christian theology. In the words of Alan Race,

> To say that we live in a religiously plural world is not new. What is new, however, is the increasing awareness that this brings with it serious theological issues for the Christian church . . . Is the presence of God to be found only within one community of faith? Or is (God) more chameleon-like than that, dancing through history, enticing men and women into faith irrespective of the cultural shape of their response? These are major questions which strike at the core of Christian conviction.[6]

The question, which we raised in this work is, "What could the atonement mean in an Indian-Visistadvaitic Hindu context?" It is precisely to this question that we attempted to construct an answer with a particular direction. Theologians of the East, living amongst people of different religious persuasions, wonder about the sense of the traditional understandings of the atonement. With the growing number of immigrants from different traditions of the East to the West, theologians of the West are also puzzled about the absolute claims frequently made in atonement theology. Hindu theologians of India, troubled by the absolute claims of atonement theology, have invited Christian theologians to engage in a reformulation of the idea of salvation as realized only through Christ's work on the cross. In this

---

5. We had already stated that, we join Dillistone in saying the more ways in which we view the doctrine of the atonement, the more we learn. However, the complexity of the atonement concept is also manifest when we attempt to penetrate into the meaning of it from more directions. Hence, one can go on pondering into the meaning of the atonement forever to make it clearer and clearer. Along with other similar works on the atonement, this work is offered as an addition by viewing the atonement from a new perspective.

6. Race, *Christians and Religious Pluralism*, 1.

book, we have constructed a theology of the atonement at a point where Christians and Visistadvaitic Hindus meet.

As we have already mentioned, we are well aware that we do not claim any finality in the understanding of the atonement. In the book of Deuteronomy, we read, "If a prophet speaks in the name of the Lord but the thing does not take place or prove true, it is a word that the Lord has not spoken. The prophet has spoken it presumptuously; do not be frightened by it."[7]

Like the prophets of Old Testament times, every theologian needs to be cognizant of the inherent jeopardy and tentativeness of all theologies of the atonement. In this sense the theology of the atonement and, for this matter, any theology will and should always remain a probe, a conversation and thus an unending task. Now, we will briefly highlight the significance of theological language in understanding the atonement and the anticipated usefulness of our study in the Indian context as well as in the world context.

Theological Language and the Atonement Creating Unions

Some final comments and observations must now be made concerning the nature of this study for the better understanding of the wider issues of the meaning and purpose of the atonement creating unions model. Each model of the atonement, which we analyzed in chapter 3, revolves around a key term. For example, "substitution" and "representation" are the key terms for the respective models. Our model revolves around the key terms "four-fold union." It is in this area that the implication of our study is to be found. The historical particularity of the atoning work of Christ portrays that Christ has already brought "salvation" to us in terms of the four-fold union. We are not kept in a position to seek for this four-fold union, but to live a practical life with the assurance and confidence that Christ has already brought about the four-fold union, which is salvation to us.

Now, what is the contribution of the key-words, "four-fold union" to the doctrine of the atonement? The key words can have explanatory as well as interpretative functions. Obviously, these key words were borrowed from the Visistadvaitic Hindu tradition to outline the atonement creating unions-model. In the Visistadvaitic Hindu tradition these words explain and interpret how and why Brahman brings about salvation. The function of these words is the same in the atonement creating unions model as well.

---

7. Deut 18:22.

Inter-Religious Theology and the Usefulness of Our Study

Inter-religious theology is a welcome theology as we live amidst various theological traditions. In this regard, it is noteworthy that there are significant works being done in comparison between Christian theology and Visistadvaitic Hindu tradition. However, theology of the atonement has not been hitherto extensively dealt with, in an inter-religious perspective, using the two aforesaid religious traditions.

In this book, we analyzed the concept of the means to salvation in the Visistadvaitic Hindu tradition. We also portrayed the inadequacy of selected models of the atonement, both in tradition and in modern theology, in that context. This motivated us to outline our model of the atonement in chapter 4. We also highlighted the potentialities and problems of our model of the atonement precisely pointing out the commonalties and differences. We also concluded that the divergences of the two different traditions are not as great as they are often assumed to be. Although there are problems in constructing a comparative doctrinal theology, with the concept of the atonement at its core, we have more or less made it obvious that comparative theology is possible between Christianity and Visistadvaitic Hindu tradition, using atonement theology. Now, we move on to point out the fruitfulness of our study in the Hindu-Christian Indian context or a similar context elsewhere.

The Hindu-Christian Indian Context or a Similar Context Elsewhere and the Usefulness of This Work

As we noted in chapter 1, India has a population about 80 percent Hindu and only about 2.3 percent of Christian. Visistadvaitic Hindus form a major sect of people within Hinduism. However, the Christian minority experience their belief and practices as life-affirming. Although colonialism has a negative side to it, most missionaries who came to India undertook their mission with good intentions. For example, William Carey, a Baptist missionary, played a remarkable role in the legal abolition of the evil practice of *Sati* (widow burning). Further, the many educational institutions, hospitals, homes for the vulnerable and the numerous church buildings will testify to their dedicated mission. Even today, Indian Christians continue the good works that were initiated by the missionaries. Hence, it is not wise to say that "India is Hindu" and that Christian belief and worship should be avoided. It may also be interesting to remember that Christianity originated in Palestine, which is part of Asia, and that Palestinian culture was, and is, closer to

Indian culture than to Western culture. In the light of the positive values that are present within Christianity we may claim that it should be appropriated and made relevant to all contexts including the Indian context.

This is not to say that Visistadvaitic Hinduism does not have life-affirming practices and concerns. Many missions are now undertaken and many Hindus work for the development of the nation. For example, the Ramakrishna Mission actively teaches moral values to Hindu children and provides free education and food to the poor. It is simply a fact that Hinduism has a long and constructive history in India when compared with the history of Christianity in India.

To move on, it is beyond dispute that Christianity in India lives in the midst of Hindu villages and cities. I have had the privilege of serving with four different churches of the Church of South India, Kanyakumari Diocese for a short period of about one year with each church. Of the four churches, three churches were built either very close or adjacent to Hindu temples. What is unfortunate is that living in such close proximity conflicts and riots between Christians and Hindus can erupt. It is also noteworthy that riots sometimes flare up for the most trivial of reasons, such as, whether or not to use loud speakers, but sometimes they arise from more significant matters related to power-politics. The burning of church buildings is a recurring phenomenon. Further, poor Christians are often deprived of government privileges allotted to low caste Hindus. At the same time, Christians may mock Hindus by saying that their gods are just stones and trees.[8] It is a pity that numerous unnecessary deaths and bloodshed have happened in the name of religion. For instance, the brutal killing of the renowned Christian missionary, Graham Staines, is just one amongst the numerous deaths that could have been prevented.

One reason for religious conflicts, riots and violence is because people of different religious traditions do not understand each other. The need of inter-religious theology which is to help people of diverse religions understand each other is apparent here. Understanding each other better, in turn, can promote reconciliation, unity and peace within and between people of different religious cultures.

Moreover, an Indian approach to Christian theology is valuable because an Indian-Visistadvaitic Hindu religious context is distinctively different from an American or a British context and can therefore make a unique contribution. Here it is the task of inter-religious or comparative religious studies to provide a holistic understanding of Christian theology.

---

8. Obviously, the list of causes for inter–religious conflicts are numerous but within the scope of this chapter, I have only pointed out two examples of the causes of inter-religious conflicts.

The impact of interreligiious theology is already seen in a few writings. For example, Vedanayagam Sastriar, a Tamil Christian poet and theologian, addresses God as *parabrahmaekova* in one of his famous hymns.[9] This word is a combination of *para* (all-encompassing) *brahman* (the Hindu term for the divine, which we had explored in detail) and *ekova* (a modified form of YHWH). Thus the traditional name of God, YHWH, is brought into conjunction with and complemented by, a Hindu concept, Brahman. Through making new conceptual connections in different contexts inter-religious and comparative theology can enrich our understanding of God as well as work for peace and harmony in very practical ways between people of differing faiths. Our work on the atonement is intended as an addition to this way of thinking and to this task in an Indian context or as similar Hindu-Christian context elsewhere.

The world context and the usefulness of this work

Apparently, the world today is increasingly conscious of being multi-religious. Migration of people from the East to the West rapidly changes the religious situation of the Western world. The process of globalization makes the existence of different religious communities ever more apparent. Alan J. Torrance says, "The contemporary world is one in which cultural [religious] diversity is becoming ever more pronounced."[10] Although globalization is often thought of as integrating religions and promoting homogeneous religions, in reality, people belonging to different religious traditions re-affirm and enhance their religious traditions in the presence of others. This phenomenon is largely known as "the invention of tradition" since the publication of a book edited by the historian, Eric Hobsbawm and the anthropologist, Terence Ranger.[11]

In fact, Christianity has extended its presence to most parts of the world, with its major concentration in the West, Israel, Latin America and Africa. There are nevertheless many Christians spread around Asian countries as well. Thus Christianity is in constant contact with other religions around the world. This also implies that other religions are in contact with Christianity as well.

It is in this context that inter-religious theology becomes inevitable and necessary. This is particularly so where the autochthonous population is not inclined to change. As Cham Kaur-Mann claimed, "none [Indian

9 Sastriar, *Kristava Keerthanaikalum Puthelucchi Padalgalum*, 115
10. Regan and Torrance, *Christ and Context*, 1
11. Hobsbawm and Ranger, *The Invention of Tradition*, 1983

Hindus] were sufficiently convinced by the message of the missionaries or inclined to reject or renounce Hinduism as a way of life."[12] Probably this is true in other parts of the world as well, particularly where Christianity is placed amidst other world religions.

As Archbishop Menamparampil says, "It is true that most wars in human history have been fought over territories, natural resources, trade, and economic and political interests. But beneath these clashes of interests there often lay, at a deeper level, ethnic, cultural and religious prejudices."[13] Further, Kosuke Koyama observes,

> The experience of the enormous violence, past and present, has placed all the world religions in the same level of importance since all have failed to stem the violence of human history. Human experience of the world religions in the 20th century has been one of confusing disappointment.[14]

How will the atonement creating unions model precisely be useful in the world context? The atonement creating unions model deals with two selected religious traditions of our world. We have analyzed the Christian doctrine of atonement using a Visistadvaitic Hindu concept. We had also seen the potentialities and problems of our constructed inter-religious model of the atonement. Our atonement model will be directly useful to promote reconciliation, unity and peace in all places where Christians and Hindus live as neighbors because we have dealt with concepts crucial to both religions. The emergence of temples in the Western world testifies to the fact that there are Hindus not only in India, but in other parts of the world as well.

However, the usefulness of our study need not be limited to handling Christian and Visistadvaitic Hindu religions alone. A similar methodology can be applied to understanding the atonement using doctrines of other religions like Islam, Buddhism, Confucianism and so on. Hence, this work is not only useful for Christian-Visistadvaitic Hindu encounters but also provides a methodology and direction in which inter-religious theology can be constructed using doctrines of other religions as well. Thus our work in inter-religious theology will be highly relevant in all those places where religious traditions co-exist which today appears to be in most parts of the world.

---

12. Kaur–Mann, "Who Do You Say I Am?," 36
13. Menamparampil, *The Challenge of Cultures*, 72.
14. Houtepen and Ploeger, *World Christianity*, 46

Graham Monteith, dealing with 'vernacular religion', says, "Theology must aim at producing a rhetoric which both captures the truth and offers adequate rhetorical tools to reflect, and correct public expressions of scantily worked out religious sentiment."[15] In fact, our multi-religious and global world continues to demand that we re-think our theology. Our interreligious model of atonement is the product of our assumption that interreligious theology is a responsible, reasonable, constructive, creative and appropriate theology in our multi-cultural world context. It is our hope that this book will not only stress the need for "union" in places of alienation but will also be an inspiration to other scholars interested in the atonement theology around the globe.

---

15. Monteith, "The Constructive use of Vernacular Religion," 426. Monteith goes on to say that academic theology sometimes gets detached from day to day realities in which people live. In his words, " . . . it is up to theologians to suggest ways in which modern beliefs can be assimilated into the church's traditions." In this work we analyze the way in which the church should formulate its theology in the light of its existence amidst people of diverse religious beliefs.

Abbreviations for Reference Works

AJT	Asia Journal of Theology
BTIJ	Black Theology: An International Journal
CC	Christian Century
CD	Church Dogmatics
CQ	Covenant Quarterly
IJT	The Indian Journal of Theology
ITS	Indian Theological Studies
JD	Journal of Dharma
MIR	Missiology: An International Review
MSJIAMS	Mission Studies: Journal of the International Association for Mission Studies
NCB	New Century Bible
R and S	Religion and Society
RS	Religious Studies
SJT	Scottish Journal of Theology
VJTR	Vidyajyoti Journal of Theological Reflection

Bibliography

Aiyangar, Sakkottai Krishnaswami. et al. *Sri Ramanujacharya: A Sketch of His Life and Times, His Philosophical System, with an Account of Ramanuja and Vaishnavism.* 2nd ed. Madras: G. A. Natesan, n.d.
Aland, Kurt and Barbara Aland et al., eds. *The Greek New Testament with Dictionary,* 4th rev. ed. Stuttgart: Deutsche Bibelgesellschaft, 1994.
Aleaz, K. P. *Christian Thought Through Advaita Vedanta.* Delhi: ISPCK, 1996.
Althaus, Paul. *The Theology of Martin Luther.* Translated by R. C. Schultz. Philadelphia: Fortress, 1966.
Amaladoss, Michael. "Dialogue as Conflict Resolution." *Vidya Jyothi Theological Reflection* 63 (1999) 21–36.
Anselm, Saint Archbishop of Canterbury. *Cur Deus Homo?* Edinburgh: Grant, 1909.
Ariarajah, Wesley S. *The Bible and People of Other Faiths.* Geneva: World Council of Churches, 1985.
Athanasius, Saint Patriarch of Alexandria. *On the Incarnation.* London: Mowbray, 1963.
Atkinson, James. "Salvation." In *A Dictionary of Christian Theology,* edited by Alan Richardson, 301–2. London: SCM, 1969.
Augustine. *On Free Choice of the Will.* Translated by Anna S. Benjamin and L. H. Hackstaff. Englewood Cliffs, NJ: Prentice-Hall, 1964.
Aulen, Gustaf. *Christus Victor: An Historical Study of the Three Main Types of the Idea of the Atonement.* Translated by A. G. Hebert. London: SPCK, 1975.
Ayyangar, C. R. Srīnivāsa. The *Life and Teachings of Sri Ramanujacharya.* Madras: R. Venkateshwar, 1909.
Baago, Kaj. *Pioneers of Indigenous Christianity.* Bangalore & Madras: The Christian Institute for the Study of Religion and Society & The Christian Literature Society, 1969.
Baillie, D. M. *God Was in Christ: An Essay on Incarnation and Atonement.* London: Faber & Faber, 1948.
Barrett, C. K. *A Commentary on the Epistle to the Romans,* 2nd ed. London: A & C Black, 1991.
Barth, Karl. *Church Dogmatics,* Vols. II & IV. Edinburgh: T. & T. Clark, 1957.
Baum, Gregory. *Religion and Alienation: A Theological Reading of Society.* New York: New York, 1975.
Berkey, Robert F., and Sarah A. Edwards. *Christology in Dialogue.* Cleveland: Pilgrim, 1993.

Berkhof, Louis. *Systematic Theology*. Edinburgh: Banner of Truth, 1958.
Bettenson, Henry. *Documents of the Christian Church*. Oxford: Oxford University Press, 1944.
Bigg, Charles. *A Critical and Exegetical Commentary on the Epistle of St. Peter and St. Jude*. Edinburgh: T. & T. Clark, 1975.
Boersma, Hans. "Penal Substitution and the possibility of unconditional hospitality." *Scottish Journal of Theology* 57 (2004) 80–94.
Boff, Leonardo. *Jesus Christ Liberator*. New York: Orbis, 1978.
Bonhoeffer, Dietrich. *The Cost of Discipleship*. London: SCM, 1959.
Bowen, Paul, ed. *Themes and Issues in Hinduism*. London: Cassell, 1998.
Bowes, Pratima. *The Hindu Religious Tradition: A Philosophical Approach*. London: Routledge and Kegan Paul, 1977.
Boyd, Robin. *An Introduction to Indian Christian Theology*. Madras: Christian Literature Society, 1969.
———. *Khristadvaita: A Theology for India*. Madras: Christian Literature Society, 1977.
———. ed. *Manilal C. Parekh, Dhanjibhai Fakirbhai*. Madras: Christian Literature Society, 1974.
Bretall, Robert, ed. *A Kierkegaard Anthology*. Princeton: Princeton University Press, 1973.
Brock, Rita Nakashima. *Journeys by Heart: A Christology of Erotic Power*. New York: Crossroad, 1988.
Brockington, John. *Hinduism and Christianity*. London: Macmillan, 1992.
Brown, Kerry, ed. *The Essential Teachings of Hinduism*. London: Ridder, 1988.
Brown, Joanne Carlson and Carole R. Bohn. eds. *Christianity, Patriarchy and Abuse: A Feminist Critique*. New York: Pilgrim, 1989.
Browning, Don S. *Atonement and Psychotherapy*. Philadelphia: Westminster, 1966.
Brunner, Emil. *The Mediator*, Translated by O. Wyon. London: Lutterworth, 1934.
Brummer, Vincent. *Atonement, Christology and the Trinity: Making Sense of Christian Doctrine*. Aldershot, England: Ashgate, 2005.
Buber, Martin. *Between Man and Man*. London: Routledge and Kegan Paul, 1947.
Buitenen, J. A. B. Van, *Ramanuja on the Bhagavadgita*, 2nd ed. Delhi: Motilal Banarsidass, 1968.
Burleigh, John H. S., ed. *Augustine: Earlier Writings*. N.p.: SCM, 1953.
Burnaby, John. *The Belief of Christendom: A Commentary on the Nicene Creed*. London: SPCK, 1959.
Buttrick, George Arthur, ed. *The Interpreter's Dictionary of the Bible*. New York Abingdon, 1962.
Calvin, John. *Institutes of the Christian Religion*. Translated by F. L. Battles. Edited by J. T. McNeil, Vols. 2 and 20. Library of Christian Classics, Philadelphia: Westminster, 1973.
Camfield, F. W. "The Idea of Substitution in the Doctrine of the Atonement." *Scottish Journal of Theology* 1 (1948) 282–93.
Campbell, McLeod. *The Nature of the Atonement*. Edinburgh: Handsel, 1996.
Carman, John B. *The Theology of Ramanuja*. New Haven and London: Yale University Press, 1974.
Cave, Sydney. *The Doctrine of the Work of Christ*, 4th impression ed. London: Hodder & Stoughton, 1956.

Chapple, Christopher Key, and Mary Evelyn Tucker. *Hinduism and Ecology*. Massachusetts: Harvard University Press, 2000.
Charry, Ellen T., ed. *Inquiring After God: Classic and Contemporary Readings*. Oxford: Blackwell, 2000.
Chaturvedi, Benarsidas and Marjorie Sykes. *Charles Freer Andrews*. New York: Harper, 1950.
Chaudhuri, Nirad, C. *Hinduism*. Oxford: Oxford University Press, 1980.
Clark, Robert ed. *Our Sustainable Table*. San Francisco: North Point, 1990.
Clarke, Sathianathan. *Dalits and Christianity*. New Delhi: Oxford University Press, 1967.
Clooney, Francis X. *Hindu God, Christian God: How Reason Helps Break Down the Boundaries Between Religions*. New York: Oxford University Press, 2001.
———. *Theology After Vedanta: An Experiment in Comparative Theology*. New York: State University of New York Press, 1993.
Cobb, John. *Christ in a Pluralistic Age*. Philadelphia: Westminster, 1975.
Collins, Arbis B. "Metaphysics" In *The New Dictionary of Theology*, 655–60. Dublin: Gill and Macmillan, 1987.
Cone, James H. *God of the Oppressed*, rev. ed. Maryknoll, NY: Orbis, 1997.
Costa, Ruy O. ed. *One Faith, Many Cultures: Inculturation, Indigenization, and Contextualization*, Volume 2. Maryknoll, New York: Orbis, 1988.
Cragg, Kenneth. *The Christ and the Faiths*. London: SPCK, 1986.
Crompton, Yorke. *Hinduism*. London: Ward Lock Educational, 1971.
Cupitt, Don. *After God: The Future of Religion*. London: Weidenfeld & Nicolson, 1997.
———. *Christ and the Hiddenness of God*. London: Lutherworth, 1971.
Das, Sisir Kumar. *The Shadow of the Cross*. New Delhi: Munshiram Manoharlal, 1974.
Dave, Donald G. and John B. Carman, eds. *Christian Faith in a Religiously Plural World*. New York: Orbis, 1978.
Davis, Donald R. "Being Hindu or Being Human: A Reappraisal of the Purusarthas." *International Journal of Hindu Studies* 8 (2004) 1–27.
Denney, James. *The Atonement and the Modern Mind*. London: Hodder & Stoughton, 1930.
———. *The Death of Christ*. London: Tyndale, 1950.
DeSmet, Richard. "Review Article: From Catholic Theology to Sankara Vedanta." *Vidya Jyothi of Theological Reflection* 58 (1994) 795–807.
Devasahayam M. and Sundarisunam, A.N, eds. *Rethinking Christianity in India*. Madras: Hogarth, 1939.
Devdas, Nalini. *Swami Vivekanada*. Bangalore: Christian Institure for the Study of Religion and Society, 1968.
Dietrich, Gabrielle. "The Educational Situation in India: Myrdal's Analysis," *Religion and Society* 2 (1973) 5–20.
Dillistone, F. W. *The Christian Understanding of Atonement*. Herts: James Nisbet and Company Limited, 1968.
Dodd, C. H. *The Epistle of Paul to the Romans*. London and Glasgow: Fontana, 1959.
Drane, John. *Cultural Change and Biblical Faith*. Cumbria: Paternoster, 2000.
Dunn, James, ed. *The Cambridge Companion to St Paul*. Cambridge: Cambridge University Press, 2003.
Elliot, A. B. *Hebrews*. Madras: Christian Literature Society, 1957.

Elwood, Douglas J., ed. *What Asian Christians are Thinking: A Theological Source Book.* Quezon City, Philippines: New Day, 1976.
Estborn, Sigfrid. *Christian Doctrine of Salvation.* Madras: Christian Literature Society, 1954.
Evans, Alice F., Robert A. Evans, and David A. Roozen., eds. *The Globalization of Theological Education.* Maryknoll, NY: Orbis, 1993.
Fairweather, Eugene, ed. *A Scholastic Miscellany: Anselm to Ockham*, Volume 10. London: SCM, 1956.
Felderhof, Marius. *Revisiting Christianity: Theological Reflections.* Surrey, England: Ashgate, 2011.
Feuerbach, Ludwig. *The Essence of Christianity*, Translated by George Eliot. New York: Harper & Row, 1957.
Fiddes, Paul. S. *Past Event and Present Salvation: The Christian Idea of Atonement.* London: Darton Longman & Todd, 1989.
Forward, Martin, ed. *Ultimate Visions: Reflections on the Religions We Choose.* Oxford: Oneworld, 1995.
Fowler, Jeaneane, *Perspectives of Reality: An Introduction to the Philosophy of Hinduism.* Brighton: Sussex Academic Press, 2002.
Franks, R. S. *The Atonement.* Oxford: Oxford University Press, 1871.
Frei, Hans W. *The Identity of Jesus Christ.* Philadelphia: Fortress, 1967.
Galloway, A. D., ed. *Basic Readings in Theology.* London: George Allen & Unwin, 1964.
———. *The Cosmic Christ.* London: Nisbet, 1951.
Gandhi, M. K. *Autobiography.* Boston: Beacon, 1966.
Gayford, S. C. *Sacrifice and Priesthood.* London: Methun, 1924.
Geertz, Clifford. *The Interpretation of Cultures: Selected Essays.* New York: Basic Books, 1973.
Gill, Robin. *Readings in Modern Theology.* London: SPCK, 1995.
Gilkey, Langdon. "Nature as the Image of God: Reflections on the signs of the sacred." *Zygon* 29 (1994) 489–505.
———. *Reaping the Whirlwind.* New York: Seabury, 1976.
Girardi, Giulio. *Marxism and Christianity.* Translated by Kevin Traynor. New York: Macmillan, 1968.
Glasser, Arthur F. *Announcing the Kingdom: The Story of God's Mission in the Bible.* Grand Rapids: Baker Academic, 2003.
Goetz, Ronald. "The Suffering of God." *Christian Century* 103 (1986) 385–89.
Gorringe, Timothy. *God's Just Vengeance: Crime, Violence and the Rhetoric of Salvation.* Cambridge: Cambridge University Press, 1996.
Goulder, M., ed. *Incarnation and Myth.* London: SCM, 1979.
Grensted, L. W, ed. *The Atonement in History and in Life.* London: Macmillan, 1929.
Griffiths, Bede. *A New Vision of Reality.* New Delhi: HarperCollins, 1992.
———. *Vedanta and Christian Faith.* Los Angeles: The Dawn Horse, 1973.
Gunton, Colin. *The Actuality of Atonement: A Study of Metaphor, Rationality and the Christian Tradition.* Edinburgh: T. & T. Clark, 1988.
———. *Enlightenment and Alienation.* Grand Rapids: Eerdmans, 1985.
Gutierrez, Gustavo. *A Theology of Liberation: History, Politics and Salvation*, revised ed. Maryknoll, NY: Orbis, 1973.
Hall, Calcin S and Gardner Lindzey. *Theories of Personality*, 2nd ed. New York: John Wiley and Sons, 1970.

Harper, Susan Billington. *In the Shadow of the Mahatma: Bishop V. S. Azariah and the Travails of Christianity in British India.* Cambridge: Eerdmans, 2000.

Harre, Rom. *One Thousand Years of Philosophy: From Ramanuja to Wittgenstein.* Oxford: Blackwell, 2000.

Hartshorne, Charles. *The Divine Relativity: A Social Conception of God.* New Haven: Yale University Press, 1964.

Hegel, G. W. F. *The Phenomenology of Mind.* London: George Allen and Union, 1969.

Heim, Mark. *Salvations.* Maryknoll, NY: Orbis, 1999.

Hewlett, David. "Substitution and Representation Patterns of Thought in Christian Atonement Theology." PhD diss., University of Durham, 1984.

Hick, John. *An Interpretation of Religion.* New Haven: Yale University Press, 1989.

———. *Problems of Religious Pluralism.* London: Macmillan, 1985.

Hick, John, and B. Hebblethwaite. *Christianity and Other Religions: Selected Readings.* London: Collins, 1981.

Higton, Mike. *Christian Doctrine.* London: SCM, 2008.

Hill, David. *God and the Universe of Faiths: Essays in the Philosophy of Religion.* London: Macmillan, 1973.

———. *The Gospel of Matthew.* London: Oliphants, 1972.

———. *The Metaphor of God Incarnate.* London: SCM, 1993.

———. *Problems of Religious Pluralism.* London: Macmillan, 1985.

Hinnells, John. R. and Eric J. Sharpe. eds. *Hinduism.* Newcastle, England: Oriel, 1972.

Hiriyanna, M. *The Essentials of Indian Philosophy.* London: Allen & Unwin, 1985.

Hobsbawm, Eric, and Terence Ranger. eds. *The Invention of Tradition.* Cambridge: Cambridge University Press, 1983.

Hodge, Archibald. *The Atonement.* London: Thomas Nelson and Sons, 1868.

Hodge, Charles. *Systematic Theology,* Volume 2. London: James Clark, 1960.

Holmes, Steve. "Can Punishment Bring Peace? Penal Substitution Revisited." *Scottish Journal of Theology* 58 (2005) 104–23.

Houtepen, Anton and Albert Ploeger. eds. *World Christianity Reconsidered.* Zoetermeer, Netherlands: Meinema, 2001.

Houts, Margo G. "Classical Atonement Imagery: Feminist and Evangelical Challenges." *Catalyst* 19 (1993) 1–6.

Hughes, Thomas Hywel. *The Atonement.* London: Allen & Unwin, 1949.

Hwa, Yung. "Theories of Atonement and the Mission of the Church." *Asia Journal of Theology* 3 (1989) 452–64.

Isherwood, Christopher. *Rama Krishna and His Disciples.* London: Methun, 1965.

Israel, Joachim. *Alienation: From Marx to Modern Sociology.* Boston: Allyn & Bacon, 1971.

Jantzen, Grace M. "Human Diversity and Salvation in Christ." *Religious Studies* 20 (1984) 579–92.

Jathanna, O. V. *The Decisiveness of the Christ-Event and the Universality of Christianity in a World of Religious Plurality.* Berne: Peter Lang, 1981.

Johnston, Robert. "Acculturation or Inculturation? A Contemporary Evangelical Theology of the Atonement." *Catholic Quarterly* 46 (1988) 200–14.

Karmakar, R. D., ed. *Sri Bashya of Ramanuja.* N.p.: n.p., n.d.

Käsemann, E. *New Testament Questions of Today.* Philadelphia: Fortress, 1969.

Kaur-Mann, Cham. "Who Do You Say I Am? Images of Jesus." *Black Theology: An International Journal* 2 (2004) 19–44.

Kee, Howard Clark and Franklin W. Young. *The Living World of the New Testament*. London: Darton Longman & Todd, 1960.
Kelly, J. N. D. *Early Christian Doctrines*, 5th ed. London: Adam & Charles Black, 1977.
Kim, Sebastian C. H. *In Search of Identity: Debates on Religious Conversion in India*. New Delhi: Oxford University Press, 2003.
Kirk, J. Andrew, ed. *Contemporary Issues in Mission*. Birmingham: Department of Mission, Selly Oak Colleges, 1994.
Klostermaier, Klaus. *A Concise Encyclopedia of Hinduism*. Oxford: Oneworld Publications, 1998.
———. *Hinduism: A Short History*. Oxford: Oneworld Publications, 2000.
———. *Indian Theology in Dialogue*. Madras: Christian Literature Society, 1986.
Klyback, Willaim. *Sri Aurobindo Ghose: The Dweller in the Lands of Silence*. New York: Peter Lang, 2001.
Knitter, Paul. *No Other Name? A Critical Survey of Christian Attitudes Toward the World Religions*. New York: Orbis, 1985.
Kraemer, Hendrick. *The Christian Message in a Non-Christian World*. London: Edinburgh, 1938.
———. *Religion and the Christian Faith*. London: Lutterworth, 1956.
Kumarappa, Bharatan. *The Hindu Conception of the Deity: As Culminating in Ramanuja*. London: Luzac & Co., 1934.
Kung, Hans. *On Being a Christian*. Translated by Edward Quinn. London: Collins, 1977.
Kurien, C. T. *Poverty and Development*. Madras: Christian Literature Society, 1974.
Lampe, G. W. H. *Reconciliation in Christ*. London: Longmans, 1956.
Lipner, Julius. *The Face of Truth: A Study of Meaning and Metaphysics in the Vedantic Theology of Ramanuja*. London: Macmillan, 1986.
Lott, Eric J. *God and the Universe in the Vedantic Theology of Ramanuja: A Study in the Use of the Self-Body Analogy*. Madras: Ramanuja Research Society, 1976.
———. *Vedantic Approaches to God*. London: Macmillan, 1980.
Macquarie, John. *Principles of Christian Theology*. London: SCM, 1975.
Mahadevan, T. M. P. *Outlines of Hinduism*. Bombay: Chetana, 1971.
Margaret and James Stutley. *A Dictionary of Hinduism: Its Mythology, Folklore and Development, 1500 BC-AD 1500*. Bombay: Allied, 1977.
Marshall, Bruce. D. *Theology and Dialogue*. Notre Dame: University of Notre Dame Press, 1990.
Marshall, Howard, Stephen Travis, and Ian Paul. *Exploring the New Testament*, Volume 2. London: SPCK, 2002.
Martin, Paul. *The Missionary of the Indian Road*. Bangalore: Theological Book Trust, 1996.
Mattam, Joseph. *Land of the Trinity: A Study of Modern Christian Approaches to Hinduism*. Bangalore: TPI, 1975.
McCormack, Bruce L. "For Us and Our Salvation: Incarnation and Atonement in the Reformed Tradition." *Studies in Reformed Theology and History* 1 (1993) 1-56.
McGrath, Alister E. *Historical Theology*. Oxford: Blackwell, 1998.
McFague, Sallie. *Super, Nature Christians. How We Should Love Nature*. Minneapolis: Fortress, 1997.
Meadowcroft, Tim. "Between Authorial Intent and Indeterminacy: The Incarnation as an Invitation to Human-Divine Discourse." *Scottish Journal of Theology* 58 (2005) 199–218.

Menamparampil, Thomas. *The Challenge of Cultures*. Mumbai: Institute of Cultural Studies, 1995.
Migiliore, Daniel. *Faith Seeking Understanding*. Grand Rapids: Eerdmans, 1991.
Moltmann, Jürgen. *The Crucified God: The Cross of Christ as the Foundation and Criticism of Christian Theology*. Translated by R. A. Wilson and John Bowden. London: SCM, 1974.
Monteith, W. Graham. "The Constructive Use of 'Vernacular Religion.'" *Scottish Journal of Theology* 59 (2006) 413–26.
Morgan, Kenneth W., ed. *The Basic Beliefs of Hinduism*. Calcutta: YMCA Publishing House, 1955.
Morris, Leon. *The Apostolic Preaching of the Cross*, 3rd ed. London: Tyndale, 1965.
Nag, Kalidas and Debajyothi Burman. eds. *The English Works of Raja Rammohan Roy*, Part VI. Calcutta: Sadharan Brahmo Samaj, 1946.
Nakamura, Hajime. *A History of Early Vedanta Philosophy*, Volume 1. Delhi: Motilal Banarsidass, 1983.
Nehring, Andreas. *Ecology: A Theological Response*. Madras: Department of Research and Publications, Gurukul Lutheran Theological College & Research Institute, 1994.
Neelamkavil, Raphael. "Reconstructing the Foundations of Vedantic Metaphysics." *Journal of Dharma* 30 (2005) 337–64.
Ogden, Schubert. *The Reality of God*. London: SCM, 1967.
Pannenberg, Wolfhart. *Jesus-God and Man*. London: SCM, 1968.
Pannikkar, Raimundo. *The Unknown Christ of Hinduism: Towards an Ecumenical Christophany*. London: Darton Longman & Todd, 1981.
Paul, Robert S. *The Atonement and the Sacraments*. New York: Abingdon, 1961.
Peacocke, Arthur. *God and Science: A Quest for Christian Credibility*. London: SCM, 1996.
Peery, William Powlas. *A Christian Understanding of South Indian Vaishnavism*, PhD diss., Duke University, 1972.
Peringalloor, Joseph. *Salvation Through Gita and Gospel*. Bombay: Institute of Indian Culture, 1972.
Persaud, Winston, D. *The Theology of the Cross and Marx's Anthropology*. New York: Peter Lang, 1991.
Podimattam, Felix. "Why Would a Good God Allow Suffering?" *Indian Theological Studies* 42 (2005) 175–211.
Pollard, Elaine. *The Oxford Paperback Dictionary*, 4th ed. Oxford: Oxford University Press, 1994.
Polkinghorne, John. *The Work of Love: Creation As Kenosis*. Grand Rapids: Eerdmans, 2001.
Popper, Karl. *Conjectures and Refutations*. London: Routledge and Kegan Paul, 1968.
Prime, Ranchor. *Hinduism and Ecology: Seeds of Truth*. London: Cassell, 1992.
Race, Alan. *Christians and Religious Pluralism: Patterns in the Christian Theology of Religions*. London: SCM, 1983.
Radhakrishnan. *The Hindu View of Life*. London: George Allen & Unwin, 1927.
———. *Indian Philosophy*, Volume II. London: George Allen & Unwin, 1927.
———. *Indian Philosophy*, Volume II, 2nd ed. rev. London: George Allen & Unwin, 1931.

———. *The Vedanta According to Samkara and Ramanuja.* London: George Allen & Unwin, 1928.
Rahner, Karl. "Sin." In *Encyclopaedia of Theology*, 1586–88. London: Burns and Oates, 1975.
———. *Theological Investigations.* London: Darton Longman and Todd, 1966.
Ramanuja. *Gita Bhasya.* Translated by M. R. Sampatkumaran. Bombay: Ananthacharya Indological Research Institute, 1985.
———. *The Vedanta-Sutras with the Sri-Bhasya of Ramanujacharyar*, Vols. I, II, and III, 2nd ed. rev. Translated by M. Rangacharya and M.B. Varadaraja Aiyangar. Madras: Educational Publishing, n.d.
Regan, Hilary, Alan J. Torrance, et al., eds. *Christ and Context.* Edinburgh: T. & T. Clark, 1993.
Richards, Glyn. *Towards a Theology of Religions.* London: Routledge, 1983.
Richardson, Alan. "Reincarnation." In *A Dictionary of Christian Theology*, 288–89. London: SCM, 1969.
Robertson, S. "Hindu Spirituality." *Religion and Society* 50 (2005) 1–23.
Robinson, R. and Helmut Koester. *Trajectories Through Early Christianity.* Philadelphia: Fortress, 1971.
Rowe, William. *Religious Symbols and God.* Chicago: The University of Chicago Press, 1968.
Roy, Virendra K., and Ramesh C. Sarikwal, eds. *Marxian Sociology.* Delhi: Ajanta, 1979.
Rupp, George. *Christologies and Cultures.* Hague: Mouton, 1974.
Russell, T., ed. *The Works of John Owen*, Vols. 5 and 9. London: Richard Baynes, 1826.
Samartha, Stanley J. *The Hindu Response to the Unbound Christ.* Madras: Christian Literature Society, 1974.
———. *One Christ-Many Religions: Toward a Revised Christology.* New York: Orbis, 1991.
Sanders, E.P. *The Historical Figure of Jesus,* London: Penguin, 1993.
———. *Paul: A Very Short Introduction,* Oxford: Oxford University Press, 2001.
Saraswathi, Swami Dyananda. "An Open Letter to Pope John Paul II-Conversion is Violence." *Indian Express*, Oct 29, 1999.
Sartori, Giovanni. "Representational Systems." In *International Encyclopaedia of Social Sciences*, 465–74. London: Macmillan, 1979.
Sastriar, Vedanayagam. *Kristava Keerthanaikalum Puthelucchi Padalgalum* (Christian Lyrics and Songs of New Life), rev. ed. Madras: Christian Literature Society, 1988.
Schacht, Richard. *Alienation.* London: George Allen & Unwin, 1971.
Schleiermacher, Friedrich D. *The Christian Faith.* Edinburgh: T. & T. Clark, 1976.
Schillebeeckx, Edward. *Interim Report on the Books Jesus & Christ.* New York: Crossroad, 1980.
———. *Jesus: An Experiment in Christology.* Translated by Hubert Hoskins. London: William Collins, 1979.
Selvanayagam, Israel. *Relating to People of Other Faiths: Insights from the Bible.* Thiruvilla: Christava Sahitya Samithy, 2004.
Sharma, Arvind. *Classical Hindu Thought.* New Delhi: Oxford University Press, 2000.
Shedd, William G. T. *Dogmatic Theology*, Volume 1, 2nd ed. Edinburgh: T. & T. Clark, 1889.
———. *A History of Christian Doctrines*, Volume 2. Edinburgh: T. & T. Clark, 1877.

Shults, F. LeRon. *The Postfoundationalist Task of Theology*. Grand Rapids: Eerdmans, 1999.
Singh, David Emmanuel. "Rethinking Jesus and the Cross in Islam." *Mission Studies: Journal of the International Association for Mission Studies* 23 (2006) 239–60.
Smith, Huston. *The World's Religions*. New York: Harper & Row, 1991.
Snook, Lee E. *The Anonymous Christ: Jesus as Saviour in Modern Theology*. Minneapolis: Augsburg, 1986.
Spence, Alan. *The Promise of Peace: A Unified Theory of Atonement*. London: T. & T. Clarke, 2006.
Solle, Dorothy. *Christ the Representative: An Essay in Theology After the 'Death of God.'* Translated by David Lewis. London: SCM, 1967.
Srinivasachari, P. N. *The Philosophy of Visistadvaita*. Madras: The Adyar Library and Research Centre, 1970.
———. *Ramanuja's Idea of the Finite Self*. Calcutta: Longmans, 1928.
Stackhouse, Max L and Peter J. Paris, eds. *God and Globalization: Religion and the Powers of the Common Life*, Volume 1. Pennsylvania: Trinity Press International, 2000.
Stevens, George B. *The Christian Doctrine of Salvation*. Edinburgh: T. & T. Clark, 1905.
Strong, Augustus H. *Systematic Theology*, Volume 2. Philadelphia: American Baptist, 1886.
Sumithra, Sunand. *Christian Theology from an Indian Perspective*. Bangalore: Theological Book Trust, 1990.
Swami Chidbhavananda. *The Bhagavad Gita: Commentary*. Thiruchirapalli: Sri Ramakrishna Tapovanam, 1975.
Taylor, Vincent. *Jesus and His Sacrifice*. London: Macmillan, 1955.
Thangaraj, Thomas. *The Common Task: Theology of Mission*. Nashville: Abingdon, 1999.
———. *The Crucified Guru*. Nashville: Abingdon, 1994.
Theissen, Jerome P. *The Ultimate Church and The Promise of Salvation*. Minnesota: St. John's University Press, 1976.
Thibaut, George. *The Vedanta Sutras with the Commentary by Ramanuja*. Delhi: Motilal Banarsidas, 1962.
Thomas, P.M. "The Authority of Hindu Scripture." *Indian Journal of Theology* 23 (1974) 85–95.
Thomas, P. T. *Vengal Chakkarai*. Madras: Christian Literature Society, 1981.
Thornton, Lionel S. *The Common Life in the Body of Christ*. Westminster: Dacre Press, 1946.
Thottakara, Augustine. "A Vedantic Perspective of Ecology." *Journal of Dharma* 26 (2001) 9–27.
Tiliander, Bror. *Christian and Hindu Terminology*. Uppsala: Almqvist & Wiksell, 1974.
Tillich, Paul. *Systematic Theology*, Volume 2. London: James Nisbet, 1957.
Tinker, Hugh. *The Ordeal of Love*. Delhi: Oxford University Press, 1979.
Torrance, Alan J. and Michael Banner, eds. *The Doctrine of God and Theological Ethics*. London: T. & T. Clark, 2006.
Torrance, Thomas F., ed., *The Incarnation*. Edinburgh: The Handsel Press, 1981.
Troeltsch, Ernst. *The Absoluteness of Christianity and the History of Religions*. London: SCM, 1972.
Tsoukalas, Steven. *The Krsnavatara Doctrines of Sankara and Ramanuja and Classical Christian Orthodoxy's Incarnation of Christ: A Comparative Study of the Body-Soul-*

Divine Relation and its Theological/Soteriological Implications, PhD diss.,University of Birmingham, 2004.

Upanisad. N.p.: n.p., n.d.

Van Gemeren, Willem, et al., eds. *Dictionary of Old Testament Theology and Exegesis*, Volume 1. Cumbria: Paternoster, 1996.

Veeramani, Thampi. "Redemption in Paul's Epistles." In *Paul Examined*, 55–57. Delhi: ISPCK, 2002.

Vince, R. M. "Alienation." In *New Dictionary of Theology*, 14–20. Leicester: InterVarsity, 1988.

Vishnu Purana: Book VI. N.p.: n.p., n.d.

Vivekananda, Swami. *Collected Works,* Volume 1 and Volume 6. Calcutta: Advaitha Ashrama, 1962.

Vyasa, *Bhagavad Gita*. N.p.: n.p., n.d.

Walker, Alan. *The Many-Sided Cross of Jesus*. Nashville: Abingdon, 1962.

Weaver, Denny. *The Nonviolent Atonement*. Grand Rapids: Eerdmans, 2001.

Weil, Simone. *Intimations of Christianity Among the Ancient Greeks*. Translated by Elisabeth Chase Geissbuhler. Boston: Beacon, 1957.

———. *Waiting on God*, Translated by Emma Craufurd. London: Fontana, 1959.

Wessels, Anton. *Images of Jesus*. London: SCM, 1990.

Westcott, Brooke F. *The Victory of the Cross*. London: Macmillan, 1989.

White, Vernon. *Atonement and Incarnation*. Cambridge: Cambridge University Press, 1991.

Williams, Monier. *A Sanskrit-English Dictionary*. Delhi: Motilal Banarsidass, 1990.

Winter, Michael. *The Atonement*. London: Geoffrey Chapman, 1995.

Wood, R. D. Hinshel. *A Dictionary of Kleinian Thought*. London: Free Association, 1989.

Wolf, William. *No Cross, No Crown*. New York: Seabury, 1957.

Wright, Tom. *Justification: God's Plan and Paul's Vision*. London: SPCK, 2009.

Young, Francis. *Can These Dry Bones Live?*. London: SCM, 1982.

Zaehner, R.C. *Hinduism*. London: Oxford University Press, 1966.

www.ingramcontent.com/pod-product-compliance
Lightning Source LLC
Chambersburg PA
CBHW051641230426
43669CB00013B/2396